THE SPIRIT OF THE UNION: POPULAR POLITICS IN SCOTLAND, 1815–1820

The Enlightenment World: Political and Intellectual History of the Long Eighteenth Century

Series Editor: *Michael T. Davis*
Series Co-Editors: *Jack Fruchtman, Jr*
     Iain McCalman
     Paul Pickering
Advisory Editor: *Hideo Tanaka*

Titles in this Series

1 Harlequin Empire: Race, Ethnicity and the Drama of the Popular Enlightenment
David Worrall

2 The Cosmopolitan Ideal in the Age of Revolution and Reaction, 1776–1832
Michael Scrivener

3 Writing the Empire: Robert Southey and Romantic Colonialism
Carol Bolton

4 Adam Ferguson: History, Progress and Human Nature
Eugene Heath and Vincenzo Merolle (eds)

5 Charlotte Smith in British Romanticism
Jacqueline Labbe (ed.)

6 The Scottish People and the French Revolution
Bob Harris

7 The English Deists: Studies in Early Enlightenment
Wayne Hudson

8 Adam Ferguson: Philosophy, Politics and Society
Eugene Heath and Vincenzo Merolle (eds)

9 Rhyming Reason: The Poetry of Romantic-Era Psychologists
Michelle Faubert

10 Liberating Medicine, 1720–1835
Tristanne Connolly and Steve Clark (eds)

11 John Thelwall: Radical Romantic and Acquitted Felon
Steve Poole (ed.)

12 The Evolution of Sympathy in the Long Eighteenth Century
Jonathan Lamb

13 Enlightenment and Modernity: The English Deists and Reform
Wayne Hudson

14 William Wickham, Master Spy: The Secret War against the French Revolution
Michael Durey

15 The Edinburgh Review in the Literary Culture of Romantic Britain: Mammoth and Megalonyx
William Christie

16 Montesquieu and England: Enlightened Exchanges, 1689–1755
Usrula Haskins Gonthier

17 The Sublime Invention: Ballooning in Europe, 1783–1820
Michael R. Lynn

18 The Language of Whiggism: Liberty and Patriotism, 1802–1830
Kathryn Chittick

19 Romantic Localities: Europe Writes Place
Christoph Bode and Jacqueline Labbe (eds)

20 William Godwin and the Theatre
David O'Shaughnessy

Forthcoming Titles

Ebenezer Hazard, Jeremy Belknap and the American Revolution
Russell M. Lawson

Robert and James Adam, Architects of the Age of Enlightenment
Ariyuki Kondo

British Visions of America, 1775–1820: Republican Realities
Emma Vincent Macleod

www.pickeringchatto.com/enlightenmentworld

THE SPIRIT OF THE UNION: POPULAR POLITICS IN SCOTLAND, 1815–1820

BY

Gordon Pentland

LONDON
PICKERING & CHATTO
2011

Published by Pickering & Chatto (Publishers) Limited
21 Bloomsbury Way, London WC1A 2TH

2252 Ridge Road, Brookfield, Vermont 05036-9704, USA

www.pickeringchatto.com

All rights reserved.
No part of this publication may be reproduced,
stored in a retrieval system, or transmitted in any form or by any means,
electronic, mechanical, photocopying, recording, or otherwise
without prior permission of the publisher.

© Pickering & Chatto (Publishers) Ltd 2011
© Gordon Pentland 2011

BRITISH LIBRARY CATALOGUING IN PUBLICATION DATA

Pentland, Gordon.
The spirit of the union: popular politics in Scotland. – (The Enlightenment world)
1. Radicalism – Scotland – History – 19th century. 2. Scotland – Politics and government – 19th century. 3. Scotland – History – 19th century.
I. Title II. Series
941.1'074-dc22

ISBN-13: 9781851961535
e: 9781851960620

This publication is printed on acid-free paper that conforms to the American National Standard for the Permanence of Paper for Printed Library Materials.

Typeset by Pickering & Chatto (Publishers) Limited
Printed and bound in the United Kingdom by MPG Books Group

CONTENTS

Acknowledgements   ix

Introduction   1
1 The Forging of Post-War Politics   7
2 Loyalism and Whiggism in Scotland   33
3 Scotland and the Mass Platform   53
4 The 'General Rising' of 1820   89
Conclusion   109
Epilogue: The Legacies of 1820   127

Notes   145
Works Cited   179
Index   199

ACKNOWLEDGEMENTS

First of all, I would like to thank colleagues at the University of Edinburgh for providing such a stimulating environment for research and writing. In particular, I am grateful to Dr Ewen Cameron and Professor Tom Devine for advice and support throughout this project and to 'The Management' of the School of History, Classics and Archaeology for providing a timely period of sabbatical leave in which to write this book. Much of the research was completed with the generous financial assistance provided by an Early Career Fellowship from the Leverhulme Trust (ECF2005/049). It is a humane funding body that allows a researcher to change tack halfway through an award and I gratefully acknowledge the Trust's flexibility and generosity. This assistance was supplemented latterly by small grants from the Carnegie Trust for the Universities of Scotland and the Strathmartine Trust, which facilitated crucial research trips to London and Devon.

I would like to register my appreciation of the kind help that was offered by the staffs of the Mitchell Library in Glasgow, Airdrie, Paisley and Dundee public libraries and the Devon Record Office. I would also like to thank the BBC and, in particular, Dr Mark Jardine, whose ceaseless labour lay behind much of their *History of Scotland* series. Mulling over some of the material contained in this book in my role as consultant for programme 9, 'This Land is Our Land', was a stimulating experience which I hope improved the content of both. I would also like to thank *Past & Present*, whose editorial board offered searching criticism that dramatically improved the presentation of the research which largely constitutes the epilogue to this book. This was published as "Betrayed by Infamous Spies"? The Commemoration of Scotland's "Radical War" of 1820', *Past and Present*, 201 (November 2008). Finally, I am especially grateful to two scholars and friends – Dr Joseph Hardwick and Dr Valerie Wallace – who agreed to read a chaotic manuscript at short notice and whose timely criticisms saved me from a number of errors. Those that remain are, of course, my own.

More personal debts are numerous. As always, my greatest thanks are to my wife, Katie, for her patience in enduring monologues about radical politics and Valentine's Day trips to less than salubrious cemeteries in the west of Scotland.

She remains a constant source of support, advice and good humour. I cannot thank her enough. Finally, my thanks go to our wonderful son, Archie 'Smudge' Pentland. He can readily be blamed for any delays to the manuscript, but he has to be thanked for the endless amounts of joy he has provided the author during its composition. This book is for him.

INTRODUCTION

The 'Radical War' – one name given to an attempted general rising in April 1820 – holds a prominent place in Scottish culture but an uneasy one in Scottish historiography. The only book-length exploration of the event, Peter Berresford Ellis and Seumas Mac a'Ghobhainn's *The Scottish Insurrection of 1820* (1970), offers an interpretation of it as both a serious rupture in Scottish society in the form of an insurrectionary attempt nourished by nationalist and class consciousness and as a piece of 'hidden' history which had been intentionally exorcized from Scottish historiography.[1] In some quarters this interpretation has been challenged, but with the paradoxical effect of reducing the social and political tensions demonstrated by the event to 'the futile revolt of a tiny minority'.[2] A more recent investigation of the 'Radical War' within the wider context of the long eighteenth century, by C. A. Whately, has gone some way to marking out a different case for the significance of the event and acknowledges its disruptive effect, but unshackles it from some of the less supportable assertions of *The Scottish Insurrection*.[3] Nevertheless, as Ellis points out in the new preface of the 2001 reprinted but unrevised edition of the book, it remains the only full-length published study of 'the last major Scottish insurrection.'[4]

The lacuna in 'academic' history is all the more striking given the frequency with which the attempted insurrection has appeared in Scottish politics and culture and its centrality to 'popular' histories of Scotland. In recent times, for example, it has provided slogans for Scottish National Party (SNP) activists and inspiration for trade unionists, while it was the fulcrum for a politically-engaged education debate in the Scottish Parliament in 2001. Outside of the explicitly political sphere, it has inspired plays, poetry, novels and paintings. Finally, calls for the commemoration of the 'martyrs' of 1820 have led to widely-publicized campaigns both to restore and amend existing monuments and to establish new ones (such as the monument to the 'battlefield' of Bonnymuir, erected in 2007). Given this pervasive presence in politics and culture, a re-examination of the event itself and its legacy provides a valuable addition to our understanding both of Scotland's past and of its political 'usability'. This book argues that a thorough evaluation of this crucial yet little understood and much mythologized period in

Scottish history makes a significant contribution to our understanding of politics during E. P. Thompson's 'heroic age of popular radicalism'.[5]

The book has three key aims. First, it aims to place the rising itself in its proper contexts. It does this by exploring the different modes of extra-parliamentary politics between 1815 and 1820 and paying close attention to events outside of Scotland. It thus shifts the focus from the 'Radical War' itself to the reform movements of 1816–17 and 1819–20 more generally and includes an analysis of the Queen Caroline agitation that followed the attempted insurrection. The dramatic appeal provided by the events of 1820 has tended to overshadow both the importance of the development of mass popular politics after 1815 and the revival and transformation of popular loyalism after this date. While some superb unpublished work has provided a compelling examination of the development of radical politics between 1815 and 1820, it has done so without addressing the interactions of radicalism and loyalism and without placing events in Scotland within a convincing British framework.[6] Other work has demonstrated that events in Scotland can fruitfully be examined in the context provided not only by events in Parliament, but other popular political activity, in particular, in London and the north of England.[7]

Existing work on Scotland in this period has approached popular politics through the categories bequeathed by social history methodologies of the 1960s and 1970s. By concentrating on issues of class formation and class conflict (either explicitly or implicitly) the tendency has been to ignore the interlocutors of popular radicals, those other groups that constitute a political culture.[8] The theoretical underpinning of the current book is provided by the 'new political history', which has been central in remodelling interpretations of English politics across the nineteenth and twentieth centuries.[9] Though there are few programmatic statements of this approach to political history its central premises are well established. First, it has been influenced by the 'linguistic turn' in the humanities, which has encouraged historians to take the study of language more seriously and to complicate the relationship between language and social being. Secondly, it has entailed emphasizing the relative autonomy of politics from underlying social structures and encouraged a sustained assault on the notion that political ideas and activities are the expressions of processes of class formation or instances of class conflict.

In terms of popular politics and radicalism the Ur-text of the new political history was Gareth Stedman Jones's influential article on Chartism, which shifted focus away from the social composition of the movement to the languages used by activists in pursuit of wide-scale political mobilization. Instead of social and economic distress being the crucial explanatory factor for Chartist mobilization, Stedman Jones reversed the equation. The key area for historians to explore, he argued, was how activists provided and disseminated languages and ideas about politics that allowed people to make sense of this distress in political terms.[10] The historiographical legacy of this approach has been a dramatic shift in focus. Political historians are now far more interested in questions of leadership, language and organization than in profiling the social constituencies of mass movements and divining their role in processes of class formation and conflict.

Stedman Jones's key insight has been applied with considerable sophistication to English radical politics for the period after the end of the Napoleonic Wars. Jonathan Fulcher's work has followed Stedman Jones in eschewing the dominance of social and economic explanations for popular radicalism: 'it is the political arena which provides the crucial context for understanding the rise and fall of mass activity'.[11] Such an approach involves not only examining the way in which radical activists sought to appeal to the people and turn them into political actors, but how such appeals related to and interacted with the language and actions of other groups within the political culture. This compelling case to take seriously other positions – most notably those of loyalists and of both Whigs and Tories inside and outside of Parliament – has influenced the approach of this book, which aims to place radicalism within its proper political context in Scotland.

Chapter 1 examines distinctive features of politics in the immediate aftermath of 1815 and highlights important continuities with the popular politics of the preceding decades. It briefly discusses the socio-economic context in which politics was pursued but emphasizes how different political groups – radicals and reformers, Whigs and loyalists – responded both to Parliament and to the specific challenges and opportunities afforded by the cessation of hostilities. One of the key arguments is that war and the challenges involved in what one radical poet called 'this swift hitch from war to peace' dominated both political discourse and aims into the 1820s. In particular, it focuses on the relationship between 'moderate' and 'radical' reformers, both of whom pursued specific goals after 1815 and developed novel strategies to do so, but whose critiques were both premised on popular understandings of the British constitution. It also explores the rhetorical and political strategies and the geographical reach of the reform movement, all of which were crucial in the movement's claim to represent 'the nation' in 1816–17. Finally, it explores the evidence for the existence of an insurrectionary 'underground' in Scotland, which provided much of the rationale for a series of repressive legislative measures (in particular, the suspension of habeas corpus) in 1817.

Chapter 2 examines how a broadly-based reform movement came to an end in 1817. Traditional explanations focus on the role of both repression and the ebb and flow of economic conditions. The argument here will focus on politics. It will explore closely both the reaction to radicalism in terms of state trials (in particular those of Niel Douglas, the Universalist minister and Andrew McKinlay, a weaver tried for administering secret oaths) and the encouragement of a revival of official loyalism across Scotland. Another part of the explanation, however, is provided by an examination of how Whigs and potentially sympathetic groups responded to popular politics and radicalism. The Whigs in Scotland were generally successful in asserting some leadership of reform during 1817, both by channelling it through a critique of the Scottish state and its assault on the liberties of the people and by linking it to the specifically Scottish issue of burgh reform.

Chapter 3 investigates the emergence in Scotland of the first genuinely popular political movement based around the 'mass platform', which reached its apotheosis during the second half of 1819. Once again, previous accounts have tended to ground explanations in socio-economic factors, on the premise that material distress necessarily produced political activism. While these factors will be explored, emphasis will be placed instead on the shifting relationships of different political groups and on the languages and strategies they used. 'Union' had been a key strategic goal and an end in itself for the earlier movement, but it became axiomatic during the movement of 1819, which was both socially and geographically more exclusive. It was in this year that the *Spirit of the Union* – the short-lived Scottish radical periodical from which this book takes its name – emerged, in part as a response to the problems of creating and articulating a national claim for radicals in the fraught context after Peterloo.

While the centre of gravity of the book lies in the mass political activity preceding 1820 its second aim is to provide the first full and referenced account of the rising of 1820 itself in Chapter 4. There are key problems with existing accounts. Ellis and Mac a'Ghobhainn's work was clearly based on extensive consultation of primary source material, but this was left unreferenced throughout. Through the careful examination of the surviving sources a different account of 1820 will be presented and the roles played by events in England and by purported *agents provocateurs* will be examined. The political context for radical activity described and analysed in Chapters 1–3 goes some way to furnishing this different interpretation of the events of 1820. The compelling case for the connections between Scottish and English radicals has been made for the 1790s and it is no less important in explaining some of the central events of the postwar period.[12] In particular, the idea that events in the west of Scotland formed part of an abortive 'general rising' across north Britain will be explored.

It is worth stating at this stage that I have been unable to identify or locate the *only* evidence cited by Ellis and Mac a'Ghobhainn in support of their assertion that the aims of the radicals in Scotland were nationalist and republican. This consisted of two letters about the Scottish radicals, allegedly sent by the Glasgow chief of police, James Mitchell, in March of 1820, stating that: 'Their plan is to set up a Scottish Assembly or Parliament in Edinburgh, likewise similar assemblies are to be set up by the disaffected in England and Ireland'.[13] Despite assiduous searching through all of those manuscript sources that appear in the book's truncated bibliography (and much else besides) I have come across neither of these letters, nor have I come across any mention of them. I make no claims or accusations. What I will say is that even if these letters do exist, they are slim testimony indeed when set against the overwhelming evidence, both in public and private statements, that radicals in Scotland generally spoke a British language of popular constitutionalism. This language was capacious enough to make room for the extensive use of the Scottish past, but its principal aim was the radical reform of British political institutions and its implications, therefore, were unionist.[14]

The Conclusion addresses two historical questions: what did the mass reform movement actually achieve; and how can historians explain the relative political quiescence of the 1820s during which, while reform projects abounded, there were no mass calls for political reform until the constitutional crisis of 1830–2? The conclusion incorporates an investigation of the Queen Caroline agitation, which should be seen as a period of transition from post-war politics to those of the 1820s and as far more than a 'footnote' to the mass platform agitation of 1819–20. Indeed, one recent account has interpreted it as a 'rehabilitation' of constitutionalist popular politics, which acted as a kind of balm after the violent episodes of 1817–20.[15] Arguably the most important impact was from this realignment of the reform platform, which provided a model for what would happen in 1832 and also rendered radicalism an acknowledged force within the state. Above and beyond this impact, the period after 1815 emerges as one of considerable political innovation that established much of the repertoire of mass political action into Chartism and beyond.

The third and final aim of this book is to examine the long-term political 'usability' of the insurrection of 1820. A lengthy epilogue argues that the 'Radical War' has a complex legacy, which has been more politically significant than the event itself. The historicity of popular politics in the nineteenth and twentieth centuries ensured that 1820 was used by a number of groups in different contexts and maintained a consistent presence in Scottish political culture (in spite of its later casting as 'hidden' or 'forgotten' history). The Epilogue thus shifts the focus to move onto issues of commemoration and the different political uses of the Scottish past. Existing literature on modern commemoration has tended to focus on the activities of states and political elites rather than within what Geoff Eley calls an 'oppositional public sphere'.[16] An exploration of how different understandings of this period have been mobilized provides an ideal lens through which to examine radical and oppositional uses of commemoration during the nineteenth and twentieth centuries and addresses a significant lacuna within modern Scottish history.

1 THE FORGING OF POST-WAR POLITICS

The first step in reconstructing the politics of the early nineteenth century is to acknowledge the sheer impact of the end of the war. The transformative nature of the long French Wars (1793–1815) can scarcely be underestimated. It was an unprecedented conflict in terms of the scale of participation of manpower (and indeed womanpower), something conveyed in part by simple but striking figures. The participation rate of men of military age was one in sixteen for the War of the Austrian Succession (1740–8); one in eight for the American Revolution (1776–83); but rose to one in five or six at the height of the French Wars.[1] The peacetime army of 1789 had stood at 40,000 – by 1814 it had reached 250,000. One of the most remarkable features of the period is the manner in which the British state proved capable of mobilizing manpower at those points at which French invasion seemed credible and imminent. In particular, the extraordinary mobilization of 1803–4, which saw volunteering on a huge scale, vastly increased the numbers of Britons with some military experience. While it avoided recourse to the novel French *levée en masse* the British state nevertheless managed to create the 'armed nation'.[2] As J. E. Cookson has demonstrated, the participation rate of Scots in all of these various forms of martial endeavour was out of proportion to the small size of their country. As well as providing more men, proportionately, for both the officers and the rank and file of the army, they were the United Kingdom's most enthusiastic volunteers.[3]

This mobilization of manpower was matched by the ability to raise resources through borrowing, and especially through taxation. Britain was the only state in Europe which, under the pressure of the French Wars, successfully transformed itself into a 'fiscal state', able efficiently to tax a large proportion of the nation's wealth and combine this with large-scale borrowing. The great innovation here was, of course, the income tax, which provided a source of direct taxation between 1799 and 1816. While there were worrying signs for ministers, in attacks on corruption and 'tax-eaters', that the legitimacy of the public revenue was increasingly being questioned towards the end of the war, it was successfully maintained.[4]

No society could have snapped from a war demanding such a level of participation and commitment and returned to the *status quo ante*. Britain's elite was faced with challenges common to the post-war experiences of other states and, indeed, other periods.[5] An economy geared to war, in which prices for marginal agricultural land had risen, was thrown into competition with Europe and became subject to repeated economic crises. Adding to this profound problem was the fact that thousands of men with military experience were thrust back into a turbulent civilian life and countless more people with exposure to years of military spectacle considered how best to promote and defend their interests in peacetime.[6]

The impact of demobilized soldiers, in particular, was dramatic and formed an oft-stated anxiety of contemporary observers. Between 300,000 and 400,000 ex-servicemen were demobilized in the years following Waterloo. In 1819, according to F. C. Mather, there were 61,397 out-pensioners registered at Chelsea, fully three times the 1792 figure. This continued to rise to a peak of 85,834 in 1828 and then steadily diminished after that point.[7] Military recruitment, of course, had been strong in populous areas and the army had been a destination for many from the manufacturing communities of the north of England and south of Scotland, as well as from increasingly landless and proletarianized rural communities. These men were thrust back into an economy which was contracting as it adjusted to post-war realities, with the predictable outcome of spiralling unemployment.[8] As Mather pointed out, to the ruling elites and nervous middle classes these ex-servicemen represented at one and the same time a threat and an opportunity. The opportunity was slowly but, in the end, successfully grasped and men of military experience were co-opted into the peacetime law and order establishment. This was, however, a gradual and uneven process with marked success only after 1819. Even if, as Cookson has argued, 'military service more obviously produced civil officers and "magistrates' men" than it did insurrectionists', it did create both, and before the 1820s ex-servicemen were a threat to the social order as much as they were a guarantor of it.[9]

This profoundly altered socio-economic landscape was matched by an utterly changed context for the practice of politics. First, new groups emerged with novel claims on the state or with old claims strengthened and given a new validity, while at the same time governments ran the risk of becoming victims of those rhetorical and political strategies they had employed to sustain the war effort. The end of the war entailed a major shift in the political languages open to different groups. Most importantly, war had been the crucial glue that kept patriotism and loyalism in close proximity. The fit had never been exact and patriotism had remained contested throughout the war. Radicals had largely lost this contest by the mid-1790s, but there were attempts to rebuild a reform consensus around a patriotic critique of the war effort after 1805.[10] The language of patriotism was, however, far more open to radical appropriations after 1815.

In existing accounts of popular politics in Scotland, the changed political context after 1815 has been overshadowed by the changed social and economic context as an explanation for the emergence of a radical political movement. A generation of historians has, however, worked with Gareth Stedman-Jones's intellectual case for assigning political causes to political phenomena.[11] This chapter will argue that a similar approach might be used within the Scottish context, and that the reasons for the form and content of the radical movement ought to be sought in the profoundly altered post-war political culture. First, popular radicalism did not emerge in isolation and cannot be removed from its immediate political context and reduced to a function of its social base. It was the result of responses to and interactions with other groups seeking to adjust to post-war problems and opportunities. Especially important were the relationships between developing popular radicalism and three other groups: a ministry, which needed to address problems within the public finances; a Whig and radical opposition in Parliament that sought opportunities to develop a distinctive critique of the Liverpool administration; and an emergent middle class which had been encouraged to believe that property taxes were a wartime expedient. Secondly, this chapter will explore post-war radicalism as in part the product of a continuous presence within Scotland. The idea that radicalism was destroyed by 1799 only to re-emerge after 1816 cannot be taken seriously and this chapter will point to some possible arguments for continuity. Thirdly, it will explore the form and the content of the reform movement itself, placing particular emphasis on the language of those petitions and meetings which sustained it.

I

The idea of radical politics emerging *ex nihilo* after 1815 ignores the dynamic post-war context provided by both a Whig opposition exploring the new opportunities offered by the cessation of hostilities and a middle class which had been politicized by issues of war and taxation. A pronounced Scottish dimension to this revival and reshaping of Whiggism was apparent in the *Edinburgh Review*, the hugely influential publication launched by a group of young, briefless Whig lawyers in 1802. It was established after a decade of considerable challenges for the small but significant number of Whig activists in Scotland, whose very political survival was no small achievement.[12] The party-political complexion of the *Edinburgh Review* was confirmed in 1808, with the 'Don Cevallos' article penned by Francis Jeffrey and Henry Brougham. The article, which praised the Spanish patriots and used events in Spain to call for reforms in Britain, alienated contributors and subscribers of a Tory hue and inspired the establishment of a rival journal, the *Quarterly Review*.[13] From its establishment to the 1830s the *Edinburgh Review* developed a global reputation and played a crucial role in both shaping and reflecting the intellectual culture of Whiggism.[14]

While acknowledging its dynamic role in the revitalization of Whiggery, the *Edinburgh Review* should not be focused on to the exclusion of other dynamic developments within the Scottish press. A key phenomenon in the early nineteenth century was the emergence of a provincial press embracing a range of political positions. In this developing press 'liberal' opinion – which questioned the war and established institutions, called for retrenchment and the abolition of taxation and was at least willing to discuss reform – was marked. While radicals and reformers in the 1790s had been largely dependent on London newspapers and would, to an extent, continue to look to English publications, there was a rash of 'progressive' newspapers established before 1815.[15] For many, such as the *Greenock Advertiser* and the *Dundee Advertiser* (1802), the *Berwick Advertiser* (1808), the *Dumfries and Galloway Courier* (1809) and the *Montrose Review* (1811) this path to reformist credentials was stuttering and uneven, but the emergence of this local press was a marked feature of the early century.[16]

One paper in particular illustrates how space was made for political discussion during the war years and also provides an example of the links between these publications and political action. The *Glasgow Sentinel* (which became the *Glasgow Chronicle* in 1811) was the progeny of reformist political activity during the war. Historians have increasingly taken seriously the revival and reshaping of reformist and radical politics during the Napoleonic wars and a crucial moment has been identified in the scandal that engulfed the Duke of York and his mistress Mrs Clarke in 1809.[17] In the context of a war which was going badly, the revelation that the duke's mistress was corruptly influencing appointments within the army was politically electrifying. There was clear interest in parts of Scotland, but in Glasgow no newspaper would run an advertisement for a public meeting on the subject. The *Sentinel* was established specifically to fill this gap and to act as an 'independent' newspaper. As a result, a meeting was held and the city sent an address with 4,000 names attached to it.[18]

The relationship between Whig politicians and this emerging 'liberal' opinion outside of Parliament was uneasy and episodic. From 1809 links were most formidable whenever the Whigs chose to focus on issues which allowed them to politicize extra-parliamentary discontent and both direct and reflect middle-class concerns. Henry Brougham played a crucial role in developing these strategies of 'petition and debate' and scored a notable success in the campaign to repeal the Orders in Council of 1812. The campaign stimulated petitions from a number of places in Scotland, including Dunfermline, Paisley, Leith and the counties of Lanarkshire and Renfrewshire.[19] The strategy only really came into its own in the changed context after 1815 and over the issue of the property tax. This was the first large-scale reform campaign in post-war Britain, but one which has received scant attention from historians of radicalism.[20] Its focus was Pitt's income tax, introduced in 1799 to address acute problems with the maintenance of public credit. Having been repealed at the Peace in 1802 it was re-established at a higher rate after 1803.

The issue of the income tax provides a key example of how post-war realities had changed the nature of political argument. For ministers the principal challenge was that of funding the national debt. Peace had not meant an end to borrowing and, having renewed the income tax for a year in April 1815, Lord Liverpool's government planned to renew it for a further two years in the 1816 session.[21] While ministers were not keen to contemplate funding the debt without this tax, they were hobbled by the fact that, from its inception, the income tax had been explicitly presented as a wartime expedient. In the deflationary slump that followed the end of the war the tax was unpopular with merchants, traders and landholders and provided a promising issue on which to build an opposition consensus. The Whig leadership was agreed on using the issue and, indeed, Brougham had mooted a campaign on the tax in the immediate aftermath of his success with the Orders in Council.[22]

It was a campaign partly initiated by Whigs and partly generated by local middle classes and had an impressive response from Scotland, which sent forty-seven petitions for repeal in the 1816 session.[23] By March of 1816 the *Dundee, Perth and Cupar Advertiser* could report, 'the whole kingdom is roused – Scotland as much as England'.[24] The importance of the campaign in encouraging the culture of public meetings was marked. Henry Cockburn, another founder of the *Edinburgh Review*, looked back on the Edinburgh meeting to oppose the income tax as a crucial step in the development of a political culture, an 'advance towards the habit of public meeting' and 'a striking indication of the tendency of the public mind'. Such meetings had analogues and precursors in, for example, gatherings in opposition to slavery and the slave trade, but Cockburn identified the income tax meeting as more profoundly important: 'the first respectable meeting held in Edinburgh, within the memory of man, for the avowed purpose of controlling Government on a political matter'.[25]

If the assault on the tax was partly premised on an appeal to economic self-interest and aimed at the politicization of economic distress, there were wider issues at stake which ensured that the campaign played a crucial role in setting the tenor of post-war politics. Central to the concerns of petitioners was the notion that wartime expedients and policies could not be indefinitely and artificially extended into the very different context provided by peace. Nearly all petitions reprimanded and reminded government, as did the inhabitants of Edinburgh and Leith:

> That it was originally proposed merely because the unparalleled War in which the Nation was engaged was said to render it necessary, and the most solemn assurances were given, and often repeated, that it would cease with the Conflict out of which it grew.[26]

This critique of a 'war system' being extended into times of peace was a trope of reform and radical politics. Similarly, the campaign on the income tax helped to establish the language of public economy, behind which lingered a hostility to fundholders, sinecurists and pensioners, whose ranks had been swelled by war and whose incomes had been fixed at a time of high prices. Again, petitions dwelt frequently on this theme of economy and the magistrates and council of Dysart called for the abolition of a large peacetime military establishment and 'the reformation of abuses, for the abolition of sinecure offices, and, in short for the most rigid actual economy, and for every possible retrenchment, in every branch of the Public Expenditure'.[27]

Alongside these concerns with the prolongation of a war system and its effects was a species of anti-statist rhetoric, which opposed the nature of the income tax itself, 'because unequal in its principle, vexatious, inquisitorial and oppressive in its practice; in its immediate consequences hostile to the independence of individuals, and in its remoter tendencies destructive of public liberty'.[28] The main contentions of the movement to repeal the income tax – that to continue it meant an extension of a wartime expedient, which was iniquitous in its implications and bolstered a system of 'old corruption' – would also constitute the main planks of the radical platform after 1816. Even though popular radicals pushed this argument in starker and often more virulent terms and with different objectives and solutions in mind, this still suggests that the movement against the income tax provided an important ideological, rhetorical and strategic model for the radicalism that emerged after 1816.

II

Whig revival and the development of extra-parliamentary politics over questions such as slavery and taxation form part of the context for explaining radicalism. The idea that popular radicalism and reform were 'dead' between the Peace of Amiens and Waterloo, however, is no longer credible. Both metropolitan and regional studies have recovered the wartime politics of radicalism and explained its reorientation.[29] As mentioned above, Scotland certainly took some part in the revived reform campaign that followed in the wake of the scandal surrounding the Duke of York and his mistress, Mrs Clarke.[30] Similarly, the political ramifications of events such as the great weavers' strike of 1812 have yet to be uncovered and studied in the same kind of creative manner as Luddism.[31]

Luddism has generated considerable controversy within English historiography, but it is clear that attempts to compartmentalize protest and to separate the 'economic' from the 'political' are unsustainable. John Dinwiddy steered a fruitful middle line between accounts which assigned little role to politics within industrial protest and those which have tended to discern the seeds of political revolution in Luddism.[32] While we should perhaps remain sceptical of the idea of Luddism as a widespread revolutionary organization, it is not helpful to throw the baby out with the bathwater. 1812 *did* play an important role in giving discontent a political dimension. From 1809, handloom weavers had been combining and making contacts across the United Kingdom. Though William Roach claims they combined 'for no political purpose' there was clear overlap between both the personnel and the objects of reform.[33] Alexander Richmond, one of the weavers' leaders, published a rather egotistical account in the 1820s that recalled how he had to take on the responsibility of organizing petitions from Renfrewshire and Lanarkshire against the Orders in Council. His claims that, despite repeated efforts to import the 'Luddite system' into Scotland, Scottish workers' protests remained legal and constitutional seems on the whole to be true.[34] There is, however, some evidence of direct action, of webs being destroyed or otherwise made redundant in Scotland in 1812, while one of Sidmouth's trusted informants communicated plans for a coordinated insurrection driven by oath-bound and salaried delegates 'all the way from Glasgow to London'.[35] Given their key role in post-war agitation evidence of the politicization of handloom weavers is significant.

Certainly the famous Scottish tour between July and October 1815 of the veteran radical, Major John Cartwright, was not some safari into an apolitical wilderness. He was able to contact and galvanize existing groups of reformers, whose activities lacked national organization. Recent work has rescued Cartwright from the fringes of radical culture. Instead of being seen as a cranky monomaniac, pushing his Anglo-Saxonist ideas *ad nauseam*, he now has a central place. Partly this has meant reappraising his role as a strategist and tactician, but his ideas have also come to seem far more representative of the historicist languages of nineteenth-century politics than they were in the past.[36] For the first decade of the nineteenth century Cartwright focused his efforts on reshaping the radical campaign on the basis of an alliance between moderates and an attempt to pursue a parliamentary reform strategy to achieve a taxpayer franchise.[37] Such schemes failed and the crisis year of 1812 helped to shift his strategy towards one of building provincial support for reform. His key weapons were an extensive correspondence, the rhetorical and physical motif of 'Union' and a series of pioneering political tours: in 1812 to the 'disturbed districts' of the Midlands and the north-west of England; in early 1813 a more extensive tour of England; and in 1815, to the lowlands of Scotland.

Rachel Eckersley has convincingly demonstrated that Cartwright was not the founder of the Hampden Club, with which he has become associated. This group was too exclusive to act as the basis of the Grand National Association, which Cartwright had been discussing since the 1770s. Instead, in the first instance, he proselytized on behalf of the Union for Parliamentary Reform, a more open body which had disappeared by 1813, when the Hampden Club fell in line with Cartwright's agenda.[38] Even before his tour of Scotland, it was clear that Cartwright had been making contacts north of the border as part of this strategy of revitalizing provincial radicalism. We get some tantalizing glimpses of these networks through the visit to Scotland in 1812 of Maurice Margarot, one of those 'martyrs' transported during the 1790s. Margarot chose this moment to throw himself back into politics with two pamphlets: *Thoughts on Revolution* (1812) and *Proposal for a Grand National Jubilee* (1812).[39] Both demonstrated that his radical sentiments remained undimmed. The latter developed the idea of a redistributive jubilee. This was a biblical concept with a key role in the metropolitan ultra-radicalism of the followers of Thomas Spence, and has been characterized as involving a kind of parish-based communism.[40] Margarot's experience of exile in Australia, where radical land schemes might have seemed more applicable, may well have moved him closer to the position held by Spence's supporters. His peregrinations in Scotland in 1812 demonstrate why historians and contemporary elites have experienced difficulty in unravelling the various strands of politics during the war.

Margarot was watched very closely by the authorities – even an overheard conversation on a coach journey from Scotland to Liverpool made it into a report. Thankfully, this close observation allows the historian certain glimpses into those circles in which he moved. First, he could clearly make contact with pre-existing and established networks of radicals. In Paisley, for example, he dined and spent considerable time with Archibald Hastie, a delegate to the 1793 convention in Edinburgh and a leader of local radicalism.[41] In Edinburgh one of his associates was the solicitor, William Moffat, who had been a friend of Thomas Muir.[42] He was able to re-establish and expand on contacts he had made in the 1790s and he reported to his associates in London that: 'He found the good old conventional & Republican Party in that part of the Kingdom to be as determined as ever'.[43]

Secondly, both his activities and list of contacts would seem to suggest that he was connected in some way to Cartwright's attempts to strengthen provincial radicalism. His contacts in Paisley were interrogated by the Sheriff of Renfrewshire, John Connell, and a number of these were found to have corresponded with Cartwright. Connell concluded that 'a Society was on the point of being established in Glasgow similar to that which has been recommended by Cartwright'. Piecing together the evidence he was in no doubt that Margarot was acting as an emissary for these Union Societies.

Finally, and perhaps less plausibly, there was some apprehension on the part of the authorities that Margarot's aim and intention was to stir up disturbances among the lower orders and, in particular to politicize the ongoing dispute between the weavers and their employers. In Paisley, for example, it was worthy of note that Margarot 'drank with about twenty persons, mostly weavers'.[44] It is more likely that Margarot was acting in a similar way to Cartwright: touring Scotland's 'disturbed districts' in an attempt to channel distress into activity for radical political reform rather than industrial violence.

Cartwright's tour was thus significant, but it was premised on pre-existing links and contacts and on networks which, in some cases, stretched back into the 1790s.[45] Cartwright did, in spite of his more egotistical moments, recognize this. In some reflections on his visit to Scotland in a published letter to Francis Burdett he declared: 'The truth is, as those experiences prove, that the soil is abundantly impregnated, but yet, for various causes, Petitions burst not forth spontaneously'.[46] Cartwright clearly had some idea that he was in part preaching to the converted. Events such as the crowd that assembled outside of Forfar to greet him and chair him into town suggest a receptive and informed population.[47] Indeed, Forfar was a case in point. Before Cartwright's arrival it already contained a population interested in and to an extent politicized by the question of the Corn Law passed in the spring of 1815. Its petition attracted attention in the House of Lords when Lauderdale complained that

> violence and intimidation had been used by the mob to procure signatures; that persons riding through the town had been compelled to sign it; that the mob had assailed a clergyman residing in the neighbourhood, with abuse and mud, because he refused to sign on compulsion.[48]

Scotland had sent seventy-nine petitions to Parliament against the measure and there was considerable printed opposition: one broadside, for example, represented it as an immoral oppression of the poor, sure to result in national judgement.[49] Efforts to politicize the issue also attracted considerable comment in the press, and 'political resolutions' adopted at Falkirk alongside the petition were put down to 'artful demagogues' using the Corn Law as a pretext for 'sowing disaffection to the constitution'.[50] The riots across lowland Scotland that constituted a popular response to the legislation brought to government attention those fears of itinerant orators and delegates and mischievous publications that would be a hallmark of the following decade. In Perth, for example, the Duke of Atholl ascribed rioting to the fact that the 'discontented' were in communication with Glasgow, from whence they received 'Inflammatory Papers' printed by the radical, William Lang, one of Cartwright's correspondents.[51]

Cartwright's tours were pioneering attempts to forge a national movement, to politicize and organize widespread but diffuse dissent, a model that would be exploited by later radicals, Chartists and others.[52] Armed with a stack of circular letters from the Hampden Club Committee and a suggested printed form for a petition, he and his servant undertook a gruelling tour of Scotland. If part of his intention was to make converts (an aim which stimulated him to offer lectures on the English constitution later in his tour) his tours are best conceived of as early attempts to overcome the limitations of localism in political campaigns.[53] First and foremost his aim was to bring the 'SUNSHINE OF ENCOURAGEMENT' to bear. In Cartwright's analysis simply 'by making known the existence of a Society of Noblemen and Gentlemen, having for its object the recovery of our Public Liberties' he would be doing great service to the cause in the north of England and Scotland.[54] It was another of his great achievements to make the language of 'Union' axiomatic within radical discourse and this was a theme of his tour as he explicitly encouraged reformers to 'become NATIONAL beyond all that is recorded in history'.[55]

The ultimate end of encouragement and the means of achieving a national movement lay in fundamentally altering people's perceptions of petitioning; no longer the act of sycophants or beggars, it should be mobilized and wielded as 'a constitutional *weapon*' and Cartwright's development of printed petition forms was intended to achieve precisely this end.[56] He was clearly encouraged in this goal by the resurgence of mass petitioning towards the end of the wars. Especially he drew explicit comparisons with the successful mass petitioning against the slave trade and challenged his audience to petition 'to redeem from slavery the white men of *England*, of *Scotland*, of *Wales* and *Ireland*' and end the 'HOME SLAVE TRADE'.[57]

If, in the long term, it was a pioneering event of political agitation, we can rightly ask how much impact Cartwright's tour had in Scotland. This is especially difficult to judge in the light of an almost overwhelmingly hostile or ambivalent press which, according to Cockburn, simply did not report on Cartwright's activities.[58] He was certainly received enthusiastically in many places, and while he himself rated his lecture in 'the political Gomorrah of our country' a resounding success, we should not underestimate the strength of loyalism in communities like Edinburgh: 'the strong hold of a court influence and an unconstitutional tyranny not conceivable by a mere English mind'.[59] He did attract some attention in the press with his well-attended lecture (the owner of the room used was subsequently persecuted) and his subsequent defence of his conduct in the *Glasgow Chronicle*, the *Caledonian Mercury* and the *Dundee, Perth and Cupar Advertiser* against an attack on him in the ministerial *Edinburgh Correspondent*.[60]

The slim testimony we have suggests that Cartwright was successful in some of his objectives. 'AN OLD FRIEND OF REFORM' in Edinburgh wrote to William Cobbett's *Political Register* and, while sceptical about the potential of a petition from Edinburgh, was still convinced that Cartwright's visit had done inestimable good:

> it maintains in the minds of men a kind of connection of common chain, by which the friends of liberty know each other more intimately, are led to a bolder and firmer hope of the fulfillment of their wishes, and the drooping of the benevolent mind, in the present state of the world, is in some degree animated to a new exertion.[61]

This was, of course, precisely Cartwright's aim.

There were more tangible results in the establishment of reform societies and the raising of petitions. Edinburgh held a reform meeting in the immediate aftermath of Cartwright's visit and its composition and conduct are revealing of the nature of the radicalism of this period. The account comes to us courtesy of an extraordinary and rambling text by John Borthwick Gilchrist, an expert in Oriental languages, who had spent much of his life in India and left Edinburgh in 1816 accusing local Tories of political persecution.[62] According to Gilchrist his book had to be taken to Glasgow to be printed by William Lang, the Scottish printer of the Hampden Club circulars, because none of the servile Edinburgh printers would touch it.[63]

The text gives a good, if idiosyncratic, demonstration of radical political development. Gilchrist rode a variety of hobby horses which demonstrated how radical principles were deployed in support of a number of local issues before Cartwright's visit. These included the projected Union canal, proposed reforms to the Court of Session and the deficiencies of municipal government. The first of these issues revolved around the proposed canal to link Edinburgh to the coalfields of the west of Scotland. It sparked vigorous debate, with Gilchrist taking the popular side, which interpreted magisterial resistance to the project as proof that they were in the pockets of the Midlothian coal proprietors, who were seeking to maintain high prices. The Union canal debate, which saw a mob stone the Lord Provost's house in 1814 and accusations that the canal's supporters were 'Jacobins', provides a prime example of how local issues acted as vehicles for wider political questions.[64]

The text also offers an account of a meeting in favour of parliamentary reform held on 3 October 1815, which had been advertised by handbill. The other speaker alongside Gilchrist was Captain William Johnston, yet another veteran from the 1790s and the proprietor of the *Edinburgh Gazetteer*, which had publicized the activities of the radical conventions.[65] This meeting and petitioning followed similar activity in Glasgow, where a meeting had been chaired by one of those correspondents of Cartwright who had attracted the attention of the authorities in 1812, the merchant Adam Ferrie. The account of the Edinburgh meeting gives some insight into the developing reform agenda and some of its peculiarities in the Scottish context. A long string of thirty resolutions followed the agenda laid down by the Hampden Club. The personnel at the meeting incorporated many existing activists and, as elsewhere, there was clear evidence that petitioning campaigns for other objects and, in particular, the abolition of the slave trade, had helped to draw them to the question of parliamentary reform: 'XIX. – That seeing the abolition of the *Slave-trade* has, after a *persevering struggle*, become almost universal *abroad*, surely equal pains will soon be taken to eradicate every degrading *vestige of slavery at home*'.[66] So too there was a clear sense that the sheer weight and repeated application of petitions following the inspiration provided by Cartwright would achieve reformist goals.[67]

While Gilchrist and the meeting lauded Cartwright's agenda and the content of his lectures on the English constitution, there were also indications of differences in the Scottish approach to political reform. Frequent references were made to the peculiarities of the Scottish political system, which should have received constitutional liberties such as annual parliaments as part of the Union with England.[68] This theme ran throughout Gilchrist's writings as well as Johnston's speech. Johnston repeated a quip of Horne Tooke in response to a question from someone facing a state trial in Scotland as to any preparations he might make: 'Leave Scotland as soon as you can, and pity all those poor devils who cannot follow your example'. Running through both men's speeches was the idea of Scotland as a place standing most acutely in need of reform, 'where the feudal system has left, to this day, very legible impressions against every thing in the shape of emancipation from vassalage and reformation of its abuses'.[69] There was clearly no problem in echoing Cartwright's historicist ideas of political rights and appealing to an English history of liberty to argue for reform in Scotland. There was, however, some attempt by Gilchrist to encourage Scots to lay claim to the shared nature of at least part of this common libertarian heritage: he suggested, for example, that Scottish reformers should establish 'Fletcher' rather than 'Hampden' clubs, while earlier George Kinloch had discussed both the idea of 'Fletcher' and 'Wallace' clubs in Scotland.[70]

III

This was the dynamic political context from which a reform movement emerged. The role of Cartwright's tour in galvanizing existing networks of reformers was marked and successful earlier political mobilizations based on meetings and petitions provided fertile models for political action. Indeed, the 'petition, petition, petition' exhortations of Cartwright had, in effect, already underpinned movements to abolish the slave trade in Europe and to repeal the property tax.

This latter campaign, in particular, had a role in widely disseminating a political critique and provided strategies for agitation. When economic distress began to be more acutely felt in 1816, there were networks of reformers prepared to explain it in political terms and to mobilize on the basis of a coherent critique of existing institutions.

Over the spring and summer of 1816 there was, however, plentiful evidence of other possible responses to widespread and increasing levels of distress. In April 1816 (in an uncanny precursor of events four years later) an anxious sheriff wrote to the Lord Advocate about the worrying state of the lower orders in Glasgow. Numerous handwritten 'inflammatory addresses' had been posted on street corners and he had been obliged to increase the military force in the city in anticipation of trouble. He enclosed a copy of one of these handbills, which addressed the weavers and asked them to look to the villas of their employers, 'look on their luxuriant tables – their concealed revels – their gluttonies – their rosy cheeks and their wallowings in wine!' and contrast this with their own sorry lot. It accused employers of having 'subverted the Moral Law' and concluded that 'Steel is the only argument left you'. Acute distress could clearly be politicized in ways outside of the dominant discourse of constitutionalism. Possibly with the failure of efforts to repeal or defeat the Corn Bill in mind, the handbill proclaimed: 'Private assassination will [*sic*] when public remonstrances fail'. The handbill sought to convince readers that the supposed constitutional remedy of petition and appeal had already failed leaving only violence as the *ultimo ratio*. To underline the point the address was signed by 'John Dirk, Secretary'.[71]

More apparent was rioting over food supply and over relief measures. Tensions in Glasgow boiled over in the summer, when rioters destroyed a soup kitchen, erected by subscription in the Calton suburb for the relief of the distressed weavers. It seems likely that the riot was a violent but reasoned response to the use of subscription money in this way and an expression of long-held views on the acceptance of charity. When weavers had persistently mobilized in pursuit of a living wage to prevent downward pressures on wages or the artificially high price of bread, the offensive connotations of a charity soup kitchen were simply too much and they were attacked elsewhere as well. In Glasgow the crowd had apparently attempted afterwards to destroy some cotton works, but had been prevented. This itinerary suggests a sophisticated critique: charity dole-outs were not the answer to economic distress. Other signs of considerable concern to those in authority became apparent in August. Those soldiers who had accosted four of the rioters were pelted with bricks and then they fired into a crowd, seriously injuring at least two of its members. Hence, there was considerable concern about growing tensions between soldiers and citizens in Glasgow.[72]

Such events were not restricted to Glasgow, though they were most prevalent in those weaving and textile communities where distress was being most keenly felt. In June of 1816 there was a violent meal mob in Ayr and an attack on a toll bar, both of which went down in the annals of local history.[73] After a bad harvest and into the winter of 1816 such events became more frequent and more serious. Anxious Lord Provosts in Perth and Aberdeen asked for augmented military forces on the basis of worrying signs among their populations. Dundee witnessed the most serious rioting in December, when a large crowd of some 500 attacked the houses of several corn merchants and meal sellers 'committing such depredations and with such a spirit as defied any force of the civil power'.[74]

Finally there was the option of attempting by repeated representations to convince elites of the scale of the distress, while beseeching them to act. An affecting letter in the Home Office correspondence from a weaver in Perth to the Home Secretary, Lord Sidmouth was one such attempt. Its author reminded Sidmouth that the weavers had already made attempts to remedy their own situation by petitioning against the Corn Law and against the exportation of cotton twist, but were now forced to seek any relief possible. In what would become one of the major appeals of radicals the author also reminded the minister of the sacrifices of many soldiers who had returned to stare poverty in the face.[75] This strategy was taken further in an address, which aimed to inspire subscriptions for the relief of the weavers and demonstrated how the post-war context made a number of different appeals possible. One lay in expanding the appeal to charity made by the letter writer:

> who were the individuals that carried the name of Caledonia beyond everything hitherto known. I am confident that an impartial enquirer will discover that the major part of our army, who have been so prodigal of their blood in their country's cause were Weavers.[76]

The great achievement of reformers at meetings, in speeches and in the press was to explain this increasing and widespread distress in political terms. To an extent the ground had been laid for this explanation by those petitions and meetings against the property tax and the demonstrations against the Corn Law. From the middle of 1816 meetings in and petitions from across Scotland began to forward a remarkably consistent critique of government. This drew on existing influences and political languages, but the critique undoubtedly reached and helped to politicize a wider audience with the 'revolution in journalism' wrought by William Cobbett's cheap, mass circulation version of his *Political Register*.[77] From November 1816, this cheap pamphlet version of his leading article circulated in large numbers across Scotland, much to the consternation of those in positions of authority. On noting a dispatch of 50,000 copies of the first number, the Lord Provost and the Town Clerk of Glasgow were horrified at the anticipated baneful influence of such publications, but were bound by law not to interfere with its distribution.[78] Cobbett's intentions in that first address 'To the Journeymen and Labourers of England, Scotland and Ireland' were simple and elegant. First, he aimed to expound a critique of the causes of economic and social distress; secondly, he aimed to highlight the effective remedy for this as lying in parliamentary reform, while demonstrating the unsuitability of other proposed remedies; and thirdly, he aimed both to publicize and be a crucial part of the means of achieving that remedy: a unified and national movement of meetings and petitions.[79]

In truth Cobbett's publication was one of a number which provided national networks of communication for the meetings and petitions, which ultimately drew their strength from local activism. The scale of Cobbett's endeavour and the audience to which his cheap *Register* addressed itself were dramatic innovations. The interaction between a national and largely London-oriented press and local meetings and petitions helps to explain some of the key features of the reform movement. The remarkable consistency of the arguments used and the messages circulated at meetings and in the seventy-six petitions presented to Parliament from Scotland in the 1817 session were marked.[80] Print as a means of forging a national movement was integral to petitioning. This relationship was most clear in the deliberate but unsuccessful attempts from 1813 onwards to establish the viability of printed petitions as a means of delivering a uniform reform message. The sense of the House of Commons remained as it had been when the question had been tried in 1793 – that printed petitions were illegitimate and the language of Cartwright's petition was deemed offensive.[81]

Nevertheless, other forms of print helped to create a coherent and consistent reform critique. Nearly all meetings and all petitions began with descriptions of economic distress, which gave some insight into the range of social perceptions that underpinned political argument. Frequently the appeal was to the middle and lower classes in aggregate, equally victims of the post-war crisis.[82] Others expressed particular concern that the political and social impact of economic distress was a dangerous levelling: 'the middle class, that main piller [sic] in the social edifice, fast disappearing and falling into the labouring class'.[83] Few speakers or petitions expressed an explicitly working-class-centred vision of the social order, although there were rare statements agreeing with Cobbett's resounding declaration that 'the real strength and all the resources of a country ever have sprung and ever must spring, from the *labour* of its people'.[84] The social vision communicated was largely that of an inclusive populist appeal. Indeed, even though Cobbett had addressed himself to 'the Journeymen and Labourers', he urged them not to pin blame on petty capitalists, on shopkeepers or farmers, whose interests were, in truth, the same as their own. An aspiring mass movement had to appeal to a wide social range – either to the 'nation' as a whole or to the 'middle and lower classes' or the 'agricultural, commercial and manufacturing interests' – to render its claims to represent public opinion plausible.[85]

This sense of a national movement was partly maintained by a common reference point found in the blanket rejection of ministerial explanations for the prevailing distress. In the address debate at the opening of the 1816 parliamentary session both Nicholas Vansittart, the Chancellor of the Exchequer, and Lord Castlereagh, the Foreign Secretary, had attributed the growing distress to the transition from a wartime to a peacetime economy.[86] This explanation was more notoriously forwarded during the summer in the first resolution of a meeting of the Association for the Relief of the Manufacturing and Labouring Poor. This body met to raise subscriptions for relief and included among its number prominent members of the royal family, senior clergy including the archbishop of Canterbury, and ministers and MPs. This meeting was widely reported, largely for the hostile response which met the Duke of York's attempt to move the first resolution:

> That a transition from a state of extensive war to a system of peace, has occasioned a stagnation of employment and a revulsion of trade, deeply affecting the situation of many parts of the community, and producing many instances of local distress.

Lord Cochrane's response, in moving an amendment, encapsulated the radical movement's angry rejection of this analysis: 'the enormous load of National Debt, together with the high Military Establishment, and the profuse expenditure of the Public Money, are the real causes of the present general distress'.[87] This intervention was widely supported and, for example, a pamphlet published in Paisley satirized the meeting of the great and good and lauded Cochrane.[88] More telling evidence of the impact of this meeting in inspiring the reform movement can be found in the near universal repudiation of the analysis of the first resolution in meetings, petitions and the press. Hundreds of references explicitly rejected that the distress could be explained as the fruit of the 'swift transition from war to peace'.[89] In this way the resolution had a similar impact in providing a national anchor for a reform movement to the Duke of Wellington's notorious statement flatly denying there was any appetite for reform in 1830.[90]

In place of this explanation reformers pushed one which explained distress not as the inevitable result of the end of war, but as a direct consequence of war and of the 'system' it had generated and fostered, which had conspired to impose an oppressive and suffocating burden of taxation. In the first instance, of course, there was the colossal national debt, the repayment of which necessitated high taxation and placed a parasitic class of fundholders in direct opposition to the people's interests. The rhetorical strategy of pitting 'the people' against this narrow faction was furthered by frequent references to 'a Debt, unjustly called National'. This burden was further compounded by 'the extravagant sums of Public Money lavished away in unmerited Pensions, Salaries, and Sinecures'.[91]

One speaker at Paisley dramatized this notion with a parody of Robert Blair's poem, 'The Grave':

> — O great tax-eaters!
> Whose every date is carnival, not sated yet!
> Unheard of epicures!
> The veriest gluttons do not always cram;
> Some abstinence is sought to edge the appetite
> But they seek none; and, like the grave, can never have enough.[92]

The final cause of misery was found in the unnecessary maintenance of a large military establishment during peacetime, sometimes vilified as the civic humanist bugbear of 'supporting an immense Standing Army in time of profound Peace', further draining resources from the productive part of the nation.[93]

If this idea of a suffocating load of taxation as an explanation for domestic distress was disarmingly straightforward, something less frequently pointed out is that it was joined by a widespread critique, which featured in meetings and petitions, of government foreign policy. Cobbett had highlighted in his opening salvo that the so-called war for liberty had only resulted in the restoration of the Bourbon monarchy at the point of a bayonet and the re-establishment of other Catholic tyrannies, including the Inquisition. Such disquiet was not restricted to radicals. In January 1816, for example, a public meeting had been held in the Trades Hall in Glasgow, which protested against the persecution of Protestants in France under the restored monarchy and similar persecution elsewhere in Europe.[94] Nevertheless, hostility to the unjust causes and unsavoury consequences of the war were developed most deeply within the reform movement and formed a constant refrain in speeches and petitions. The Kilmarnock petition gives some idea of the virulence with which such sentiments were communicated:

> His Majesty's Ministers publicly told us, that it was for religion and social order, the status quo ante bellum, indemnification for the past, and security for the future ... the Petitioners would ask these Ministers, if to restore the Pope to all his former splendour, and the Inquisition to all its racks and fiery horrors, be Religion? do they call it Religion, their having forced three bigoted Catholic Princes back upon the people who deposed them, with all the mummeries of Popery, or palliating with palpable untruths the massacres at *Nismes* [sic] and the chains and dungeons which assailed the *Spanish* Patriots? ... can social order, or the social relations, subsist betwixt the arbitrary Princes whom we have forcibly restored, and their unwilling subjects?[95]

Such sentiments were widespread and indicative of a movement the attentions of which were not solely focused on domestic distress, but incorporated a coherent critique of foreign policy. This held that the ministry's course not only deepened distress at home but contravened both the universalist 'liberties of mankind' as well as those more particularist 'principles which placed the illustrious House of *Hanover* on the British throne'.[96] Given the apparent centrality of religious and ecclesiological issues to the languages of popular politics in Scotland and elsewhere, this critique of foreign policy contributed to the powerful appeal of radicalism.[97]

The solutions to this compound crisis were correspondingly straightforward: retrenchment and reform. All meetings and petitions identified the first as crucial. The military establishment, salaries, pensions and sinecures all had to be stripped back immediately to ease public burdens. To make this possible, however, petitioners argued that more a fundamental remodelling of the relationship between people and Parliament was required. This, according to reformers, needed to be rendered more effective in a case where, according to the Hampden Club's suggested petition distributed by the Glasgow printer William Lang, the House of Commons 'doth not, in any constitutional or rational sense, represent the nation'.[98] Many petitions from Scotland cited both this passage and the example of the Corn Law of 1815 as a proof of the contempt of Parliament for the opinion of those people it nominally represented.[99]

In suggesting *how* this revised relationship might be achieved there was considerable diversity. The common umbrella solution was 'reform' but there was less agreement as to what this meant. Some petitions, notably those emanating from local elites of town councils, recommended reform and left it to ministers to decide how best this might be achieved.[100] Some of these more moderate recommendations were accompanied with explicit rejections of 'wild and impracticable notions of annual parliaments and universal suffrage'.[101] Perhaps the most prescriptive solutions came from places whose resolutions and petitions had been motivated by and were closely modelled on the Hampden Club's recommended solution, which had been reiterated by Cobbett: annual parliaments and a franchise co-extensive with the payment of direct taxation.

This linking of representation to taxation was a key feature of the post-war debate and while relatively few of the meetings advocated universal suffrage, those that did based their argument less on an idea of universalist rights than on the link between taxation and representation.[102] The Inhabitants of Elderslie, for example, coupled this idea of contribution in terms of taxation to the patriotic idea of military service and asked that 'every man, not disqualified by crime or insanity, arrived at the age of twenty-one years, should possess a vote for his Representative in Parliament, for every man being liable to be taxed to support the State, and to be called upon to arm in its defence, are surely sufficient proofs that he has a right to choose the Representative who is to vote away his money and demand his services'.[103] On the question of representation, in the interests of unanimity many recommended simply that the people be 'more freely, fairly, and equally' represented in Parliament and eschewed a detailed suggestion of a franchise. There was far more unanimity, in fact, on the length of parliaments. While a few petitions were ambiguous and simply called for shorter parliaments or for at least triennial ones, the vast majority of petitions called for annual parliaments.

The analysis of the petitions and meetings of 1816–17 does suggest a couple of distinctive features of the reform movement in Scotland. First and foremost there was some recognition that the politics of Scotland were different. Since the 1790s a critique of Scottish institutions, which saw them as more corrupt and less representative even than their flawed English counterparts, had been developed as the bedrock of Scottish radicalism.[104] This came across in petitions which suggested that reform was urgently required in Scotland and urged the Commons to:

> take into their immediate consideration the state of the representation generally, and more particularly that of *Scotland*, where the elective franchise is confined to the self-elected Councils of Royal Burghs, and to a small number of landed proprietors, and feudal superiors, many of them without landed property in the Counties.[105]

These sentiments were often echoed by those Whig and radical MPs who presented petitions, and the tone was set by Lord Archibald Hamilton who presented petitions from Kirkintilloch and Rutherglen at the very start of the session: 'Whatever opinion prevailed in England on the subject of an alteration in its representation, there could, he presumed, be none as to the imperative necessity of such a change in the representation of Scotland, in a rational and practical sense'.[106] Another area of distinctiveness could be found in some of the petitions from town councils, which pushed burgh reform as a particularly urgent species of parliamentary reform, a question which would be developed in earnest after 1817.[107]

Finally, there was some distinctiveness in the languages reformers used in pursuing their goals in Scotland. As they had done in the 1790s, Scots appealed to their own history for exemplars of the struggle for civil and religious liberty. At one of the most famous meetings, that at Thrushgrove near Glasgow, this Scottish pantheon was fully present. One speaker urged the audience 'let us not forget that the glorious Patriot William Wallace, bled and conquered on this very ground. The descendants of Wallace, Bruce, Buchanan, Knox, Belhaven, and Fletcher still inhabit our dear native country'. He was followed by a speaker who invoked the later Covenanters as the only absentees from this patriotic roll-call: 'You are this day met in the open fields, and not far from the tombs of the Martyrs, who in former times lost their lives for the cause of civil and religious liberty'.[108] As it had been in the 1790s and would be in the 1830s, these Scottish events and figures were written into an essentially English history of liberty and appeared, uncomplicatedly, alongside heroes of this narrative, such as Hampden and Sidney. The anonymous author of *Thaumaturgus*, for example, drew a lengthy comparison between the meeting at Thrushgrove and the meeting of Barons at Runnymede to obtain the Magna Carta.[109]

Such a British approach was indispensable as reformers attempted to create through resolution, press and petitions a national movement around the critique outlined above. There were, of course, some references to specifically Scottish national pride, but far more frequent were demonstrations of a consciousness of acting alongside 'the great body of the people throughout the United Empire' and of speaking in 'the voice of the British nation'.[110] The essential glue in this aspiration to be a national movement was an appeal to the language of patriotism. Space and opportunity for this had been provided by the cessation of the war. While the 1790s had allowed reformers to be smeared as anti-British Jacobins, the plausibility of this demonization was much reduced after 1815. Reformers were able to lay claim to the high ground of patriotism, to paint a narrow clique of sinecurists, pensioners, fundholders and ministers, whose tentacles reached down to corrupt civil life, as the anti-national force. In supporting the Bourbon restoration and other uncomfortable Catholic bedfellows it was they, not radicals, whose patriotic credentials were suspect.

The idea that the reformers were a national movement was rendered more plausible by the genuinely national reach of the petitioning movement. While there were, of course, concentrations of petitions from the dense network of communities in the west and few from the more rural areas in the Highlands, the petitions did come from across Scotland. This was strengthened by the social inclusiveness of a movement which could plausibly claim to represent all interests: manufacturing, commercial and agricultural; middle and working classes; householders, heritors, burgesses and inhabitants; even provosts and magistrates. This expansive social and geographical reach, coupled with the fact that there was little or no attempt to secure loyal or anti-reform addresses, which might have contested reformers' claims to represent public opinion, contributed to the strength of the movement.

The appeal to patriotism was rendered even more effective by repeated references to the national sacrifices involved in waging this unjust war. Again, the theme was broached by Cobbett in his initial address, when he pointed out that 'the victories were obtained by *you* and your fathers and brothers and sons' and was developed further within the radical movement.[111] The fillip that the French Revolutionary and Napoleonic Wars had given to an idea of military Scottishness was susceptible to a number of political borrowings and did not remain the sole property of any one political group. Radicals mobilized it to back their own claims to patriotism and claims such as that from Glasgow that 'thousands of the Petitioners have carried arms, and fought and bled for what was called the cause of the Country' were common.[112] The same language was apparent in an emotive appeal made at the Greenock meeting:

> England is in a grand effort to maintain her independence, and shall Caledonia cringe behind? No! Let them point to the flower of the army, and recall to memory their feats at the fields of Alexandria, Corunna, Barossa, Vittoria, and at the immortal conflict of Waterloo. Are the Caledonians (after indenting the brightest gem in the British Crown, by struggles both by land and sea,) to undergo the calumny of wretchedness? Must the mother, whose son died covered with wounds, maintaining what is falsely called 'the cause of his country,' must she too, trembling with cold and hunger, die while such women as Mrs Fox, Lady Grenville, Miss Hann, and old Mother Hann, are receiving what would relieve all the distressed matrons in the nation.[113]

For this claim to patriotism to remain plausible and powerful, two further requirements were needed: that the radicals achieve unanimity and so defuse charges of factionalism and that they retain the ability to argue that they were operating within the boundaries of the constitution. Unanimity was the goal of all leading radicals and a *leitmotif* of the movement. The Hampden Club's exhortation in its circular was reiterated by Cartwright and Cobbett and at countless meetings: 'UNANIMITY is the ONE THING NEEDFUL. Wanting this, the People of course fail; while a Nation that is of ONE MIND assuredly succeeds'.[114] As Kevin Gilmartin has shown, this theme of union highlighted some tensions within popular radicalism. While their publications shared the common goal of creating and sustaining this unanimity, the egos and personality clashes of leading radicals did often militate against unity. The desire to maintain a unified front was so great that meetings themselves became means to the end of generating and maintaining unanimity across a wide range of local circumstances rather than democratic and deliberative events.[115] On the whole, however, this crucial strategy of presenting a unified message was successfully pursued.

Finally, popular constitutionalism – that range of understandings of those rights and activities protected and sanctioned by the British constitution, nourished by the blood of ancestors and underlined by a history of British liberty – was the principle guide to radical language and action.[116] It entailed radicals dissociating themselves from anything that could be regarded as unconstitutional action. Just as reformers during the 1790s had tried to join loyalist societies, such as the Goldsmiths' Hall Association, and had eschewed the actions of the mob, resolutions, petitions and the medium of print were used to trumpet reformers' attachment to the constitution after 1815. The radicals of Greenock, for example, met in December 1816 and repudiated two recent examples of what they vilified as unconstitutional politics – the Spa Fields riot in London and a meal mob in Dundee:

we contemplate with horror the late atrocious proceedings and depredations of a misguided population at London and Dundee; and we do consider it individually, as our imperative duty, to assist the civil power, if called to do so, in suppressing mobs or unlawful assemblies of every description.[117]

It was in this constitutionalist language and its associated claims to patriotism that the real strengths of the popular movement lay. By arguing explicitly for the restoration of rights and following Cartwright and Burdett rather than Paine in presenting annual parliaments and a wider franchise as a constitutional inheritance rather than a claim to universal natural rights, radicals stuck to powerful rhetorical ground and gave meaning to their claim that they supported 'no revolutionary principles'. Appealing to a shared national past and reminding legislators that the seventh article of the Act of Settlement excluded placemen and pensioners from Parliament, as did petitioners at Johnstone and Thrushgrove, was less divisive than basing such claims on ideas of natural rights (though radicals at meetings often did both).[118] If popular constitutionalism afforded reformers a number of powerful things to say, James Epstein has also pointed to the equally powerful range of things it allowed radicals to *do*. Public meetings and petitions, while the limits of these were never entirely settled, were used self-consciously as the constitutional 'weapons' of Cartwright's description.

IV

The discourse of popular constitutionalism entailed an ongoing argument over the limits of constitutional speech and action. It was in reaching and breaching these limits that lay the movement's greatest weakness. Part of the context for events across the winter in Scotland was the important series of meetings held at Spa Fields in London on 15 November, 2 and 9 December 1816. These meetings demonstrated the tensions between what have largely been interpreted as two competing radical analyses. First, Henry Hunt's developing mass platform which played on ambiguities in the constitution but determined, nevertheless, to remain within its limits.[119] Secondly, the partly-submerged currents demanding insurrection and physical force as the only means of addressing political and economic problems, most commonly identified with 'Spencean' radicalism.[120]

In reality, it is not easy to draw any kind of rigid physical versus moral force dichotomy for the radicalism of this period. Radicals such as the Spenceans were certainly advocates of the idea of an insurrectionary strike emanating from London, but Hunt's self-consciously constitutional language and actions constituted a threat as much as they did a promise of orderly protest. Both languages had, in fact, an anchor in the important idea of petitioning within British political culture. The first Spa Fields meeting had deputed Hunt to present a petition to the Prince Regent and the second meeting, which was the most eventful, was called to receive his answer. The anger and outrage, which spilled over into raids on some gun shops, was focused on the breaking down of this relationship between a petitioning people and their sovereign. In the words of Dr Watson, a leader of the Spenceans, it was this rupture that provided the rallying call for insurrection:

> I have to inform you, however, that the Prince Regent has resolved to give no answer – it is useless, therefore, for us to pursue that course. We are now called on, then, to see whether the people of England will suffer themselves to be treated with contempt.[121]

Such tensions were not restricted to London, and across the reform movement, the key question in the winter of 1816 to 1817 was what course was open to reformers in the event that the constitutional weapon of petitioning failed to hit its mark. Just as the meetings at Spa Fields took place in the context of spiralling economic distress, especially among the silk weavers of Spitalfields, such discussions in Scotland intersected with the acute distress of the handloom weavers of Glasgow and its neighbourhood. By December, such demonstrations were taking an ominous form. In the eastern suburbs, a meeting of some seven or eight hundred petitioned the minister of the barony parish and demanded immediate and permanent relief and matured plans to approach other members of the civic elite and 'according to some of our accounts, said that if they did not get Bread, they would have blood'.[122] While a successful subscription was launched in response for the relief of the distressed, it did little to soften the sense that relationships at parish, city and national levels were breaking down.[123]

One response was, of course, to continue to petition and to remonstrate in the expectation that an answer would come. Another was to conclude that these relationships *were* fundamentally broken and to represent violence as the only means of effecting political change. Radicals did still try to fit such recommendations into the framework of constitutional language. They could, of course, use Britain's libertarian history to highlight previous efforts at violence, when the relationship between prince and people had failed. Conveying a spy's report on a radical meeting in Kilbarchan in December, the sheriff substitute for Renfrewshire highlighted the veneration of Bonaparte as an enemy to tyranny and reported:

> another thing was plainly enough stated viz that force was the means to which the people had to trust in case of their petitions being refused; and that by so doing they would imitate the conduct of their ancestors, and discharge their duty to posterity, however dreadful the consequences.[124]

Similarly, a speaker at a meeting in Kilmarnock, who would find himself on trial for sedition the following year, framed his remarks with the idea that a just prince *must* receive and answer the meeting's petition: 'But, should he be so infatuated as to turn a deaf ear to their just petition, he has forfeited their allegiance'.[125]

It is in this context of increasingly exasperated and desperate calls for relief and an increasingly radicalized constitutionalism pushing the need to move beyond petitioning that we need to locate the treasonable conspiracies in and around Glasgow. The authorities in Scotland had some vague indication of treasonable activities around the beginning of December, when Andrew McKay, the head constable of Linlithgow, learned of the manufacture of weapons in Glasgow and was encouraged by the Lord Advocate and the Home Secretary to procure further information.[126] From December onwards, different sources of authority – the Lord Advocate, the Glasgow magistrates in consultation with the MP for the city, Kirkman Finlay, and the sheriff-depute for Lanarkshire – attempted to test and put flesh on McKay's skeletal account of a treasonable conspiracy. Three principal sources of information were used: first, Captain Brown of the Edinburgh police toured Glasgow with one McKenna who he made efforts 'to disguise as a reformer'; secondly, Alexander Richmond, who had been a leader of the weavers during 1812 and 1813 and was outlawed for his involvement, but had become a confidante of Kirkman Finlay, used his contacts to ascertain the shape and nature of the radical underground; and thirdly, the Sheriff of Lanarkshire, Robert Hamilton, recruited his own man, George Biggar, who successfully infiltrated the Central Committee of the organization and sent textured reports and detailed information.[127]

Efforts to untangle this twisted intelligence network have met with considerable success and have demonstrated the definite existence of a radical underground.[128] Richmond's subsequent account placed its genesis in the Calton district of Glasgow in the immediate aftermath of Thrushgrove. It was, in his reckoning, the brainchild of men who were already convinced that petitioning would not work.[129] Some reports do indeed confirm that it was inspired partly by a radicalized constitutionalism among those who had attended the mass meeting at Thrushgrove and had determined that petitioning would be ineffectual. Richmond's information continued to stress that the radicals remained focused on the upcoming parliamentary session and on the outcome of petitions.[130] It was also partly a response to distress or rather to perceptions of how that distress was being managed by those in authority. The conspiracy emanated from those areas which were presenting an increasingly intransigent case for relief to the local authorities. One of the men arrested at the end of February traced the links between the efforts to obtain relief and insurrectionary plotting.[131]

It was its roots in these communities that gave the conspiracy its character and whatever strength it can be said to have enjoyed. The secret organization was particularly associated with the weavers, who were suffering the worst of the economic dislocation, and reports highlighted beaming houses as the venues at which political information was communicated.[132] In its own way, however, the conspiracy was socially inclusive and its members reflected the social composition of the communities from which they came. Of the thirty-two men questioned over the events the majority was, indeed, composed of weavers or those involved in weaving. Also present, however, were cotton spinners, teachers, a mechanic and a grocer.[133] It prospered in a culture where the language and rituals of masonry, large numbers of men with military training, and a significant Irish community with both memories and personnel from the insurrection of 1798 were all present.[134]

What is clear is the very limited nature of the organization; it existed, but its plans were not developed and there is little evidence that it had made much headway in manufacturing arms or in firming up contacts with radicals in England or Ireland. There was fitful intelligence relating to both activities but by early February the Scots had apparently given up on sending delegates south owing to lack of funds, though the organization had attempted to expand to include communities in Dundee and Perth.[135] Overall, the evidence affords an insight into the key weakness of insurrectionary movements in this period: though strong at their community bases, it was extremely difficult and hazardous to make contacts and networks beyond these.

Attempts to caricature the events as the product of *agents provocateurs* (in this case, Richmond) or as the figment of the authorities' imagination certainly do not fit the available evidence.[136] The authorities were concerned to find out the precise extent of the conspiracy and were not quick to jump to alarmist conclusions. Richmond's evidence was deemed untrustworthy unless it could be independently corroborated: his claim in early January that five thousand men had been sworn in and were armed with cutlasses and crude recycled ammunition was disproved by the end of the month when the extent of the conspiracy was reckoned at 500.[137] The Lord Advocate did demonstrate a keenness not to move until he had evidence of a seditious or treasonable conspiracy and assessments that passed between the key men were seldom very alarmist. They knew by the end of January that the conspiracy was not very extensive, that its main movers were being watched and that there were no very mature plans for insurrection. Biggar helped to fill in the details across February, furnishing the text of the oath which constituted the legal evidence required by the Lord Advocate, and arrests were made towards the end of February.[138]

The impact of this conspiracy was far greater than its extent would seem to warrant. While it exposed the weakness of insurrectionary planning in this period, it also accelerated a process of polarization. Those petitioners who supported reform but had eschewed wild and 'visionary' politics, were alienated from the cause of popular reform. In this context it is easy to see why the idea that the government acted through *agents provocateurs* to provoke treasonable conspiracies is an attractive one. It became a key trope in reform arguments of the 1820s and 1830s that constitutionalist agitation needed to be upheld in the face of ministerial attempts to seduce the people into violence. Ultimately, it benefited ministers to tie together events in Glasgow, the north of England and Spa Fields into a connected threat to the state. There was certainly a difference between the cool and measured way in which those in the know discussed the extent of the conspiracy in Glasgow and the deliberately melodramatic manner in which the Lord Advocate made its existence known in the House of Commons. The real significance of the treasonable conspiracy of 1816 and 1817 lay in inspiring a qualified loyalist revival.

2 LOYALISM AND WHIGGISM IN SCOTLAND

> I apprehend that Loyal Associations will soon be necessary to counteract the gathering storm and to preserve the Constitution and Peace of the Country.[1]

Historians have, by and large, remained uninterested in the idea of loyalism after the end of the Napoleonic Wars. In contrast to the now rich literature on loyalism during the 1790s, which has been fruitful of a number of debates, the period after 1815 is still seen in more binary terms, with a heroic mass radicalism pitted against the government-directed forces of reaction.[2] There are, of course, some obvious reasons as to why this should be the case. First, just as the shift from war to peace profoundly altered the terrain on which radicals operated, so too it shifted the available languages and strategies of would-be loyalists. Crudely, if the end of the war opened up to radicals (or at least expanded) the possibility of a plausible, patriotic and constitutionalist mass appeal, it closed opportunities for the expression of loyalist politics. Powerful rhetorical resources – in particular, the claims that all reformers were tainted by 'French' ideology and that an existential military conflict was not the time to be discussing reform questions – were simply not available or would ring hollow after 1815. This has contributed to a second reason for the lack of historical interest: the loyalism that did emerge after 1815 was not marked by the same dynamic mix of activism and ideas that had characterized organized anti-radicalism during the 1790s.

This should not, however, blind us to the very good reasons for continuing to take loyalism seriously as a phenomenon after 1815. The first, as indicated by the quote from the town clerk of Glasgow above, is that some people were apt to see the period after 1815 as a re-run of the 1790s. The problems of radical insurgency and ideological contamination were, by this reading, the same and needed to be met with the same arsenal. Secondly, and more importantly, the work of Mark Philp, Jonathan Fulcher and others has demonstrated how impoverished the study of radicalism is when it is examined in isolation from its rhetorical 'other', loyalism. Instead of exploring loyalism and radicalism as 'movements', built from identifiable constituencies of activists, organized through societies and premised on certain distinct ideologies, a more fruitful approach has been

– 33 –

to treat them as 'developing political practices'. Simply put, both loyalists and radicals were involved in a creative dialogue in rapidly shifting circumstances. Radicalism and loyalism need to be examined as rhetorical positions within a single political culture: to isolate either from its proper political context is to risk misunderstanding both phenomena.[3]

I

If there are good reasons to take loyalism seriously, there are also reasons for thinking about loyalism in Scotland as a 'special case'. As Bob Harris has demonstrated for the 1790s, loyalism was not the same thing in Scotland as it was in England. It was, by his account, considerably more elitist and statist in both its personnel and its ideology. It was more reliant on the 'top-down' activities of law officers, courts and governing elites than the more robustly 'popular' phenomena of loyal mobs, Paine burnings and the like, which characterized loyalism south of the border.[4]

Explicating loyalism demands the investigation of a number of different contexts. The legacies and memories of the 1790s was only one factor, albeit a powerful one, which determined and shaped the content and the form of organized antiradicalism after 1815. There was a wider British context to the development of post-war loyalism and two events loomed large in a new demonology of popular politics. First, the meeting and attempted insurrection at Spa Fields in London in December 1816. Secondly, the 'shot' fired at the Prince Regent's carriage on his journey to the opening of Parliament in January 1817.[5] Nationally, both of these events exercised the loyalist imagination and could be represented as a dangerous reprise and expansion of the politics of the 1790s. The year 1795, in particular, had witnessed mass outdoor meetings orchestrated by the London Corresponding Society and the stoning of George III's carriage.[6] To Whigs and many radicals, they were, instead, the specious pretext for a spasm of 'alarmist' measures similar to those pursued in 1795, such as the suspension of habeas corpus and its Scottish equivalent and restrictions on freedom of assembly.[7]

These events had their equivalents in the Scottish context. Loyalism north of the border was, of course, concerned about the implications of the Spencean doctrines alleged to have been behind events at Spa Fields, but remained far more focused on disturbances within its own urban communities, in particular, the riots in Glasgow, Dundee and Dumfries. Nevertheless, phenomena such as the mobility of radical 'emissaries' and the supposed connectedness of events across the country were important spectres haunting the loyalist imagination and the inflation and connection of apparently discrete events was common. William Kerr at the General Post Office in Edinburgh, for example, reported to his superior in London, Francis Freeling, that he initially suspected the food rioting in

Dundee in December of 1816 to be connected to the Spa Fields meeting.[8] The first reports of the Committees of Secrecy of the House of Commons and the House of Lords both pointed to the existence of insurrectionary conspirators in Scotland who sent 'emissaries' south and whose plot was dependent on 'the simultaneous rising of the disaffected in England'.[9] This sense of the connectedness of events worked in both directions. The second secret report of the House of Commons would allege that part of the reason for insurgency in England was a widespread belief that the 'Scots were on the march', while newspaper reports had this as one of the falsehoods industriously circulated ahead of the meeting at Spa Fields.[10]

In the Scottish context this fear of a connected conspiracy received its greatest boost in responses to the developments discussed at the end of the previous chapter. The physical force, oath-bound conspiracy was numerically and geographically constrained, but it was nevertheless a major resource for those who sought to underline, emphasize or inflate the danger from an insurgent radicalism. In spite of clear indicators from their sources of intelligence that the conspiracy was neither very widespread nor very well advanced, public statements attempted to weave together all of these disparate strands.

This was done to electrifying effect by Alexander Maconochie, the Lord Advocate, on whose testimony some of the report of the Secret Committee of the House of Commons had been built. He had produced a copy of the oath provided by Biggar and Richmond, but had asked for it not to be included in the Committee's report. In a debate on one of the resulting measures, for the suspension of habeas corpus, on 26 February 1817, Henry Bennet attempted to devalue the report of the Secret Committee by pointing out that only one witness, the Lord Advocate, had been examined. In response, Maconochie delivered his maiden speech, which painted an alarming picture of the state of Scotland. The publications which had tended to bring government and governing institutions into contempt and the numerous petitions for reform were linked together into 'a settled system ... for inflaming the discontented and distressed into open violence'. This in itself justified his having taken further actions, in particular, keeping watch on those men who had played a conspicuous role in 1795. The result of this, he informed the house, had been the discovery of the 'secret conspiracy', which was connected with the disaffected in England and 'widely extended in Scotland and not confined to Glasgow'.[11] His reading of the oath during this speech received cheers from the House and helped to set the tenor of loyalist reaction.

Despite this alarmist speech, what is striking about the loyalism that developed throughout 1816 to 1817 was its relative weakness, both in comparison to the 1790s and to events south of the border. Part of this was down to the considerable scepticism among elites as to the scale of the alleged threat and uncertainty as to the best means of addressing it. There were, from the winter of 1816, a number of panicked calls for armed volunteers to be reconstituted on the model of the 1790s. In early December, in the immediate aftermath of the disturbances in Dundee, Maconochie had written to Sidmouth with a bleak estimate of how effectual unarmed civilian special constables could be and suggesting he 'authorize in some of the larger towns the embodying, as armed Volunteers, such of the more respectable inhabitants as might incline to involve themselves ... to serve without pay'.[12] He aired these plans on the basis of reports he was receiving from elites in the localities, who were lamenting both the paucity of available military assistance and the inadequacy of those civilian contingencies which government had suggested should fill the void. James Reddie from Glasgow was especially persistent. He continually called for an armed volunteer force in Glasgow, in particular a reconstitution of the Glasgow Sharpshooters, who he claimed were prepared to act. He did so not only on the basis that 'any mob we shall have to encounter will not be an ordinary mob, but one so far disciplined and armed', but also because he suspected that the 42nd regiment, stationed in Glasgow, as 'fathers, brothers, cousins &c' of the local people, would not prove to be dependable: 'To oppose the insurgents here we ought clearly to have English not Scotch Regiments'.[13]

While there was clearly some appetite to see 1790s measures adopted, ministers, through Sidmouth, offered 'strong objections' to the embodiment of armed volunteers. These objections were partly to the cost of any such project at a time when retrenchment was badly needed but also demonstrated a preference that solutions to these problems be found locally. His responses demonstrate a clear scepticism about both the viability and the desirability of armed citizen volunteers in the post-war context: with the war over, their rationale would be no more than as an armed domestic police force.[14] The furthest he would move would be to recommend the reconstitution of the more socially-exclusive yeomanry corps and he sent a circular to Lords Lieutenant and to Reddie in Glasgow encouraging such a force.[15] It seems probable, however, that both the unpopularity of government measures with a wide range of the population and the economic fluctuations after 1816 had sapped the possible foundations of a mass armed loyalism in any case. The Lord Advocate, for example, was apprehensive that 'the pressure of the time has so much reduced in this part of the Empire the number of persons either who keep riding horses or who can afford the expense of their equipment as Yeomanry cavalry' as to render the tool suggested by Sidmouth an ineffective one.[16]

Indeed, this sense of isolation compounded by the fear that available military force and suggested civilian alternatives could be unequal to the policing activities that might be asked of them, encouraged the Lord Advocate to explore other, more constitutionally dubious tactics. He was clear in communication with the

Sheriff of Lanarkshire, that in the event of trouble, no half measures should be taken. He advised against firing over the head of riotous crowds and suggested a more effective strategy: 'to select some of the best marksmen of the corps and direct them to take aim at the persons who may be most actively engaged or appear, or are even privately known, if present in the riot, to be ringleaders & engaged in seditious practices'.[17]

This hesitancy and sense of weakness was no less marked in other areas of conspicuous loyalist endeavour from the 1790s. There appears to have been no attempts to establish loyal associations specifically to counter reform bodies, as there had been during the French Revolution. There was little activity in terms of preparing and voting loyal addresses, even on such critical occasions as the assault on the Regent's carriage in January. One concern that did form a constant refrain in the letters both sent received by the Lord Advocate was the belief that 'seditious publications' and, in particular, Cobbett's second *Register*, needed to be combated.[18] One approach, which would eventually be adopted in 1819, was to make cheap publications such as Cobbett's subject to a stamp, which the Lord Advocate urged as an effective means of crushing 'the wholesale vendors of Sedition at Glasgow'.[19] Simultaneously, however, both he and Sidmouth were exploring the possibilities of encouraging loyalist publications from London and Edinburgh, respectively, and Maconochie was attempting to engage 'men of the very first talents'.[20] Walter Scott was involved in these early attempts to get a loyalist press up and running as was one of his patrons, the Duke of Buccleuch. Buccleuch's efforts were focused on another friend of Scott's, the solicitor Joseph Gillon. He had acted in support of government during the 1790s and had been clamouring to edit a loyalist paper since 1812, but his 'unfortunate aptitude to convivial society' had somewhat retarded his career. Buccleuch suggested a loyalist Sunday newspaper to counteract radical papers, such as the *Examiner*, a project which met with Sidmouth's encouragement on the basis that 'there is no Day of the Week, on which Poison is so widely circulated thro' the Medium of the Press'. Despite such powerful backing, the paper never seems to have got off the ground.[21]

There was, of course, a loyalist and pro-ministerial voice embodied in papers such as the *Edinburgh Evening Courant*, the *Edinburgh Weekly Journal*, the *Glasgow Herald* and the *Glasgow Courier*, which supported suspension of habeas corpus and offered robust opposition to reform.[22] Literary big guns, such as the Tory *Quarterly Review*, developed the intellectual case against reform. Robert Southey's lengthy and phlegmatic article on 'Parliamentary Reform' aimed to lay down a framework on which this wider loyalist press could draw and received the approbation of Lord Liverpool who considered it 'a Masterpiece, and if generally read calculated to do the greatest good'.[23] Even here, however, the medicine was too strong for a fledgling Tory publication, *Blackwood's Edinburgh Maga-*

zine, which criticized the article's 'strain of violent exaggeration and reproach' even while it approved of its general drift.[24] Such efforts did inspire attempts to debunk arguments for political equality based on ideas of natural rights and to explain that taxation was not in fact oppressive.[25] There is no evidence, however, that such tracts had a wide circulation or much impact.

Overall there seems to have been little attempt to disseminate material that made a genuine effort to communicate with the 'lower orders', an activity which had been such a marked feature if the loyalism of the 1790s. There were, of course, satires on radical aims, such as 'Carlop Green; or, Equality Realized', a riff on a Drydenesque satire from the 1680s, which had initially been published in 1793.[26] Its sophisticated satire and substantial price tag, however, rule it out as a genuine attempt to communicate with the audience radicals sought to engage. More promising were endeavours such as that of the energetic minister of Ruthwell, Rev. Henry Duncan, an evangelist for self-improvement and savings banks. His *Scotch Cheap Repository* had been founded in 1808 and was modelled explicitly on Hannah More's famous series that had pushed a homespun case for political quietism informed by evangelical religion.[27] One such tale on the virtues of education and self-improvement, *The Cottage Fireside*, was successful enough to be published separately and went into a third edition in 1816 and a sixth in 1821.[28] Other formats, such as chapbooks, offered similar encouragement to political abstinence without the moral exhortations. One example, printed in Falkirk, provided a mix of patriotism, loyalty and fatalism, with songs celebrating the Scottish contribution to the victory at Waterloo and her martial prowess and a popular folk song 'We've Aye Been Provided For'.[29] Such chapbooks, however, do not seem to have been issued in such numbers as to suggest a sustained campaign.

The challenge to loyalist propagandists was to find a credible lower-class voice. As Mark Philp has pointed out, success in that area often meant constraining or diluting the loyalist message of a text and offering hostages to fortune.[30] For example, a moralizing text by another of Scott's protégées, John Struthers, recommended that the poor abstain from the 'intoxicating cup' of radicalism and eschew meetings and parliamentary reform. Such behaviour, however, entailed reciprocal obligations from rich men and the setting of standards by which *their* conduct might be measured:

> The rich man must rise to something more truly noble than improving ... the breeds of sheep, of horned cattle, and of horses ... and recollect that he is a steward of the bounties of heaven, not exclusively for hares and partridges, but for a great proportion of fellow-men whose happiness or misery is placed in his hand.[31]

This ambiguity was an obstacle to loyalist efforts and could be exploited by radicals. One pamphlet from Dundee was a clear attempt to echo the dialogue format of both loyalist and radical propaganda of the 1790s. Apparently authored by 'A Forfarshire Justice of the Peace' and selling at 2*d*., it *looked* like a loyalist pamphlet. The contents were complete with characters whose names were familiar from loyalist dialogues of the 1790s – Freehold the laird, Fallowell the farmer, Seizestill the exciseman and Clinker the smith – but whose conversation recommended rigorous retrenchment and embodied much of the radical platform.[32]

Similarly, successful evangelical exhortations to loyalism could not be anything other than double-edged. The death of Princess Charlotte in November 1817, in particular, inspired a flood of printed sermon literature and a burst of loyalist ceremonial. This did not go uncontested by radicals, and at Paisley the proposed procession was subjected to 'the most indecent and malignant abuse'.[33] Even apparently loyalist responses, however, could be ambiguous. Thomas Chalmers, in a sermon that was much reprinted, took the opportunity to preach on the virtues of civil obedience. In common with other evangelical sermons, however, the call to obedience was tempered by a critique of the morals and conduct of the higher orders, which, if it did not prescribe the same remedies as the radical critique, at least agreed on the nature of some of the problems. Chalmers's sermon caused a considerable stir and he claimed it was an act of self-defence when he published it in December.[34] Even in its published form, however, parts of the sermon did approach close to some aspects of radical ideology. Radicals whose petitions and remonstrances had been dismissed contemptuously might certainly agree that: 'It is the distance of the prince from his people which feeds the political jealousy of the latter'.[35] Similarly, radicals were just as vehemently opposed as Chalmers was to 'the base and interested minions of a court' and to:

> those men, who, with all the ostentation, and all the intolerance of loyalty, evinced an utter indifference either to their own personal religion or to the religion of the people who were around them – who were satisfied with the single object of keeping the neighbourhood in a state of political tranquillity.[36]

II

Efforts at persuasion were limited and double-edged during 1816-17 and seem to have been less of a preoccupation than they were during the 1790s. The attempts at coercion of the radical movement by political elites reveal similar weaknesses in post-war loyalism in Scotland. The series of state trials held between March and July of 1817 provided the law officers with an opportunity to prosecute the entire range of political activities that had appeared over the previous year: speaking, writing, petitioning and secret associations. Trials have been recovered as important political fora and historians, such as James Epstein, have examined state trials as key sites of conflict. Such contests were, of course, asymmetrical, but processions to the court, the relationship between the court and the press, even defendants' choice of dress could all demonstrate radical attempts to challenge the claim to dominance which lay at the core of legal language, ritual and spaces. Above all, trials afforded opportunities for reformers and radicals to narrate a history of British liberty and dramatize their own role within it.[37]

The first trial focused on a meeting held in Kilmarnock in December, one of the many petitioning assemblies held over the winter of 1816–17. The prosecution, for sedition, was aimed at Alexander McLaren, a weaver, and Thomas Baird, a local merchant. McLaren had delivered a speech at the meeting, which had celebrated the previous defeat of tyranny at Bannockburn and, crucially, seemed to have broached the question of what reformers should do if their petitions to both Houses of Parliament and, in particular, to the Prince Regent himself should be rejected. McLaren had allegedly stated that were this to be the case then 'to hell with our allegiance'. Baird was accused of being part of the reform committee, which had sought to defray the expenses of petitioning by having the speeches of the meeting printed so that they could be sold around Kilmarnock, including from Baird's own shop.[38]

Accounts of the trial of McLaren and Baird were widely circulated and the speeches of their counsel provided a sustained critique of government actions. Both McLaren and Baird, their counsel argued, had been patriotic Britons, who had served in the volunteers and had only been tempted into politics by their experiences and awareness of the extreme distress following on from the end of the war. The hinge of the defence's case rested on the assertion that all of their activities had been constitutional and fell within a reasonable interpretation of the limits of British liberty.[39] This was made partly by drawing comparisons with the more forceful language and actions of some English radicals, who had been left unprosecuted. All that the defendants had intended to do was to petition and, if that failed, to petition again.[40] The key statement about allegiance was explained and defended in a number of ways: as a quotation from *Hamlet*;[41] as simply demonstrating the faith the people had that their generous prince would redress their grievances; and, in the last resort, as exemplary of that theory of resistance which lay at the heart of the British constitution.

This latter defence saw counsel refer to the Scottish precedent that James II and VII had '*forfeited* the throne in consequence of his proceedings' and the more general argument that, while talk about resistance might be indecorous, it was not seditious: 'The law and the constitution have pronounced that resistance is lawful for the people in certain circumstances'.[42] Government's actions, it was argued, represented an unwarrantable attack on the sacrosanct right of subjects to deliberate and petition.[43] Francis Jeffrey went so far as to link the reform petitions to those other agitations over the slave trade and the property tax – all of these campaigns had been opposed by ministers and had tended to 'throw odium on our rulers', but only parliamentary reform petitions were vilified as seditious.[44] This broad constitutional defence was widely circulated, but in immediate legal terms it was unsuccessful. McLaren and Baird were found guilty, but recommended to clemency and sentenced to six months imprisonment with securities for good conduct thereafter.

After that point the luck of the Crown law officers ran out and the next trial, of Niel Douglas on 26 May, was an unequivocal defeat.[45] Douglas was a popular universalist preacher, compared later to a Victorian Baptist preacher who had attracted record-breaking crowds as 'the Spurgeon of Glasgow on a grander scale'.[46] He was an advanced radical, who had been an active delegate from Dundee to the conventions of the 1790s and had kept up his political activism from his platform at the old Andersonian institute in Glasgow.[47] The indictment and the Crown evidence made it quite clear that Douglas was prosecuted not only for the content of his sermons but also for the nature of his audience, which consisted of 'crowded congregations, chiefly of the lower orders of the people'.[48] Douglas was thus one of those key figures in loyalist demonology, an educated man attempting to poison the minds of the lower orders. The specific charge was that, in offering a lesson from the fifth chapter of Daniel, Douglas had made seditious statements about both the royal family and the legislature. George III had been compared to Nebuchadnezzar 'driven from the society of men for infidelity and corruption' and his son to Belshazzar, 'a poor infatuated devotee of Bacchus', who had failed to learn from the lessons of his father and would reap a similar reward. The House of Commons had allegedly been called corrupt, its seats openly bought and sold and its members 'thieves and robbers', while the laws of the land were unjustly administered.[49]

The case itself starkly revealed the problems inherent in prosecuting radical speech. These had been apparent in the earlier trial, when the defence had pointed out that McLaren had 'delivered his speech during a storm of wind, rain and hail; from the noise of which, and particularly from the rattling of the hail on umbrellas, it was almost impossible to hear what was said'.[50] In that case, however, the notes from the speech and the pamphlet based on these had formed part of the Crown's evidence. In Douglas's case the prosecution had to rely on the recollection of witnesses, in particular of town officers sent by magistrates to take down what was said. This was undoubtedly the weak point in an inept case by the prosecution and Jeffrey seized on the law officers' strategy of not asking each witness exactly what had been said 'but what was his impression, and his imagination of what Mr Douglas had said'.[51] The flimsy recollections of witnesses persuaded the Crown to throw up the case and ask for a verdict of 'not proven'. This would at least have vindicated their assertion that Douglas was a 'political preacher', a trait especially dangerous in 'a sectarian like the panel' and the more general point that 'the discussion of daily politics is equally a criminal departure from his duty as a Christian pastor, and from his duty as a British subject'.[52] Douglas's defence disputed this narrow conception of the duties of a clergyman, defended his privilege of alluding to government and successfully represented Douglas as someone who had stayed well within the bounds of the constitution, recommending petitioning and simply falling prey to a malicious prosecution.[53] The jury returned a unanimous verdict of 'not guilty'.

Douglas had been politically suspect for other reasons. One was that McDowal Pate, who was heavily implicated in the secret associations that had emerged in Glasgow, has acted as a precentor in his church, while other suspects attended his sermons.[54] It was in the prosecution emerging from this area of radical activity that the Crown law officers suffered their most signal defeat. Indictments for the capital charge of administering unlawful oaths were drawn up against William Edgar and Andrew McKinlay, a teacher and a weaver, respectively, both from Glasgow. The legal defence presented was a sophisticated and powerful one, grounded on the interpretation of this statute (which had been passed to deal with Luddite organization in 1812) in Scottish criminal law and the nature of the indictments drawn up by the Crown law officers. The defence counsel painstakingly argued that the oath, which had been read with such drama in the House of Commons, by binding its takers to the use of 'physical force' in pursuit of annual parliaments and universal suffrage was not necessarily treasonable.[55] Such an undertaking did not bind the oath-takers to specific treasonable acts and Cranstoun clarified the point by suggesting that it would be bold to accuse of treason a set of gentlemen who bound themselves 'to support septennial parliaments and the elective franchise as now established, by moral and physical strength'. In and of itself, the oath did not imply treasonable acts and it was instead 'the imagination of the public prosecutor' which was at fault in attempting to develop a charge of constructive treason alien to Scots law.[56] The arguments succeeded in embarrassing the law officers, who had to revise the indictment a number of times and seek advice from the Attorney General.[57]

As well as the legal argument, defence counsel aired complaints about the manner in which the case evidence had been handled, especially pointing out the Lord Advocate's tight restrictions on access to witnesses. It was this aspect of the case that issued in considerable drama when John Campbell, one of the principal prosecution witnesses, was examined. On the question being put 'has anybody given you a reward, or promise of a reward, for being a witness?' Campbell responded in the affirmative. He went on to narrate a long story of the inducements – a post in the excise, help for himself and his pregnant wife and the possibility of passage and a post in the empire – which had been dangled by Home Drummond to persuade him to give testimony.[58] Campbell, however, had been heavily implicated in the conspiracies of the winter and the most reliable information, that of Biggar, had him as 'the soul of the business in Calton

& an Irishman who has staid long here & thinks concerned in the Irish Rebellion'.[59] Different stories circulated subsequently as to the course of events, but both Peter Mackenzie and Cockburn related that Campbell had sent McKinlay a note in a quid of tobacco ahead of the trial intimating that he was being bribed but remained true to the cause.[60] While legal spaces, rituals and state trials were designed for dominance, they could still provide opportunities for radical agency. Campbell's intervention was crucial in the outcome of the trial and had wider reverberations.

Following this disaster for the law officers, there was more uncertainty from witnesses, some of whom had been drinking ahead of the alleged meetings. James Finlayson, for example, admitted that 'if I had not seen the oath in a newspaper, I could not have remembered it' and this effectively sunk the Crown's case.[61] It was thrown up and a verdict of 'not proven' was returned. This gave the Lord Advocate some narrow ground to claim victory and the Lord Justice Clerk could advert to the highly questionable activities in which McKinlay had clearly involved himself. In this narrative, the verdict was rescued as proof positive that McKinlay was indeed the citizen of a country enjoying liberty and just laws:

> you now have an entire and perfect conviction of the happiness and security under which the people of this country at present live, that you are now fully convinced that the constitution of your country affords a complete safeguard to its subjects.[62]

The radical press was less eager to represent the trial as a victory for liberty and Maconochie realized that the miscarriage of the trial would 'be made the handle for much abuse and misrepresentation of the Servants of Government in this Country'.[63] In the British context, state trials were key events in 1817. Radicals, prevented from meeting and discouraged from petitioning had recourse to other outlets. One strategy was insurrectionary plotting, for which Brandreth and the Pentrich rebels were hanged. Another arena was the press, to which the *Black Dwarf*, launched in January 1817, was a notable addition. After the suspension of habeas corpus and the passing of the Seditious Meetings Act, the nexus formed by the press and radical trials became crucial as 'a key forum for radical assembly' and a way of maintaining crucial links between the spoken and the written word.[64] Courtrooms provided numerous discussion points across the year, ranging from trials for treason to sedition and blasphemy trials of radical journalists. In the immediate aftermath of his trial, Douglas published an impassioned ideological defence of his actions, which he had intended to deliver in court had he been found guilty. The pamphlet excoriated ministers for the use of spies and the suspension of habeas corpus and profits from its sale were to be used to defray the expenses of exculpatory witnesses appearing in the conspiracy trials.[65] McKinlay's trial also fitted well into the developing narrative of a sustained alarmist assault and was widely reported in the press.[66]

The radical press was, of course, apt to celebrate the acquittal as a victory. To William Hone, whose own celebrated trials would come at the end of the year, the acquittal of McKinlay provided 'another and most signal defeat of Ministerial machination'.[67] Thomas Wooler, whose own trial for sedition had seen his triumphant acquittal in June, lambasted the 'theatrical display of cant and absurdity' in the Lord Advocate's attempts to develop constructive treason and linked McKinlay's case to his own: 'Thus defeated in London, they return again to the charge in Scotland'.[68] Indeed, Wooler's experience demonstrates how trials and the publicity surrounding them provided opportunities for the expansion of radical networks. The publisher of the Glasgow edition of Wooler's trial issued thanks to ministers: 'The *Black Dwarf*, of the existence of which we were ourselves wholly ignorant, has been thereby happily advertised'.[69] Needless to say, its readership in Scotland was constant thereafter. The state trials in Scotland thus demonstrated some of the weaknesses and vulnerabilities of loyalism and provided opportunities for radicals – through their own defences, from the witness stand, and in the expanding press – to confirm and extend their analysis. They, as representatives of 'the people', were waging war against a narrow, unprincipled and unpatriotic faction.

III

While the radical press could represent the Scottish trials as a vindication of their own political analysis they could equally be portrayed as a success for a revived Whiggism. In the 1790s, self-defence had provided a powerful opportunity for radicals to dramatize and publicize their conflict with the state, and it continued to do so in the English courts. In Scotland after 1815, however, defendants universally employed the assistance of legal counsel. There were no heroic self-defences like those of William Hone, T. J. Wooler and Richard Carlile south of the border. This absence of self-defence makes it more difficult to interpret these trials primarily as examples of radical counter-theatre. Instead, the group that used the trials to tell its own history of liberty and deliver its own verdict on the nature of politics was the Scottish Whig party. The trials were an opportunity for a resurgent Whiggism to push its own narrative into the public sphere. They were, in fact, a venue for Whig counter-theatre, something which attracted consistent complaint from Maconochie: 'being made a party question we have either 8 or 9 counsel for the prisoner in all the cases & speeches of inordinate length'.[70]

The defence counsel in all of the trials was drawn from the ever more confident body of Whig advocates in Edinburgh: prominent were George Cranstoun, J. P. Grant, J. A. Murray and John Clerk (the last of whom had defended Thomas Fyshe Palmer in the sedition trials of the 1790s). Perhaps most notably, Henry

Cockburn and Francis Jeffrey, two of the moving spirits behind the *Edinburgh Review* and the eventual architects of Scottish political reform in 1832, took leading roles. The *Review* itself has been seen as the fruit of frustrated legal ambition and demonstrates the links between court and press. With few briefs and little chance of preferment within the heavily politicized Scottish legal system of the early nineteenth century, a group of talented Whig advocates – including Henry Brougham as well as those mentioned above – turned to journalism as an outlet. Criminal trials provided another very public forum for the development and mobilization of Whig ideas.

These 'new Whigs' – as some historians have labelled them – played a critical role within the ideology and activity of the party as a whole and helped to shape the Whig revival to 1830. The *Review* became both the principal Whig weapon for shaping public opinion and 'a radicalizing force on the progressive wing of the Whig party'.[71] In doing so, the periodical developed the intellectual case for moderate reform, while it maintained an open hostility to any demands for universal suffrage or annual parliaments. In particular, there was a rejection of a rights-based argument for reform, summed up by the Scottish librarian at Holland House, John Allen:

> We are convinced that real representation and frequent elections are the best means of securing good government; but independent of their utility in this way, we see no ground for giving them the name of rights; and it is very remarkable, that among those Reformers who have this word most frequently in their mouths, and who found their creed in deductions from it, there has always been the least accommodating spirit.[72]

As this quote demonstrates, the intellectual case was matched by a critique of radical strategies and leadership: 'Because we are friends of Reform, we lament the course lately pursued by Reformers. We can neither agree with them in their plans for Reform, nor applaud the measures they have taken for the attainment of their object.'[73] The *Review* addressed the reform movement and chided the adoption of Cartwright's form of petition as having alienated 'the cooperation of many reformers very superior in information and talents' and provided 'a pretence for the senseless clamour of the poor against the rich'. Instead of confrontational petitions with 'choice metaphorical expressions' they argued that 'the object of Reformers should be to convince, not to irritate'.[74] While the reviewers were reformers this was not a ground on which the party as a whole could yet be united. Far more auspicious in that respect was the attack on ministerial 'alarms', especially as demonstrated in the Secret Reports of 1817 and the measures which were based upon these.[75] Reform, even responsibly-led and moderate reform, remained a divisive issue: the Foxite ground of defending the liberties of the subject was much more reassuring.

Against the backdrop of their journalistic activity, Scottish Whig advocates successfully used all of the state trials in Scotland to push both of these analyses. There was, of course, some common ground with more advanced radicals – both were suspicious, for example, of Crown attempts to develop doctrines of constructive treason. The Whigs, however, grasped the opportunity to offer opinions on other aspects of politics. Ideas worked out in the pages of the *Review* informed the rhetoric at the trials. For example, in McLaren and Baird's trial, both Clerk and Jeffrey pointed out that it was not necessary to discuss the merits or otherwise of annual parliaments and universal suffrage. The question at issue was whether it fell within constitutional limits to *petition* for these.[76] Having established that legal point, however, Jeffrey did go on to offer his own sentiments: 'They wished for annual elections, and that all should have votes. You may think such a plan mischievous ... I rather think so myself'. He followed this with an explanation of his opinion on the flawed intellectual and historical justifications for annual parliaments and universal suffrage which was virtually a *précis* of Allen's *Edinburgh Review* article on the subject, the appearance of which coincided with the trial.[77]

Perhaps even more marked was a Whiggish contempt for the democratic operations of a movement which lacked 'respectable' leadership. Clerk, in defending McLaren, found it unexceptionable that:

> warm or intemperate expressions, not sufficiently respectful to their superiors, occasionally fell in the course of their deliberations, from people in the lowest ranks of life, unable to express themselves with that delicacy which is required from men in higher situations.

Similarly, Jeffrey described the seditious pamphlet as 'foolish, ridiculous specimens of rustic oratory'.[78] While the Crown officers made it plain that their case against Douglas was partly based on his preaching politics to the lower orders, Whigs could be equally contemptuous of the ability of the vulgar to participate in politics. Without leadership and education they simply were not equipped as political subjects. This atitude to working-class radicals was taken to its logical conclusion in McKinlay's case, where Cranstoun opened by pointing out that the life of the prisoner depended on judgements on the use of words and their meaning. If the court allowed room for the construction to be placed on the words of the oath, this should err in favour of the accused, because these words had 'been used not by a person well educated, and critically acquainted with language, but by one who is in the lowest situation of life, and who must be presumed to be totally ignorant of the force and delicacy of terms'.[79] A prosecution based on the subtle interpretation of an oath could not be used against someone who was simply too ignorant to understand the nuances of political language: i.e. someone who did not subscribe to the *Edinburgh Review*.[80]

Whig counsel used trials and their links to the public sphere to air more obviously party-political questions. Scottish Whiggism was in part premised on an evangelical idea of amending Scotland's unfree, feudal institutions.[81] Frequently the model for doing this might be found in English institutions and Scottish Whigs at the time and, subsequently, with greater clarity, saw their mission as 'to bring Scotland within the action of the constitution' – hence their subsequent historiographical reputation as dogmatic Anglicizers.[82] Legal questions and the separate legal system provided one profoundly important forum in which to pursue and develop these ideas. Reform of the Court of Session to include trial by jury in civil cases had been mooted since the 1780s and was explored in Nick Phillipson's early work as a window into politics and intellectual currents in Enlightenment Scotland.[83] There were also very profoundly political questions involved in the administration of criminal justice.

One recurrent set of issues revolved around the somewhat ambiguous role of the Lord Advocate within Scottish politics and society. The Lord Advocate, as both chief prosecutor and the government's man in the north – a kind of minister for Scotland – had both legal and political functions. These extensive powers had been attacked by Whigs on a number of occasions. In 1804 it was done on libertarian grounds by the advanced Whig Samuel Whitbread. His attack encouraged the then Lord Advocate, Charles Hope, to deliver a worrying description of his office which formed the basis of subsequent Whig criticisms: 'he possesses the whole of the executive government of Scotland under his particular care'.[84] Criminal trials and especially state trials offered a politically-charged space in which to develop this critique and to attack the Lord Advocate in the execution of his legal functions. Such concerns featured across all of the trials. In McKinlay's trial, for example, counsel attacked the Lord Advocate for denying access to one of the key prosecution witnesses. The language used demonstrates how the courtroom was used to dramatize this conflict as one taking place between Whig advocates and a potentially despotic state:

> How can we know who the witness is from anything yet told us? He is a man shut up in a sealed casket to whom we can have no access. He is still an egg in the shell, and is not to come out until the proper process of incubation be gone through by his majesty's advocate. The public prosecutor has been hatching this evidence in the Castle of Edinburgh, and it is not yet disclosed. If we go to the castle, and approach the sentinels to ask admission to the witnesses, they ask, who goes there, and present their muskets to us.[85]

During the 1790s, the Whigs had used Scottish state trials as an opportunity to defend the liberties of the subject in Parliament. The debates surrounding the sentences of transportation passed on Thomas Muir and Thomas Fyshe Palmer gave parliamentary Whigs such as Charles Fox an opportunity to denounce this evidence of 'the infamous fabric of Scottish persecution', while Charles Grey had claimed that 'Scotland had no more liberty, than it had under the race of the Stuarts'.[86] State trials after 1815, in particular Maconochie's somewhat inept handling of McKinlay's case, provided similar opportunities for a resurgent Whiggism. Lord Archibald Hamilton, the brother of the tenth Duke of Hamilton and Whig MP for Lanarkshire, launched an attack on the Lord Advocate on 20 June, three days before the Crown's third indictment against McKinlay was to be read in Edinburgh. Hamilton raised the question during the Lord Advocate's absence, in the context of the debates on the suspension of habeas corpus bill, and used McKinlay's experience – arrested and indicted for the same offence on three separate occasions – to argue that it would be 'especially unsafe to extend the power of the Crown in that quarter'. He received support from Brougham and, more unexpectedly, from Kirkman Finlay, who was convinced of McKinlay's guilt but lamented 'that an individual should be confined to a solitary prison, and tried over and over again, merely because the lord advocate was unable to draw an indictment'.[87]

Maconochie came down from Edinburgh specifically to answer these charges during a later debate, but, after the acquittal the case and the conduct of the Lord Advocate continued to provide a useful lever for Whig arguments about the liberty of the subject.[88] Lord Archibald Hamilton moved for an inquiry in February of 1818 and used the opportunity to indict not only the Lord Advocate's handling of the case but also the entirety of his conduct in dealing with the radical reform movement. The dramatic reading of the oath to excite alarm and spread prejudices; the use of spies and informers in collecting evidence against radicals; and the attempted tampering with witnesses were all used to launch a general assault on the state of liberty in Scotland.[89] As such, the trials stood as only part of a co-ordinated Whig critique, which was prosecuted in Parliament and the press as well.

These aspirations to marshal a range of opposition opinion around notions of moderate reform and the defence of the liberties of the subject had received a further boost with the foundation of the *Scotsman* in January 1817. The newspaper had its origins in the reform movement of 1816 and its prospectus was placed before the public on 30 November 1816. It was the project of Charles Maclaren and William Ritchie and aimed at providing an independent newspaper in an Edinburgh press dominated by broadly pro-ministerial papers 'a deliverance from the slavish sycophancy of the other newspapers'.[90] Its reform critique stretched from purely local concerns to amend corrupt mismanagement of the Edinburgh Royal Infirmary, to national and international questions. Its early history thus marked it out as a reformist journal aimed at men of middling rank, exactly the kind of constituency around which Whig tacticians were seeking to build an alliance.[91] It followed a similar line to the Whig lawyers and, for that matter, other liberal newspapers such as the *Glasgow Chronicle*, by keeping ideas of universal suffrage and annual parliaments at arm's length, while supporting more moderate versions of parliamentary reform and entertaining high hopes of parliamentary and Whig leadership. The *Scotsman*'s coverage of McKinlay's trial, for example, was unsparing in its criticism of the conduct of law officers and of ministerial alarmism, but refused either to condemn or to endorse radical politics.[92]

In conformity with such an agenda, the *Scotsman*'s greatest zeal and activity in the first two years of its existence was focused on the issue of burgh reform. The movement for reforming the mode of electing to Scotland's royal burghs was of long pedigree, and predated the movement for parliamentary reform in the eighteenth century.[93] A select committee had reported on the issue in 1793 and had highlighted major grievances before it became a casualty of the political reaction to the outbreak of war with France in 1793. The most frequently aired complaint concerned the system of self-election, whereby councillors, on the authority of a statute dating from 1469, elected their own successors, thus confining municipal authority and burgh representation to a narrow oligarchy.[94] This system was not only seen as rendering the burgh representation easily susceptible to management, but also as a recipe for mismanagement and maladministration of burgh affairs.

The question of burgh reform has been almost absent from accounts of popular politics in this period. Its presentation from the 1780s onwards as an essentially moderate, even conservative effort to amend internal municipal government, seem to make it a strange fixture in the heroic age of popular radicalism. While a conservative appeal *was* part of the rhetoric and the public presentation of burgh reform, this does not mean we should ignore its effects in politicizing large parts of Scotland. The rationale for and attraction of such reform might be based just as easily on the basis of natural right or on the same foundations as parliamentary reform: it was simply not always prudent to say so. When he introduced the topic at a meeting of the Edinburgh Merchant Company, Adam Black, an advanced liberal in favour of a wide range of sweeping reforms, recalled this dynamic: 'The word "Reform" was so obnoxious to timid ears that it was thought wise to avoid it, and instead of "Burgh Reform" the thing was called "Improvement in the Burgh Polity".'[95]

The movement was revived almost immediately after the end of the Napoleonic Wars, and was given a significant boost by the government's actions over the burgh of Montrose. In 1815 and 1816, the town council elected its successors by ballot at the Michaelmas elections. When this innovation was brought before the Court of Session in the summer of 1817 it was found to be illegal and the elections were duly pronounced void. In previous similar cases, the election had been thrown open to the burgesses on the authority of a poll warrant granted by the Crown. The burgesses of Montrose exploited the situation to press for a reconstitution of their council on a more popular basis and the Lord Advocate, observing a precedent in the 1781 case of Stirling, acceded to their demands in October of 1817. The burgesses were to elect all nineteen councillors in the first year and then annually to elect the ten vacancies. In this one instance it seemed that burgh reform had been granted and petitions for a general measure replicating the settlement for Montrose soon began to appear.[96] The burgesses of Inverness, Aberdeen and Dundee, observing that reform could be achieved on the strength of a legal technicality, managed to unseat their councils by having elections declared invalid. The government, however, had realized the implications of its decision for Montrose and decided to grant no more poll warrants.[97] Using spurious precedents derived from quite exceptional conditions of 1716 and 1746 they revived the last legally elected councils in these burghs by crown warrants for the purpose of electing successors.[98]

Nevertheless, reformers had been presented with an opportunity to achieve parliamentary reform of a sort in Scotland, at a time when the mass movement of 1816–17 was in abeyance. Burgh reform was capable of attracting a constituency that was as socially and geographically diverse as that which had emerged in the second half of 1816. Town councils, incorporations, burgesses and inhabitants were involved in its prosecution. The leading lights of the Whig bar offered their services for free in raising an action in the Court of Session to declare Edinburgh's election of magistrates illegal.[99] Reformers were particularly dismayed that ministers refused to grant a poll warrant in the case of Aberdeen, which, owing to financial mismanagement by its council, had declared itself insolvent in 1817. At the election of 1818 only six of the nineteen burgesses elected could be induced to accept office, and even the outgoing council attributed its financial collapse to the 'radically defective' system of self-election. The case of Aberdeen was taken up in Parliament by Lord Archibald Hamilton. In April 1819 he moved for an investigation into the Aberdeen case and for the production of papers showing how the ministry had arrived at its policy, but lost the motion by five votes.[100] The following month, however, he moved for a committee to report on the petitions for burgh reform, which had been accumulating since 1817. When he demonstrated that these petitions showed that in nearly half of the royal burghs in terms of number, and some 80 per cent in terms of population, the town councils themselves desired reform, his motion passed with a majority of five.[101] It was a significant defeat for ministers.

After the autumn of 1817, burgh reform was an issue in Scotland capable of mobilizing a wide range of interests. While petitions and pamphlets on the whole avoided making any explicit links between burgh reform and wider parliamentary reform, the analogies between an unreformed House of Commons and radically defective local government were hard to ignore. Imagery of corrupt and closed systems, whose beneficiaries rioted in luxury at the expense of the people, were interchangeable.[102] Indeed, a number of the reform petitions of 1816–17 had pointed to burgh government as only a particularly egregious defect in the Scottish political system. As simply one component of a corrupt system municipal government was easily joined to a radical critique and radicals took clear interest in the question. One correspondent from Dundee claimed in the *Black Dwarf* that his letter on the subject, claiming burgh reform on the same natural rights basis as he argued for parliamentary reform, had not been printed in the *Scotsman*, because there was 'not enough of the Whig in it'. Nevertheless, he and others saw burgh reform as an important campaign taking a step in the right direction and an attack on 'the system':

> We are just now trying our strength with the pigmies [*sic*] of corruption. We shall soon join the standard of the main army. Call us what you please – the sappers and miners of the cause – I think the epithets belong to us for our exertion in favour of borough Reform.[103]

It would be too simple to see the legislation and trials of 1817 as signalling the 'end' of the reform movement until 1819. Within Scottish and wider British politics there was a rebalancing as different groups responded to changed conditions. What emerged after 1817 was a revitalized Whig party assault on what Whigs characterized as the unconstitutional alarmism of ministers and a broadly supported local and parliamentary assault on the constitution of Scotland's burghs. Such issues surfaced only fitfully in the general election of 1818, which saw the opposition numbers in Scotland overall remain unchanged.[104] Other than the triumphant return of Lord Archibald Hamilton once again in Lanarkshire, the highlight for reformers in Scotland was the return of the reformer Joseph Hume for the Montrose group of burghs. This was welcomed as proof positive of the transformative and liberating effect that burgh reform might have, and Hume presented himself as 'the independent, unshackled representative of the only free and independent burgh in Scotland'.[105] Burgh reform was the perfect platform from which Whigs might seek to exert responsible leadership of an extra-parliamentary movement. It was unassailably constitutional in its form, sending petitions and operating through recognized channels, such as the Convention of Royal Burghs, but it was supported nevertheless by a reformist press and wider sections of the population. The political, constitutional and economic situation which all of these groups – radicals, reformers, Whigs, Tories and loyalists – would have to respond to explain and control, changed dramatically during the summer of 1819.

3 SCOTLAND AND THE MASS PLATFORM

It is very curious how this Evil Manifests itself in Scotland, England & Ireland, according to the Character of each People, & the local Circumstances it meets with.[1]

A time of great rages and absurd terrors and expectations. A very fierce Radical and anti-Radical time.[2]

1819 has always constituted a central year for historians of popular politics. It was the pivot of E. P. Thompson's *Making of the English Working Class* (1963) and has recently been recovered by historicist literary criticism as an epoch-making year for men of letters.[3] The above recollections of the minister, Edward Irving, adequately characterize the polarized politics that had emerged by the end of 1819. Explaining that process of polarization is more challenging. One approach would be to regard a revived radical movement in that year as a direct response to the recurrence of extreme distress in manufacturing districts. Distress was certainly acute and it clearly played a prominent role in the politics of radicalism. Such an explanation would also follow some contemporary and near-contemporary analysis. Henry Cockburn characterized radicalism, or 'sedition of opinion', as a product of 'sedition of the stomach' with radical politics and orators as the waste products of a chemical process: 'They are the froth that rises and bubbles on the surface, when the mass of the people ferments'.[4] Frederick Primrose, MP, was one of many to draw an explicit connection during the winter of 1819: 'if they were permanently out of bread, they would be permanently seditious'.[5] However, to accept this explanation of political action not only ignores the complex nature of political motivation, but takes on their own terms elite attempts to disarm radicalism rhetorically, by ignoring its political claims and instead characterizing it as a 'social pathology'.[6]

In fact, much hostile contemporary comment was prepared to see the problem of radical activity in 1819 in slightly more complex and nuanced terms. The new Lord Advocate, William Rae, for example, highlighted the problem that, while great numbers of the distressed 'had suffered without a murmur', political discontent had 'spread among those who were not feeling the pressure of want'. His particular examples were relatively affluent occupational groups, such as cotton spinners and colliers, the latter of which had an additional reason to have faith in parliamentary institutions, having been emancipated from their own serfdom by Parliament in the 1790s. Their politicization offered strong proof that 'distress, or real grounds of complaint, were not essential to the reception of seditious discontent'.[7] Distress was a factor in 1819, but there is clearly a need to explain why, for some at least, radicalism was a movement of aspiration rather than a response to desperation.

This certainly was the perspective of many radicals themselves, though their public statements and self-examinations should be treated with similar caution to those of political elites. Radical speeches and writing undoubtedly highlighted distress, but they were far from restricted to this theme and often included ideological explanations of their cause, critiques of foreign policy and other motivating factors. Other work has also emphasized the role of radical politics as both an expression of and a mechanism for community cohesion or as a late flowering of a vibrant and long-lived 'custom of disobedience'.[8] What such approaches have in common is in interpreting popular political activity as not simply a response to distress or a natural expression of a political ideology. As one prominent participant in the events of 1819–20 later bore testament, there were many reasons for becoming involved, including an idea of politics as leisure: 'It must be acknowledged that fun, or diversion, or amusement had a considerable influence on the adherence of vast numbers to the popular will'.[9]

Any exploration of the popular politics of the period must then balance this range of explanations both for political motivation and for the eventual shape of radical activity. Some of these challenges can be addressed by exploring Scottish politics in wider contexts. First, a reliance on 'Scottish' sources, especially on those newspapers produced by and for Scottish radicals, would give only a partial view of a movement which saw itself in a British context. Radicals were consciously part of a British movement: events and personalities in England and in Ireland could have a dramatic impact on events in Scotland.[10] Secondly, in exploring radicalism and loyalism as political phenomena, we need to establish the centrality of Parliament to their ideologies, cosmologies and actions. Jonathan Fulcher has pointed to Parliament as a crucial missing context for English popular politics, a casualty of the concern to write 'history from below': it was no less important in Scottish politics.[11] The final missing context is that of loyalism. Organized anti-radicalism had been a relatively weak presence during 1816–17, but events that galvanized radicalism in 1819 and help to explain its nature also help to account for the emergence of a more assertive loyalism. As has been suggested above, this developing 'logic of confrontation' has important consequences, not only for understanding radical and loyalist politics, but also for explaining the position of the Whigs in Scottish politics. Just as they had at the end of the 1790s, the Whigs once again found themselves occupying a rapidly-diminishing middle ground. The main aim of this chapter is to provide an analytical account of the polarized politics of 1819, placing these within the contexts outlined above. It will then go on to explore the nature and strategies of both radicalism and loyalism in this critical period.

I

While increased distress and unemployment were apparent in Scotland from February 1819, the crucial political context for the emergence of a mass reform movement was provided by ministers' approach to public finances in the summer of 1819.[12] Only then would a mass movement premised on explaining distress in political terms emerge. On 6 June the Chancellor of the Exchequer moved a series of resolutions embodying his plans to raise an additional £3,000,000 in taxes. The revenues were to be raised from increased duty on the import of foreign wool, but principally from increased taxes on some key items of consumption: malt, British spirits, tobacco, coffee and cocoa, tea and pepper.[13] The Whigs, led by George Tierney, argued the impropriety of voting additional taxes, which must have 'the most alarming effects on discontented persons in this country' and urged the government to explore more significant retrenchment as a means of addressing the gap, in Brougham's words to 'make a better bargain for the public'.[14] The new taxes, however, sailed through the House.

These measures were, of course, widely reported in the press and provided a dramatic confirmation of the radical critique developed since the end of the war: that distress could be explained in terms of rapacious taxation emanating from a corrupt and unrepresentative Parliament. Some parts of the radical press, such as the *Black Dwarf*, which was steadily increasing its circulation in Scotland on the back of Wooler's trial, almost gleefully welcomed the news as putting to rest any idea that the boroughmongers might not quite be the villains of radical demonology: 'It is now evident that nothing is secure from ministerial rapacity ... The poor are particularly marked out for its harpy claws ... But they may determine to resist the oppression, and rise to vindicate themselves'.[15] To underline these arguments being made in the radical press, Francis Burdett's motion for a reform of Parliament came towards the end of the session, on 1 July. He made similar links between reform and taxes, dismissing the hopes borne on the back of the general election that ministers could not continue their 'career of corruption' and must adopt or give way to measures of retrenchment and economy. The new taxes were proof positive that no such hopes could be entertained from 'a new parliament constituted like the old'.[16] Burdett's motion met defeat, but the minority of sixty included seven members for Scottish constituencies; an impressive showing for an opposition vote given the state of the representation north of the border.[17]

As this muster suggests, the attack on the new taxes was not restricted to radicals alone. The *Scotsman* and other sections of the liberal press followed the Whig line of recommending retrenchment instead of taxation as the proper means of generating the required surplus.[18] And while the radical press interpreted the taxes as an emphatic confirmation of their world view and a question over which people might mobilize, the liberal press struck a fearful note for exactly the same reasons: 'Such conduct must do more to degrade the House of Commons in the estimation of the country than all the writings of all the PAINES and COBBETS [*sic*] that ever existed'.[19] The hopes of radicals and the fears of moderates were quickly borne out as meetings began to be held across the summer. These remained localized, in the first instance, to the weaving communities of western Scotland. There is little doubt, however, that the sense of weavers in Kilsyth or Airdrie being part of a wider movement was supplied by the press, which reported widely on meetings across Britain. The press was the principal vehicle of radical organization and was exploited as such. The 'Friends of Reform' in Paisley, for example, in planning a meeting in July used the pages of the *Black Dwarf* to 'announce to our suffering brethren in England'.[20] A correspondent from Falkirk also dwelt on this mutually supportive relationship. The meetings in England had a transformative effect in stimulating similar efforts in Scotland, but he claimed the servile nature of the Scottish press, including such apparently liberal papers as the *Glasgow Chronicle* and the *Scotsman*, meant that these activities were underreported.[21]

The first and most widely reported Scottish meeting took place in Glasgow on Wednesday 16 June and was attended by some 35,000 according to the *Glasgow Chronicle* (a correspondent of the *Morning Chronicle* put the attendance anywhere between 20,000 and 60,000) and was also attended by the 40th regiment, cavalry and police.[22] It demonstrated two competing solutions to the problems of distress and increased taxation. The resolutions drawn by the committee embodied a solution based on an appeal to the Prince Regent to furnish the means of emigration to Canada. Emigration had been widely discussed since 1815 (and before) as an effective means of addressing the problem of surplus labour, but it had been vilified in much of the radical press:

> let every man who would ensure permanent security, and permanent prosperity for himself and his posterity – let him remain and contribute what lays in his power to cleanse the Augean stable at home, and to render Britain once more the land of liberty, and the abode of plenty.[23]

The resolutions were received with marked hostility by a large part of the crowd. One speaker intervened to argue that in the unlikely event that government listened to and answered their petition, emigration provided no solution. Emigration from Ireland over the previous twenty years had done little to improve its economy. Instead, he urged a radical analysis and moved an amendment in favour of annual parliaments, universal suffrage and the reduction of taxes.

He was followed by a speaker who had 'come from distance' and whose speech demonstrated considerable scepticism about the utility of petitioning at all. His suggestion was that they take any petition to London themselves. He argued further that the only people who should be forced to emigrate were boroughmongers, sinecurists and 150,000 of the clergy. It seems probable that this last speaker, who was called to order repeatedly by the crowd, was a man from Bolton who had been identified as a possible spy or *agent provocateur* in Carlisle. Certainly, in recommending tumultuous petitioning, he appeared to be overstepping the bounds of constitutional politics (a boundary recently redrawn by the government response to the march of the Blanketeers from Manchester).[24] In any case, the amendment dispatching with the 'Canadian resolutions' was enthusiastically endorsed by the crowd and a new committee appointed to pursue a radical reform petition.[25]

At this first meeting in 1819, then, all of those conflicting strategies which would shape politics in Scotland over the next year were apparent. First, there were those who sought to divorce the question of material distress from that of political reform and to propose solutions to the former without broaching the latter. The original committee published an address 'expressive of their grief and disappointment that politics should have been introduced at the Meeting ... convened solely for the purpose of devising the best mode of procuring immediate relief'.[26] Such measures were to continue with meetings of weavers craving public works or for the activation of the Scottish Poor Laws, parliamentary sponsors seeking relief from English sources and printed pleas for the lower classes to abandon politics and seek relief.[27] The second strategy was that of the radical mass platform, based around a political explanation for economic distress and seeking to protest within the bounds of a radicalized constitutionalism. The emphasis was on numbers and unanimity and, in this instance, the acclamations of the crowd pushed the more radical set of resolutions. Finally, the tendency to lose faith in constitutional politics of meeting, debating and petitioning and the desire to explore other, extra-legal strategies based on the creation of links across Britain was apparent. The suspicion with which the speaker 'from distance' was received suggests some of the tensions between this approach and the aspiration to muster a mass national movement.[28]

Press comment and the correspondence of elites allow us to map out other positions being taken on the question of the tax measures. Whig conduct in Parliament was aimed at countering ministerial measures by suggesting retrenchment as an alternative to new taxes. They were, however, in something of a political corner, having engineered the repeal of the property tax and thus the shortfall in the public finances that ministerial measures sought to address. The

Chancellor did not omit to remind Parliament that the need for new sources of revenue had emerged 'out of the repeal of the property tax and other war taxes in 1816'.[29] A wide section of the press supported this position of calling for retrenchment and public economy as opposed to fresh taxation, most powerfully in Scotland the *Scotsman* and the *Glasgow Chronicle*. While they remained critical of ministers, both newspapers (in common with other liberal metropolitan and provincial newspapers such as the *Morning Chronicle*, the *Manchester Gazette* and the *Leeds Mercury*) expressed a profound unease about the nature of the emerging reform movement.

Such unease was part product and part sponsor of one of the key differences between the reform movements of 1816–17 and 1819. The first had encompassed a wide range of social groups and, while many petitions had called for radical reform, there had been a range of proposals and a range of petitioning bodies. To self-defined 'moderate' opinion the movement emerging over the summer of 1819 was denuded of 'respectable' leadership and built almost entirely upon distress and a misguided idea of appropriate remedies. While there were attempts to suggest and sponsor alternative solutions, such as emigration, the liberal press also attempted to modify the aims and strategies of radical reformers. In early July, for example, the *Scotsman* ran a lead article under the title 'Moderation Recommended to the Advocates of Universal Suffrage and Annual Parliaments'. The article attempted to pour oil on increasingly troubled waters and began by agreeing with a central plank of radical analysis, that distress could at least partly be explained as the result of the unjust taxation of a corrupt Parliament. It argued, however, (neatly forgetting the successful campaign to repeal the property tax) that 'there is no single class in the community' that could force change on the government. All reform plans, especially visionary schemes for annual parliaments and universal suffrage, were useless if they were not such as 'great numbers of all classes will concur in' and in fact represented a retrograde step by shocking 'the prejudices of the powerful classes' and thus solidifying resistance to reform. While they would not discourage the lower orders from discussing politics, the time to do so was not propitious. Instead the working classes should present their distresses in open and honest terms so as to 'obtain a hold on the sympathies and command the respect of the other branches of society, and concessions would be made from a sense of justice and pity, which will never be obtained by intimidation'.[30] It was this developing critique that led to criticism by radicals that the liberal press, which had begun so promisingly, was apostate. A meeting at Paisley later damned the *Glasgow Chronicle* 'not because it will not advocate Universal Suffrage, but for abusing the great leaders of radical reform, and for upholding a degrading and fallacious plan of emigration'.[31]

Part of this developing liberal critique was that meetings of the lower orders strengthened loyalism and provided opportunities for ministers to pass alarmist measures and employ spies.[32] The authorities in Scotland seemed not to live up to this alarmist caricature in the early stages of a revived radical movement. While concern over meetings did steadily build among those in authority over the summer and into August, Rae could report that: 'The state of Scotland still continues such as, as I trust is not calculated to create serious alarm'. He went on to recommend that the best means of avoiding disorders was to have sufficient force available, but to urge 'the utmost moderation' in its use.[33] The reports coming from Glasgow were more febrile and calls for an armed association in Glasgow were revived, but the Lord Advocate remained convinced that such reports were exaggerated. With the events of 1816–17 clearly in mind he warned that such alarmist information came from defective intelligence in Glasgow where spies 'in order to make the information they give appear valuable ... are but too apt to exaggerate the danger'.[34] The sense from the Home Office correspondence overall was that distress, if acute, was localized and hopefully ephemeral.

If realignment began with the political context created by taxation measures, it was the news of and responses to the events at Manchester on 16 August that really polarized loyalist and radical positions. The attempted arrest of Henry Hunt on the platform at St Peter's Field and the subsequent action against the crowd by the local yeomanry forces and regular troops – which left eleven dead (a toll which would later rise to seventeen) and over 650 injured – radically altered the political terrain.[35] The nature of this event and its consequences suggest the indispensability of adopting a perspective on radicalism and loyalism that views them not as programmatic ideologies, but as political practices developing in opposition to one another in a rapidly shifting context. The events of Peterloo had a dramatic impact on the radical movement. Rhetoric sharpened quite acutely and different strategies were explored. While radical actions and language were shaped by arguments about what the yeomanry and magistrates with ministerial support had sought to achieve at Manchester, so too loyalist rhetoric and activity were defined against an apparently escalating radical presence. This left the Whigs – as they had in the 1790s – occupying an uncomfortably diminishing middle ground. If Peterloo was the real catalyst of this dangerous polarization, it was something which was accelerated at local level under local circumstances. In explaining the actions and strategies of radicals, the presence or absence and the activities of militant loyalism become important.[36]

Especially important in the Scottish context were the disturbances that occurred in Paisely and Glasgow in September, which set the tone for much of the heated politics that followed. Ahead of a meeting of radicals at Meikleriggs Muir called for 11 September for 'taking into consideration, the late Proceedings at Manchester' the local authorities issued a proclamation. Having received information that radicals would be coming from adjacent towns, including Glasgow 'with Flags, bearing Inscriptions and Devices of a political and inflammatory nature, a measure unauthorized and illegal in itself' the authorities promised to take action against anyone taking part in such processions.[37] Given the widely reported shout of the yeomanry at Manchester to 'have at their flags', no more potentially explosive line could have been drawn by the civic authorities. In censuring the magistrates for their 'mischievous imbecility' the *Scotsman* reprinted a *Morning Chronicle* article that highlighted a crucial problem in the claim that flag- or banner-carrying was an illegal act in itself. Many aspects of the confrontation between radicals and loyalists were over exactly these questions of where the boundaries of legal and constitutional action could plausibly be drawn. The author suspected that the magistrates and local loyalists had been inspired by ministerial prints to target radial flags as 'a slavish piece of imitation' of the events at Manchester.[38] The publicity of the proclamation, the fact that both radicals and loyalists operated within conflicting versions of what had occurred at Manchester and the recent confiscation of 'a paltry green flag or banner' from the Glasgow radicals, which had resulted in a 'slight tumult', all conspired to lend radical flags a supercharged significance.[39]

The meeting itself, by all reports, went off peacefully as a crowd of 14,000–18,000 voted the resolutions. On the return through Paisley, however, the Glasgow contingent had their flags taken by the special constables lining the High Street. This incident triggered three days of rioting in Paisley as the crowd attempted to rescue the prisoners who had been taken. On Saturday evening this lasted until 1 a.m., when the cavalry arrived from Glasgow. On Sunday morning the magistrates were assailed on their way to church and members of the crowd were arrested. Disturbances continued throughout the day, as houses of prominent loyalists and clergymen were targeted and the railings of the Methodist chapel were torn up to be used as weapons. The rioting continued on the Monday, when the civic authorities spoke to the reform committee, who recommended peace. Crowds, however, continued to call for the release of the prisoners and for the authorities to 'give up the flags'.[40] On Monday evening rioting also broke out in Glasgow. There had been close communication and coordination between the towns and when the cavalry had assembled to ride to Paisley on the Saturday night it had been assailed with stones and bricks in Glasgow. The rioting in Glasgow was serious and caused considerable damage. For the civic and military authorities, there was also the suspicion that such activities were coordinated rather than spontaneous. One officer wearily reported in his early morning account from the Black Bull Inn:

> The magistrates are in the knowledge of this night being a diversion in favour of Paisley. Indeed the Mob were heard to call out 'help Paisley'. The two places are certainly in concert, and there is information that there is to be a constant system of harassing the Troops by these nightly disturbances in the hope of wearing them out.[41]

The riots were widely reported in the Tory, Whig and Radical press, both north and south of the border, and so had an impact in confirming radical and loyalist suspicions across Britain.[42] Their most profound impact was in Scotland. The Lord Advocate was quick to interpret the events as a confirmation of the dangerous confrontation that had been seen at Manchester: 'The proceedings of the Reformers at Manchester have been imitated at Paisley'.[43] Ministers were concerned enough at the state of Scotland to rush two regiments to Leith on frigates specially commissioned from the Prince Regent's own squadron.[44] It is not necessary to accept the idea pushed by the Whig press that disturbances among reformers were met gleefully and even encouraged by the authorities, to see the political usefulness of the riots:

> I am inclined to think that this exhibition will be of no material disservice. It proved to demonstration what the objects of these Reformers are and will open the eyes of many. It will promote the formation of the Military Association which was getting on slowly and will lead to all good men of whatever ideas in politicks [*sic*] to unite their endeavours to restore tranquillity.[45]

Rae's analysis and expectation of the polarizing impact of such disturbances was perceptive. Calls for military associations and the filling of those already underway accelerated in the aftermath of the disturbances. It was in the immediate aftermath of the riots that the Duke of Hamilton, who had contributed to the subscription for the Manchester victims, accompanying his donation with a note proclaiming his reforming credentials, was evidently dislodged from this position and called a county meeting in Lanarkshire to establish a yeomanry corps.[46] At the same meeting Thomas Hopkirk, one of the Glasgow magistrates, who had read the riot act and had been surrounded and attacked, offered a sobering estimate of the strength and organization of the radicals and supported the establishment of the yeomanry.[47] At the end of September Sidmouth suggested to Melville the encouragement of loyal addresses to the Prince Regent and these began to come in from county meetings and town councils throughout October.[48]

As an extension and confirmation of the events at Manchester the riots at Paisley and Glasgow also tended to confirm the political analysis of radicals. The pre-meditated plan to seize flags was characterized as an unprovoked assault on people exercising their legal rights and the natural outcome of Sidmouth's circular to Lords Lieutenant and the Prince Regent's public approbation of the conduct of the authorities at Manchester: 'The former incited magistrates to stretch their authority beyond the law – the latter proved to the people that justice was closed against them, and they had no hopes of redress except by taking summary vengeance against those who commenced upon them an unprovoked attack'.[49] Events in the west of Scotland also helped to underline the language of physical resistance being pursued by Wooler in the *Black Dwarf*:

> And if they are to witness around them *armed associations* for the express purpose of exterminating them, they will also form armed associations to protect themselves. It is as legal for one set of men, as for another, to enrol themselves for the purpose of protecting the laws, and defending themselves from violence.

This was partly a battle over the legal rights enjoyed under the constitution. For Wooler, the 'illegal seizure of some flags' as much as the attack launched at Manchester demonstrated the planned violation of the people's rights and justified radical organization for self-defence. Events at Paisley also demonstrated how the 'Pitt faction' sought to provoke tumults to give themselves a pretext for 'taking up arms against the principles of reform, under the pretence of protecting property that has not been attacked'.[50] After Peterloo a new feature in radical meetings was battle axes surrounding the flags and considerably increased tempo in rhetoric about weapons and arming. If Peterloo accelerated a process of polarization it was reinforced and furthered under local circumstances.

Radical reformers continued to hold meetings and, as the after-effects of Peterloo began to reveal fissures among leading radicals, some began to explore the more confrontational idea of holding simultaneous meetings. This policy, which had the support of Richard Carlile and committed revolutionaries such as Watson and Thistlewood, seemed to take the mass platform one step further and revived the hopes of ultra-radicals that it might form the springboard for a wider insurrection. It was denounced by Hunt in an open letter as the work of spies and informers and the initial date set for these simultaneous meetings, 1 November, was continually delayed. There was evidence of such meetings being planned in Scotland, in Lanarkshire and Renfrewshire. The Lord Advocate later reported that simultaneous meetings had indeed taken place on 1 and 15 November, coinciding with events in England, but in his private correspondence he remained relatively unconcerned about their impact.[51]

The key strategy of radical reformers remained the maintenance of ordered protest, but this was joined by further disturbances, especially where loyalism was noisiest and most active. Frequently it was those communities where both loyalism and radicalism were strong that proved most volatile. Airdrie was a case in point. It contained both a strong social and community basis for radical mobilization and a large military presence, a violently loyal yeomanry, and a parish minister who denounced radicalism from the pulpit as 'an attempt on the part of the "scum of the earth" ... to become rulers of the Nation'.[52] Airdrie took part in the simultaneous meetings and before the 15 November meeting inhabitants staged a 'mock fast', presumably directed at their fiercely anti-radical minister. Radicals also attacked magistrates attempting to swear in citizens as special constables in November.[53]

Both the spectacle of mass and peaceful protest, the reports of radicals drilling at night, and the occasional resort to physical violence did all, as the Lord Advocate predicted, act as recruiting sergeants for the volunteer and yeomanry corps and the special constables. Parliament reassembled towards the end of November, charged by the Prince Regent with devising 'such measures as may be requisite for the counteraction and suppression of a system which, if not effectually checked, must bring confusion and ruin for the nation'.[54] The measures that were moved would eventually become the 'Six Acts', aimed very pointedly at those features of the mass platform that loyalists found most frightening. By this point the open and peaceful mass constitutionalism of the St Peter's Field meeting was losing ground to a more forceful rhetoric of resistance.

II

The preceding narrative has aimed to demonstrate how flawed it would be only to look at radicalism or loyalism in isolation given how far radicals, loyalists, Whigs and Tories shaped the strategies, rhetoric and actions of one another. Political contest and argument was largely conducted through a shared constitutional idiom. In 1819 this space contained a number of debates, the prosecution of which was a crucial part of the developing conflict between radicals and loyalists. What or who constituted 'the people' at the centre of numerous political appeals? What was the role of 'spectacle' in politics and could it be reconciled with a constitutional debate that privileged manly rationality above all other qualities? And what boundaries, if any, existed to the constitutional rights of meeting, speaking and writing? The following sections will explore some of the positions taken up by radicals and loyalists and Whigs on these and other questions and those strategies pursued by both across the winter of 1819–20.

Radical language largely retained its focus on a critique of 'corruption' and the high taxes and other baneful measures that were its consequences. There was, however, an increased tendency to present resolutions that were more discursive and revisited ideas of natural rights. The lead here was given by the Paisley radicals, whose resolutions embodied more obviously French Revolutionary principles, such as: 'That all men are born free and equal in respect of their rights'.[55] Radicalism remained, of course, a protean phenomenon and some of these more obviously universalist values did appear in public pronouncements. Similarly, there were some anti-clerical sentiments and, as the *Spirit of the Union* complained, some small following for the astringent republicanism of Richard Carlile 'and similar impious trash'.[56] Booksellers taken up on suspicion of seditious and blasphemous libel do demonstrate that these ultra-radical works were circulating from a couple of shops in Glasgow and some of this material did make it into the speeches of radicals.[57]

Broadly speaking, however, the language of the movement, certainly in public, remained resolutely constitutionalist.[58] Following the 'alarms' of 1817 and the events of 1819, however, this constitutionalism became further radicalized.

In particular, following Peterloo it came to centre on the idea of resisting an active attack on the people's liberties. At Kirkcaldy, for example, a meeting in the fraught first week of November (when government expected simultaneous meetings) voted a first resolution, which claimed the spirit of the British constitution meant that people could meet for the discussion of public measures and that any interruption to this right was illegal, unconstitutional and tended towards despotism 'resistance to which is the duty of every one who is not willing to become a slave'.[59] This escalating rhetoric of resistance was compounded by an idea that reformers now faced a threat not only to their liberty but to their lives. When William Rodger, a leading radical in Airdrie, was taken up in connection with an attack on the magistrates swearing in special constables in the town, he was unequivocal and unguarded in his conversation with Sheriff Aiton:

> it is the Declarants [sic] private opinion that soldiers are murderers by profession at least he thinks some of them are so – and he alluded particularly to the Manchester Yeomanry cavalry who murdered the people at Manchester ... it is his own private opinion that every man should be possessed of arms to defend himself against Robbers and murderers.[60]

This radicalization was driven by events. Radical leaders, such as William Cobbett, Henry Hunt and Major Cartwright, evinced an unshakeable faith in the efficacy of petitioning and this had been the very bedrock of the reform movement of 1816–17. By 1819 there was considerable scepticism that ministers would acknowledge let alone answer petitions and as early as July the Paisley radicals had ridiculed the Glasgow Committee's 'Canadian resolutions' on those very grounds. More inflammatory was the accusation that Sidmouth was in fact acting to block the channel of communication between the prince and his people. At a meeting at Smithfield, Henry Hunt publicly accused Sidmouth of having refused to communicate remonstrances drawn up by meetings in London and Manchester to the Prince Regent.[61] For radicals this represented another dangerous incursion on the liberties of the subject and Paisley's resolutions echoed the idea that Sidmouth was guilty 'of treason against the nation' for keeping their appeals from a just prince.[62] This breach of contract was a constant refrain within the radical movement as it developed across the autumn and winter and a mass meeting in Dundee in November passed perhaps the most trenchant of the reported resolutions:

> That as Lord Sidmouth has presumed, in some instances, to refuse to present to the Throne the petitions of the people, we deem it equally unnecessary to attempt to offer any petition to that quarter, – aware that, in all probability, it would only go to increase his Lordship's store of waste paper. And farther, we are of opinion, that in thus preventing the voice of the people from reaching the throne, the said Lord Sidmouth has been guilty of the highest species of treason, – namely, treason against

the people; and that dismissal from the office which he so unworthily fills, would be far too lenient a punishment for him.[63]

The decline in general confidence in petitioning encouraged a search for alternative strategies. Convinced of the inefficacy or the impossibility of making representations to the Prince Regent, the press became even more important as an idealized forum for communicating with the nation at large. It provided a short-circuit around these corrupt institutions and provided a space in which to explore what radicals at Clayknowes called 'the only alternative that remains, an appeal to the people'.[64]

If radical language in Scotland was centred on a radicalized constitutionalism which was, in origin, an English language there was a similar orientation towards the radical press in England to make this national appeal. From trials of vendors and radical testimony about what formed radicals' reading material, we know that much of the literature that circulated came from the south. The popularity of Cobbett has already been noted, but on his departure for America the *Black Dwarf* rose to particular prominence. Within loyalism it became a byword for those seditious and blasphemous publications that were 'poisoning the minds of the people'. Thomas Hopkirk, who had read the riot act in Glasgow, was ridiculed for his horror at having seen a couple of masons reading the paper on their lunch break.[65] There was considerable Scottish input into the *Black Dwarf* including reports of meetings, correspondence, comments on events in Scotland and a large Scottish presence in the poetry section. Parodies on 'Scots Wha Hae' from Scotland and elsewhere were something of a staple and demonstrated the 'blending of Britain' in radical discourse.[66] The ways in which Scottish radicals sought to insert the Scots into a wider British history of liberty was apparent in a 'Caledonian Appeal to the Friends of Freedom' from Glasgow. This appeal both cited 'Scots Wha Hae' and offered a poem penned by 'Caledonius' and entitled 'To Britons', which deftly referenced the heroes (Washington, Wallace, Hampden) and the villains (Charles I and James II) of a shared British history.[67] The *Black Dwarf* was not, however, the only English publication that circulated. Contemporary accounts suggest that the *Manchester Observer*, which was sent direct to booksellers in Glasgow by James Wroe, and John Wade's cheap instalments of the *Black Book* were also staples.[68] Radicals frequently gave thanks to English radical editors as heroes of this British movement.[69]

Given the radical emphasis on union as an end in itself the press played a crucial organizing role in 1819. While radicalism remained strongest at the community level and weakest at the national level the press remained really the only effective way of supplying a deficiency in national leadership.[70] This was all the more important given the geographically and socially more restricted appeal of radicalism in 1819. It would be a mistake to see radicalism as simply a phenomenon of the 'west' – communities in Angus, Fife and Stirlingshire, for example, were host to strong groups of radicals, while Dundee provided an alternative urban centre to Glasgow. Nevertheless, there is no doubt that in terms of radical meetings, societies and remonstrances, activists could not claim to represent a national constituency in the same way that reformers had in 1816–17. The press allowed for what was a localized movement to conceive of itself as a truly national one.

Radicals set great store by the press and in Scotland the deficiency of a radical journal that could reflect both the wider British movement and the particular Scottish circumstances was keenly felt by some. This lay at the root of the profound disappointment with the growing hostility of the reform-minded press. An attempt to supply this deficiency was launched at a Glasgow meeting in August, when a speaker argued for a subscription to a Scottish radical publication that would be based explicitly on Wooler and Sherwin's productions. The argument was premised on the positive contribution such a publication might make to the cause by superseding and drowning out the *Glasgow Chronicle*, which was either 'corrupt or servile'.[71] The projected paper would be a reaction to the moderate line being taken by liberal papers such as the *Chronicle* and the *Scotsman* in the aftermath of Peterloo and in the face of a radicalizing reform movement.

The resulting publication – Gilbert Macleod's *Spirit of the Union* – was issued in October and ran until the arrest of its conductors in January of 1820. It offers a unique insight into some of the activities of radicals in the west of Scotland and a density of coverage not repeated elsewhere. It needs, however, to be treated with caution: its content made it plain how important news from England was to Scottish radicals and this filled most of its pages. Many radicals must have continued to read the *Manchester Observer* and the *Black Dwarf* for largely the same news, although one Union Society certainly took up the *Spirit of the Union* in preference to the English publications.[72] All of these papers allowed radicals to see themselves as part of a larger movement, without which a sense of isolation might easily have developed. The *Spirit of the Union* provided an outlet for the reviling and ridiculing of local enemies, such as Glasgow town-hall alarmists, the 'sevenpenny editors' of the liberal press and recusant Whigs such as John Maxwell and for the celebration of local heroes and victories, such as the liberation of the Airdrie radicals, William Rodger and William Miller. It attempted to create a national reform constituency and, in its second number, dedicated a long letter to 'the repressed spirit of Reform in Edinburgh', chiding the men of the east for their servility and inactivity.[73]

The proposal at the Glasgow meeting also demonstrated the various and complex relationships between assembly, speaking, writing and reading. One characteristic and important form of radical organization, the Union Society, was a product of these relationships and was based in part on the missionary activity of English radicals. From Autumn 1819 Joseph Brayshaw, a radical reformer from Yeadon near Leeds, had toured Scotland, much to the alarm of the authorities.[74] His mission, however, was an open one, and he subsisted as a new type of professional politician, funding his advocacy of reform through the sale of a penny pamphlet he had written.[75] A later pamphlet more specifically addressed his Scottish market by appending a lengthy letter to the Lord Advocate. In this letter Brayshaw outlined the cellular form of reading society, which his tours had been intended to promulgate:

> I propose that you should form Union Societies, for the dissemination of political knowledge. When I speak of Union Societies, I do not mean any kind of secret associations; on the contrary, I advise you to have no secrets of any kind whatever ... I would advise you simply to meet as a school, for the purpose of obtaining knowledge.[76]

We have some accounts of these clubs – of two in Strathaven and one in Kilmarnock – which offer some insight into their activities. With between twelve and twenty members the emphasis was on self-education and self-improvement coupled with the kind of uncompromising radicalism which was fast becoming a dictum of Richard Carlile and his acolytes. The tenor of this was summed up by one of the weaver members of the Kilmarnock society: 'All were clear that there should be no king, no lords, no gentry, no taxes!' The drive for political information seems to have been paramount and James Wilson of Strathaven was designated 'Class Leader' rather than 'President' of a Society whose meetings principally revolved around the reading of the *Manchester Observer*, but also took in the *Black Dwarf*, the *Spirit of the Union* and the *Black Book*. The declaration of one radical arrested in 1820 claimed that the club meeting in the house of a shoemaker in Strathaven 'had no other object except to read newspapers, and they discussed no political subjects there'. The first part of his statement rings true: the second does not.[77] Union Societies certainly did allow for wholesome entertainment, political education and the collective abstinence from taxable goods, but they were also a highly effective form of local political organization. The Societies were useful in mobilizing radicals for meetings, to which individual Societies often marched as a group, but they could also become the sinews of less legal forms of organization.

The very name of the Union Societies underlined the continuing emphasis on the indispensability of unanimity to the reform cause. Mass meetings were, of course, the most visible and, to the authorities, the most alarming of the strategies pursued consistently by radicals to that end. To contemporaries the most notable aspect of the meetings was less the content of the speeches and resolutions than the impression that such meetings made. Two key features emerged: first, their disciplined and orderly demeanour, a source of pride for reformers but of alarm for the authorities; secondly, the rich mix of spectacle and symbolic display which was the hallmark of radical meetings. The work of James Epstein and others has vastly expanded perceptions of what constitutes the 'political': symbolic practices and what might broadly be called the political culture of popular movements have become crucial and fruitful areas of inquiry.[78] One excellent recent account has focused on the complex range of meanings in the reformers' 'march to Peterloo' and characterized it as 'part military parade, part club outing, part village festivity'. According to Poole, in taking this cultural approach to popular politics a focus on non-verbal communication and the visual aspects of reform movements is an integral part of reconstructing their political appeal: 'the form *was* the argument'.[79] With this in mind the crucial question is what kind of rhetorical and symbolic purchase did mass meetings, with their elements of popular festivities and militarized forms, offer proponents of collective action in developing a 'logic of confrontation' with loyalists?

Militarized symbolic action formed an important part of the strategies of the mass platform which emerged after 1816.[80] This was most obvious in the numerous reports of mass drilling in 1819, which so alarmed the authorities and of which Samuel Bamford has left perhaps the most memorable account:

> Our drill masters were generally old soldiers of the line, or of militia, or local militia regiments; they put the lads through their facings in quick time, and soon learned them to march with a steadiness and regularity which would not have disgraced a regiment on parade [...] We mustered, we fell into rank, we faced, marched, halted, faced about, countermarched, halted again, dressed, and wheeled in quick succession, and without confusion.[81]

Bamford's retrospective account is similar to many contemporaneous accounts, both hostile and friendly, which dwelt on the militarized nature of the mass movement. It was not only drilling but the entire military panoply of fife, drums, flags and martial music which was remarked upon. It was, for example, a constant refrain in the diary of Charles Hutcheson, a private in the Glasgow Sharpshooters volunteer regiment between 1819 and 1820, who made frequent reference to the presence of 'flags, drums and fife' and the 'regular military step' with which radicals attended and left meetings.[82]

While Bamford undoubtedly overstated the novelty of ordered protest, which drew on a number of sources, the military inflection of the mass platform was something qualitatively new.[83] How should we account for it? The presence of ex-military personnel must clearly be a central part in any explanation. As Bamford's account suggests, and in spite of Castlereagh's confident denial that any more than a few ex-soldiers were involved in the drilling of radicals, numerous accounts emphasized that it was ex-soldiers who rallied radicals into a 'military step'.[84] Part of the reason for the adoption of the 'military step' was certainly practical: it was the only way to move large numbers of people from one place to another without disorder. It was, however, the concern to avoid not only the actual occurrence but also the impression of disorder that provides the most convincing explanation for the militarized nature of the mass platform.

Bamford claimed that drilling without arms was simply for this purpose of moving with regularity. He also claimed that drilling provided communities with a wholesome day out, in short, that it was fun: 'These drillings were also, to our sedentary weavers and spinners periods of healthful exercise and enjoyment'.[85] Men and women, old and young attended these events. Before we dismiss Bamford's claims, we should note how frequently these claims were made. John Parkhill, who was involved in the plans for an attempted rising at Paisley, believed that less than a third of those who drilled were in earnest: 'The great proportion of them were below thirty years of age, and their turning out was through excitement and what they termed *fun*'.[86] Similarly, a witness, an ex-volunteer who had drilled radicals in and around Johnstone, when cross-examined during the treason trials of 1820, attempted to convince the court that what they called drilling could be called something else. When asked what the two or three parties he had observed were doing, he replied: 'Running up and down the field, as if they appeared to be in diversion to me, or playing'.[87]

Political mobilization depends on a number of things: on community relations, on political messages being crafted to speak to individuals and groups, but also on politics and political activity being rendered fun and exciting. Drilling certainly offered this. It also made for an immediate emotional appeal, as radicals could place themselves in a national history of liberty, incorporating figures such as Wallace and the Covenanters. These figures suffused the recorded speech of radical meetings, and sites associated with them were part of the itinerary of radical marches and meetings. A party in Renfrewshire fired shots at the site of Wallace's tree, and startled a grocer in Elderslie, who had a bust of Wallace above his door, by firing shots there too.[88] Similarly, for Parkhill nocturnal excursions were exhilarating experiences and his committee at Gleniffer 'dived into the heart of the gorge in the hills, in the same manner and with the same instincts that prompted the old covenanters'.[89] A common and meaningful reference point for Scots was a comparison between Peterloo and the massacre of Glencoe.[90]

If it was fun and exciting, drilling and the self-consciously ordered conduct at meetings was most important in allowing radicals definitively to reject the idea that they constituted a 'mob'. It promised to defuse the principal rhetorical ploy of those who sought to delegitimize popular political action, or, as Bamford put it in addressing the Middleton radicals ahead of marching in step to Manchester:

> I hoped their conduct would be marked by a steadiness and seriousness befitting the occasion, and such as would cast shame on their enemies, who had always represented the reformers as a mob-like rabble: but they would see that they were not so that day.[91]

From the Gordon Riots of 1780, mass political action had been rendered synonymous with the excesses of the mob and all of its associated images of infantilism, popular licence, anarchy and bloodshed. Radicals had struggled against these charges in the 1790s, but to little avail, so that going into the post-war period 'the tumultuous mob was the spectre haunting the radical movement'.[92] The militarized display of the mass platform attempted to exorcize this spectre by echoing those spectacles of order and control with which Britons had become increasingly familiar in the early nineteenth century.

This was part of what Fulcher has called 'the rhetorical game', where radicals contested the language of patriotism and constitutionalism with armed loyalists and the government. In the aftermath of Peterloo the strategy of peaceful, disciplined and ordered protest – and, in particular, the presence of women and children – allowed reformers not only to exorcize the demon of the tumultuous mob but set it loose among its begetters. The presence of women, in particular, was another feature much noted by contemporaries. The mass platform saw an expansion of the political space available for women, who were incorporated, in albeit quite obviously gendered ways, in the ritual and display of radical politics. The emphasis on the achievement of 'mass' and on the politicization of hunger and economic distress helped to effect a shift in radical strategies, which created political opportunities for working women. By dressing in white or by making and presenting caps of liberty to radical leaders, they symbolized the community values underpinning the movement as a whole and provided a virtuous counterpoint to the common enemy of 'old corruption'.[93] This ordered and socially inclusive mass platform staked out a powerful claim that it was the radicals whose ordered demeanour and respectable behaviour rendered them fit for citizenship. It was the loyalists, the Manchester Yeomanry and the regulars, who had rioted on St Peter's Field and engaged in a wanton orgy of dehumanizing and Jacobinical violence.[94]

This was, perhaps, an unforeseen advantage and there is no doubt that the militarized nature of collective action was not only intended to present radicals as orderly and disciplined, but also constituted a threatening and intimidating gesture. During the war Luddite drilling had often been done consciously in full view of the authorities.[95] In spite of Hunt's regrets that weavers were 'playing soldiers' and Bamford's later attempts to sanitize such activity as simply an opportunity for healthy exercise and pleasant diversionary leisure time outdoors, drilling constituted both a challenge and an assertion of physical strength. Parkhill confirmed that intimidation was a crucial part of the fun for drilling radicals: 'the causing of alarm became an important feature in the matter'.[96] This consciousness of the effect of such activity on opponents was underlined by the openness with which radicals drilled and had their activities witnessed and even by such gestures as clapping in order to imitate the report of musketry.[97] If loyalists and the authorities sought to act against 'the people' they would not be suppressing a riot or quelling a mob, but facing an army. As a strategy it was designed to play on elite fears current during the war that 'the armed crowd was the all too likely concomitant of the armed nation'.[98] It certainly exerted an effect on Lord Althorp, who argued in Parliament:

> The people had been taught to march in military array; they had been instructed to wheel, to form in column, and to go through other military evolutions in large bodies: and, would any persons say that, with arms in their hands, these men, though not capable of contending with regular forces, would not be excessively formidable?[99]

More level-headed commentary identified intimidation as the key purpose of military display. By December the *Glasgow Chronicle* was convinced that drilling and persistent rumours of risings were not indicative of actual insurrectionary movements:

> We have reason to believe that the Radicals in the city and suburbs do not amount to one eightieth part of the population; and we believe that but a small proportion of this small fraction meditate violence. It ought not to be forgotten that it is their object to intimidate.[100]

Orderly protest was a crucial facet of radical symbolic display, but it was not the only one. Recent work has dwelt on the spectacular and visual nature of mass platform politics and it has been demonstrated that a thriving visual culture in radicalism depended on radicals overcoming their own and others' traditional association of the visual and the irrational.[101] Only when this was done could visual display become an important, even an integral part of the radical platform. Marching in an orderly way was one part of this visual display, but it was joined by many other visual markers of union and unanimity. Some contingents added to the sense of union and military display by wearing uniforms. Based on placards that had preceded Hunt's meetings in London and Manchester, boards bearing the words 'Order, Order' were common.[102] In both England and Scotland radicals marched with laurel in their hats as a symbol of regeneration and to betoken their peaceful intentions. In Scotland, laurel could be replaced with thistles, as at Kilmarnock, to demonstrate the idea of submerged resistance.[103]

A similar message was conveyed by the frequent presence of 'Nemo me impune lacessit' on the flags and banners that were a ubiquitous presence at radical meetings.[104] Their importance both to radicals and to loyalists had been inflated by events at Manchester and Paisley. At Manchester, witnesses famously attested that the soldiers' normal emotional investment in capturing the enemy standard had been translated into an obsession to take the radical banners and symbols: 'Have at their Flags' was the cry from the cavalry.[105] After the events of Peterloo, observers in Scotland noted that radicals became even more ostentatiously concerned to assign armed men as 'guards to the women and colours' and were 'determined that the flags should not be touched'.[106] Their importance is underlined by the assiduity with which their inscriptions, images and number were recorded by reporters. The *Scotsman*, for example, counted between thirty and forty silk and cotton banners at a Glasgow meeting and provided detailed descriptions of a number of them.[107] Whereas written reports of the speeches at radical meetings are often scanty, the flags and banners provide a crucial resource for the historian. Even the way in which banners were made – with collections taken from door-to-door by men and women – gives us good evidence of the powerful community dynamic behind radicalism.[108] In turn they helped radicals and journalists to identify particular localized contingents of reformers at mass meetings.

Some banners bore eloquent testimony to how radicals identified themselves with a wider British movement. Scots identified with the British leadership of radicalism and at Paisley, the Ferguslie party carried a banner bearing a full-length portrait of Major Cartwright, which had been paid for by local subscription.[109] Banners bearing 'Hunt and Liberty' were carried at Rutherglen, while at Kilmarnock an observer noted flags with the inscriptions, 'Major Cartwright for ever', 'Hunt for ever' and 'Sir Francis Burdett for ever'.[110] At Paisley and Glasgow in the aftermath of Peterloo a number of commentators noticed an elaborate banner showing a Manchester yeoman sabring a fellow citizen.[111] At Dundee a flag bore a British standard reversed and a small boat upside down as a comment on the anti-national nature of the faction opposed to the radicals and the ruin of British commerce.[112] Others could uncomplicatedly place Scottish heroes next to reform icons such as Cartwright. The Calton Unions could be recognized by their banner depicting 'Wallace pushing his sword through an enemy to Scottish freedom', while another common inscription invoked 'the Muckin' of Geordie's Byre', an old Scots song with Jacobite associations, which had been re-written as a popular anti-monarchical song by the radical poet Alexander Rodger.[113] Other banners advertised and encouraged political strategies: the paraphernalia of taxed items of consumption atop flagpoles, for example, became a common feature after radicals had begun to explore abstinence as a political strategy. At Dundee, poles were topped with broken tea pots, cups, dram glasses, tobacco pipes and an empty spleuchan.[114]

Other features of this rich mix of symbolism indicated the more radicalized discourse after Peterloo. These included threats of physical resistance, such as a flag at Dundee that proclaimed 'BREAD OR BLOOD' or an inscription at Kilmarnock: 'He that hath no sword let him sell his garment and buy one'.[115] Many observers indicated that this message was underlined by radicals carrying sticks, clubs, axes, halberds and swords. The ambiguity of these symbolic displays was, however, a crucial part of their strength. The carrying of axes, for example, could be done in a number of ways: as a statement about protecting women and children from unprovoked attack; as a defence of flags and banners from seizure; or, when accompanied with bound rods, as 'fasces' a Roman republican symbol of unity. Other apparently republican symbols included caps of liberty, which were frequently displayed at meetings in Scotland. As in England, these were often made and presented by female reformers in a ritual incorporating women into the radical platform.[116] Tricolours too made occasional appearances. The leaders of the Airdrie radicals, William Rodger and William Miller, were released from Hamilton tollbooth in December 1819 and were 'chaired' into Airdrie by a crowd. Reports noted that they wore 'the insignia of the order, displayed in the same manner as the Waterloo medal' or three pieces of ribbon, red, white and blue, on the left breast.[117]

This rich symbolism underlined the radicalized constitutionalism of the movement and was among the most contentious features of the movement. What linked together radical words and deeds was the struggle to demonstrate both what fell within the bounds of popular understandings of the constitution and that these boundaries were being consistently violated by ministers and loyalists rather than by radicals. The *Glasgow Herald*, for example, ridiculed and highlighted the dangerous symbolism of the caps of liberty and the fasces carried at radical meetings. Just as Hunt would later claim the cap of liberty was a British symbol and point at his trial to its appearance above the door of the York court as proof of this, so could the *Spirit of the Union* point out that the fasces – a symbol of revolution to the *Herald* – featured above Glasgow's jail and public offices.[118] This was a distinct and radicalized version of what the British constitution offered but the strength and the focus of the radical movement lay in staying within its limits. Visual display as well as making for spectacle, allowed for ambiguity and full exploration of these limits.

III

The general resources for the study of loyalist ideas and practices are clear: the press, sermons, speeches, resolutions and attempts to revive armed associations in defence of liberty and property. Loyalism was every bit as protean a phenomenon as radicalism. One complicating factor was the presence of the issue of 'party' in political disputes in Parliament and the localities. Self-identifying loyalists (and some, such as 'The Warder' in *Blackwood's Edinburgh Magazine* and the Lord Chancellor Eldon, were even keen to embrace 'the true praise in the epithet' of

'Alarmists') aimed at least as much fire at those men they interpreted as the Whig abettors of radicalism as they did at the radicals themselves.[119] For their part, the Whigs and the liberal press forwarded an analysis and acted in ways that tried to maintain a delicate balancing act: proclaiming their own loyalty while simultaneously criticizing ministers as the authors of the nation's misfortunes, expressing sympathy for the distresses of the lower orders and rejecting radical solutions to these distresses. What both Tories and most Whigs had in common was a range of criticisms of both the content and the form of radical politics as it was being practised from the summer of 1819. As with radicalism, it makes sense to treat loyalism less as a coherent body of political ideas than as a range of political positions and practices taken up within the context of debate and a rapidly changing political situation.

The now quite voluminous historiography of loyalism during the 1790s has recovered a complex phenomenon comprising a number of ideological traditions and political practices.[120] Much of the rhetorical content of loyalism remained unchanged: there were panegyrics on society as a 'great chain'; rejections of the 'visionary' schemes of reformers; and an emphasis on the results rather than the theoretical underpinning of political institutions that secured liberty and property. Loyalism sought to counter radical perceptions of the social order and its modes of political reasoning. A large part of the emphasis of loyalist language during 1819 was on countering the radical claim to represent 'the people', who were the source of political sovereignty and national wealth and were just claimants for the rights of citizens. Loyalists contested this central claim of radicalism with a particular idea of who 'the people' were and should be, which encompassed a vision of their proper role within the constitution and a critique of how radical practices acted to subvert this role.

The idealized loyalist vision of 'the people' had them as peaceable, quiescent and Christian. A hierarchical vision of society – expressed through 'the great chain' or through a language of interests – had formed one plank of loyalist language in the late eighteenth century and retained a powerful hold.[121] John Wilson offered one such idyllic vision of 'the people' to contrast with the horror of 'The Radical's Saturday Night' in *Blackwood's*:

> For in Scotland alone, and I say so with a due sense of the virtues of England, does there exist among the peasantry a union of knowledge, morality, and religion, so universal, and so intense, and so solemn, as to constitute National Character.[122]

That piety provided the crucial foundation of loyalty was key to the language of loyalism in 1819. The speeches of the Lord Advocate and the content of many of the loyal resolutions and panicked letters to the civil authorities identified the gravest political danger in Scots being led away from their religious duties. Rioting in Paisley on a Sunday would later be cited by the Lord Advocate as proof positive of how a previously religious people had been seduced from their sense of duty by seditious and blasphemous literature.[123]

'Seduced' was a central word for loyalists. An axiom of loyalist rhetoric was that the lower orders did not so much act as they were acted upon. Reference has already been made to the numerous pathological metaphors which peppered loyalist speech and writing. Radicals were frequently described as 'deluded', 'distempered', 'poisoned' or 'fevered'. Distress weakened the people and made them susceptible to manipulation. In particular, they were ready soil for 'ill-designing' demagogues, who could convince them to reject all established institutions and embrace radical reform as a ready remedy for distress. Visionary schemes of reform were simply a stalking horse for plots to achieve social equality and the threat to property and the spectre of 'levelling' was the bedrock of loyalism as it had been in the 1790s.[124] Loyalist language thus often spoke, as in the loyal resolutions of Haddington, of 'the pretence of reform'.[125] There was palpable relief in the correspondence of the Lord President, Charles Hope, when he could claim: 'even the flimsy pretence of Radical Reform is laid aside, & complete Revolution and plunder is avowed to be their object'.[126]

Enhanced receptivity to pernicious and visionary ideas could also be enlisted in the language of party. In Scotland this was at its most virulent in *Blackwood's*, which blamed the increasing infidelity and radicalism of the lower orders on a kind of percolation of ideas first aired in the *Edinburgh Review*: 'To say the truth once more, the worst of all the features in the present convulsed countenance of the affairs of our country, is, to our mind, the behaviour not of the Reformers, but of the Whigs'. Not content with providing the source of the malady in the *Edinburgh Review*, the Whigs compounded their crimes by the dangerous conduct of opposing ministers and trying to secure place instead of rallying round throne and altar: 'It is not now, who is a Tory? – Who is a Whig? But it is, who is a Briton? – Who is a Christian?'[127]

If a key part of loyalist rhetoric was an attack on the sources of those ideas, seditious and blasphemous, which were seducing the minds of the lower orders, perhaps a more important focus was the means by which these ideas were communicated. If novel developments in the form of protest were crucial features of popular radicalism, they are no less important in explaining the nature of loyalism and its arguments, which responded directly to these radical innovations. First and foremost, the seducers of the lower orders were identified as 'itinerant orators'. Itinerancy was a frequent subject of loyalist rhetoric, which expressed disquiet about the disruption of visions of a stable social order and a perceived threat from the real itinerancy of radical 'orators', 'demagogues' and 'emissaries'. Alexander Boswell's complaint was typical: 'itinerant orators from Manchester and Leeds have in this country succeeded in fomenting the spirit of evil'.[128] Such a critique extended to radical meetings attended by people from great distance. For radicals, dislocation and mobility were the necessary implications of attempting to knit together a national movement. For loyalists, such meetings breached constitutional norms for meeting and petitioning on the basis of stable and recognized social, institutional and administrative units and posed a direct challenge to the state's attempts to 'preserve its monopoly on national organization and limit radical protest to a series of aberrations'.[129]

Linked to this was the idea that the mechanisms by which the lower orders were seduced at these meetings moved beyond the rational appeal of the written word to encompass attempts to stir their senses. Itinerant pamphleteers were bad enough, but the radical embrace of spectacle as a means of seducing the lower orders was a qualitatively new threat. The use of a vocabulary of irrational sensation – of 'intoxication' and 'phrenzy' – was common and sought to defuse radical claims to be rationally and deliberatively demanding their rights. 'The Warder' gave one such account of the sights and sounds of a radical meeting and its imagined impact on a member of the audience:

> The clamours of public meetings – the noise, and the music, and the dissonance – and the brawlings of orators and the applauses of multitudes – and the solemnity of processions, and the intoxication of huzzas – all these things may for a time appear to awaken new life and new delight – and unexpected importance – and unexpected triumph: but when the poor man that has partaken in all these elements of phrenzy returns home weary ... when he contrasts the glare and tumult that has been dazzling his own imagination, with the quiet thoughts of comfort and repose that fed the spirit of his fathers ... is it possible ... that he should not feel that he has been among scenes that were strange to his nature, and among men with whom he had nothing to do.[130]

The attack on the spectacle of radicalism was a common feature of loyalist language and a shift from the 1790s, when radicalism had not embraced visual culture to the same extent.[131] Newspapers and observers frequently dwelt on the visual impact of meetings rather than the content of speeches. In descriptions of meetings 'hearing' and 'listening' were verbs less frequently employed than 'seeing' or 'viewing', as in this hostile diary entry by a Glasgow volunteer:

> the meetings here attended by the thousands ... who marched to the place of attendance, with silken Banners waving over their heads, and bundles of Rods on the ends of poles emblematic of unanimity, and large brooms to sweep away corruption and caps of liberty of all colours, men and women four and four arm and arm – these were all to be seen at a meeting which I attended at the East end of Gallowgate. I was too late of arriving to hear the speeches made but mixed with the procession at its departure and although I was struck with the order that prevailed and apparent good humour of all parties such a display in defence of such principles could not be viewed with indifference.[132]

Hutcheson here identified another aspect of radical spectacle which featured largely in loyalist denunciations. If flags and music assaulted the senses of the people, for the constituted authorities perhaps the most alarming aspect of radical activity was its very orderliness. The Lord Advocate made the point at length in a speech in the Commons, for which he was ridiculed in the radical press. For him the ordered conduct and the 'military discipline' of the radicals were portentous: 'The very silence, and order, and regularity, with which the business of these assemblies was conducted, excited in his mind the strongest apprehensions'. He based his fears on an understanding of Scottish national character, which ensured that riot was the natural and normal outcome of large assemblies of his countrymen. By this analysis, the riots at Paisley, while serious in themselves, were salutary proof that radical leaders had not obtained sufficient command over their audience:

> Now, however, they had acquired that control, and (contrary to the nature of Scotchmen) 5,000, 10,000, and even 20,000 persons of the lowest order assembled together, without the slightest disturbance, moved with precision, and separated with regularity; implicitly obeying every command of the orators who harangued and deluded them.

Such order and tranquillity, he argued, must demonstrate 'that a great though secret purpose was entertained'.[133]

Finally, all of these preoccupations of loyalists were discussed within the framework of constitutionalism and linked to understandings of the liberties of Britons. If radical strategies involved the exploration of the ambiguous boundaries of rights of petitioning, speech, writing and assembly, loyalists in turn were compelled to confront these same ambiguities. 'The Warder', as the pseudonym might suggest, was one of many loyalist voices seeking to police and to define these boundaries. If the people were, of course, empowered by a right to petition for redress of grievances, radicals had moved beyond this right to 'the means of making their sentiments *known*' to embrace ideas of intimidation of the executive and the legislature. The intimidation by a regular 'system' of meetings fell well outside the rights and duties of subjects – no man could claim such events were not dangerous and harmful 'and how dare he to declare they are constitutional?'[134] Walter Scott employed similar language to reject the constitutionality of large meetings, while rebuking James Ballantyne for an overly-critical appraisal of the Manchester magistrates in the *Edinburgh Weekly Journal*: 'It is an obvious thing that 50,000 armed men are not a deliberative body – they cannot be assembled for any proper or useful purpose and they are in the case in hand avowedly assembled for the overthrow of the constitution'.[135]

Most Whigs would not have agreed with these narrow interpretations of the boundaries of constitutional rights, nor would they have agreed with Scott's interpretation of Peterloo. There was, however, a considerable amount of common ground between their own arguments and language about popular radicalism and that of more ardent and self-proclaimed loyalists. The area of this common ground increased towards the end of 1819 under the process of polarization discussed at the beginning of this chapter. The events of August to October, when a large county meeting in Yorkshire and the dismissal of Lord Fitzwilliam from his Lord Lieutenancy of the county convinced many lukewarm Whigs that they were playing with fire, certainly did much to enliven the reforming zeal of some younger Whigs.[136] If the overall effect was to encourage some Whigs to embrace and ultimately to lead moderate reform and to oppose some aspects of the Six Acts it also sharpened the Whig and liberal critique of radical reform. Those who had always been opposed to reform or uncertain as to the consequences of reform were pushed in the other direction and Peterloo began the irreparable split between the Whigs and their more alarmist Grenvillite allies.[137]

Overall, there was much in the avowedly loyalist press which could command broad Whig assent and might not be incompatible with moderate reform. The analysis of a distressed people being seduced and deluded by itinerant orators was a common trope. The Whig leader in the Commons, Tierney, was apt to play down its consequences:

> True it was, that men marched from one town to another; but they were the same men at both places, and they were to be looked upon like a company of strollers, who travelled about to perform their parts in different situations.

Itinerancy could be a sign of the absolute numerical weakness of radical reform rather than a source of immediate danger.[138] As the radical threat seemed to increase, however, such rhetorical minimizations of it proved less and less convincing and, in Scotland, Whig defections from the banner of moderate reform came thick and fast. Towards the end of the year, some of these were accompanied by elaborate ideological justifications. John Maxwell summed up his reasons for abandoning reform in letters to the press and a separate pamphlet:

> Myself a reformer, who wished neither to be without God nor law in the world, I have been deeply grieved to find, by the recent meetings in Glasgow and Paisley, that I have been engaged in a cause that has for its object to destroy authority, divide property, and do away with religion.[139]

What followed was an impassioned defence of property, religion and established institutions and a denunciation of 'ill-designing men', 'Editors and Orators who mislead' and itinerant 'animals' from London and Manchester roaming the country spreading sedition.[140]

Another Whig strategy was to maintain that there was a good case for moderate reform but that this was being irreparably damaged by a movement dangerously composed only 'of the lower orders of the people, that is to say, operative tradesmen and labourers', whose distress was being manipulated by visionary reformers whose plans would not and could not amend economic circumstances.[141] In this way Whigs and others interested in moderate reform could share a loyalist analysis of the dangers represented by the current crisis, while maintaining a different prognosis of its causes. Even if, as many argued, ministerial measures had caused or exacerbated distress among the lower orders, there was an attempt to break the idea that economic problems had constitutional solutions: 'the depression now prevailing in our manufactures, is of a nature beyond the reach of any government'.[142]

A final difference in the Whig approach to popular radicalism was to encourage the use of language more sympathetic to the lower orders, notably in Scotland in their attempts to amend the loyal addresses that were being voted during the winter. Such an analysis was also apparent in the most spectacular of the Whig defections in Scotland, that of the Duke of Hamilton. His support for the Manchester sufferers, in particular his letter accompanying his £50 subscription in which he claimed to be 'a firm friend to Reform', elicited considerable comment and some vituperative attacks.[143] One of these came from the Prince Regent, who suggested that he be stripped of his Lord Lieutenancy like Lord Fitzwilliam: 'Is nothing to be done with respect to Lord Grovesnor & the Duke of Hamilton the subscribing Lords Lieutenant to the Manchester sufferers? For I cannot dismiss from my mind the offensive Letters which accompanied their subscriptions'.[144] The disturbances in Glasgow and Paisley and dialogue between himself and the radicals had a transformative effect on Hamilton's politics and he quickly began to subscribe to loyalist measures. Those employed by the duke on public works as a means of relief had allegedly hoisted a tricolour flag within view of Hamilton Palace. His conversion elicited considerable gloating from those in authority: Rae suspected that his new-found loyalism represented fear for his own position as Lord Lieutenant after the dismissal of Fitzwilliam; Scott and Hope saw it as a case of the duke being frightened into loyalism by the conduct of radicals; and the Tory satirist, J. W. Croker, launched his new loyalist newspaper with a piece on 'The Lanarkshire Radicals, and the Duke of Hamilton'.[145] It is clear that Hamilton, like many Whigs, did rally to the cause of social order in the face of an increasingly assertive radical movement, but he continued to represent in his letters to Liverpool that relief – even of known radicals – was the only effective means of addressing the danger.[146] Such efforts to meet distress by public works were a common response of men of property to the radical movement and came from across the political spectrum.[147]

Loyalist discourse embodied an analysis that the danger from the lower orders (with a party inflection that this danger was abetted and ultimately caused by the Whigs) required all men of property to rally to the defence of throne, altar and constitution. Whig discourse was premised on the idea that the danger came not only from the lower orders, but from ministers and their supporters and the relation of their actions to the radicals. Over the winter of 1819 for many Whigs and moderate reformers, the danger of the former became the more immediate concern and the incentives to rally to the defence of property and the constitution became more and more compelling, especially as they did not preclude continued criticism of ministers. The Whig leadership, for example, coupled continued hostility to the popular reform movement with considerable opposition to the Six Acts, over which they managed to force sixteen divisions before the legislation was enacted.[148]

IV

If one response to popular distress was to encourage public works, loyalists did not completely throw up the idea of persuasion as a powerful tool. There was a reprise of some of the loyalist dialogues of the 1790s, which had reached down to the lower orders in a caricatured Scots in an attempt to tell them, in their own language, that radical reformers were wolves in sheep's clothing.[149] In *The Marrow of Radical Reform* (1819), for example, the virtuous 'John Turnip' converts the phlegmatic but shallow radical 'Tam Shuttle' with a mixture of argument, good sense and threats.[150] A common strategy, as in the poem *Patie and Nelly* (1820), was to revisit and recycle themes from the 1790s, especially Hannah More's efforts to push an evangelical, domestic ideal symbolized by a 'clean fireside' and untainted by the intrusions of radical politics.[151] Works that were advertised at a penny or a halfpenny each with discounted rates for bulk purchases demonstrated attempts to meet the key challenges of popular radicalism: its visionary schemes of reform and its perceived infidelity and blasphemy.[152] They also demonstrated more committed loyalist attempts to circulate such propaganda, in contrast to the rather perfunctory efforts of 1816–17. The *Spirit of the Union* reported disparagingly on attempts to distribute loyalist propaganda in the west of Scotland, such as a circular blaming distress on the Whigs and one of many attempts to point to the alleged hypocrisy of William Cobbett by publishing extracts from his early anti-Jacobin writing.[153]

Loyalist propaganda also made efforts to address more directly some of the marked features and innovations of the radical movement of 1819. In *The Marrow of Radical Reform*, for example, John Turnip fastened on two of the more novel features of radical reform and criticized the embrace of visual spectacle and the presence of women on the platform:

> Wha is it that pays for a' thae glittering colours, an' liberty caps, an' bands of music that ye hae been frighten fo'k wi' sae meikle? Wha gies thae jads thae fine claes that they hae been flouncin' about wi' and encouraging you in your mischief?

He went on to attempt to contest radical appropriations of William Wallace, claiming that in defending his countrymen from a foreign enemy: 'He did the very opposite of what ye want to do'.[154] Similarly, loyalist pamphlets could be issued in response to particular events. *A Half Hour's Crack with a Glasgow Radical Reformer* was written as a direct defence of loyalist principles in the face of the suspected radical activity on Monday 13 December.[155]

Other formats sought to expand the loyalist pamphlet and Rev. Henry Duncan penned an anti-radical novel, *The Young South Country Weaver*, which was published in Edinburgh in ten parts in 1820 and as a single volume in 1821. The novel tells the story of William Webster, a weaver from a pious and 'well regulated' family in Dumfries, who moves to the Calton district of Glasgow to live with his uncle. The uncle's disordered house – he is a drinker tainted with infidelity, whose disobedient son attempts to murder both his father and his cousin – is portrayed as a function of his radical politics. While the cousin James, through his associations with the thinly-disguised demagogue Thistlethorn, hurtles to his own destruction, the pious and loyal William resists the wiles of radicalism and acts as a mouthpiece for monologues on the glories of the British constitution, the duty of political quiescence and the merits of Christian domesticity.[156]

Duncan's preface to the single-volume edition highlights the limitations of loyalist efforts at persuasion in 1819. His work was initially to have been published by a group in Edinburgh specifically established for the purpose of 'defraying the expence [sic] of printing and circulating such tracts grave and humorous religious and civil as may best meet the madness of the times'.[157] Duncan attributed the delayed publication of his tract to the weakness of this association:

> intended to form one of a series of Tracts which a loyal society in Edinburgh proposed to publish, with a view of fighting Disaffection with her own weapons. This society, however, although it commenced its labours with great zeal, and numbered among its members some of the first names in our northern metropolis, finding difficulties which it had not anticipated, became discouraged after the publication of a few Tracts, and when this tale was presented for its acceptance, it was already extinct.[158]

The society had been set up in November, with the encouragement of both the Lord Advocate and the Home Secretary. It included Scott in the background as a kind of *éminence grise*, while John Forbes, an advocate and scion of the Edinburgh Tory banking family, acted as secretary and Rev. John Inglis of Edinburgh was engaged 'to superintend the religious part of our department'.[159]

Perhaps the best explanation for the lacklustre performance of this association is that loyalists, including some of the projectors of the association itself, had less faith in persuasion as a reasonable tactic to win over the lower orders: 'I have no faith myself in the effect these paper pellets may produce on the enemy, but they are supposed to encourage our friends'.[160] This was a significant shift in emphasis from the efforts of the 1790s. In 1819 efforts were more likely to be directed at men of property – aimed to encourage friends rather than to convert enemies. This was almost certainly the intended audience for Scott's own piece of loyalist propaganda, *The Visionary*, which appeared as a series of letters in *Edinburgh Weekly Journal* in December 1819.[161] Its appearance in a stamped newspaper, its eightpenny price tag as a separate pamphlet, its tone, language and satirical style all suggest that it was aimed at an audience well above the 'vulgar'. Other productions demonstrated attempts to engage with the same audience to the same ends. The fourpenny *Use and Abuse of Charity* was necessarily aimed at those in a position to offer charity and highlighted the pitfalls of offering radicals paid relief. Master manufacturers should watch their workmen, tradesmen their apprentices, while the rich, in joining relief societies, should serve the public good:

> by withholding the hand of charity from those who chuse [*sic*] to give us their labour in return, only under the tri-coloured banner of rebellion, who devote their hours of leisure to the practice of military discipline in order to support that standard, or who misemploy the money given them by devoting it to the purchase and the study of the sedition of Paine, or the blasphemy of Carlile.[162]

Dror Wahrman sees the year 1819 as crucial in a kind of 'tug of war' between radical and loyalist languages over the designation of the 'middle class'. The influence of the concept of 'public opinion' was becoming such that whoever could make the most effective and plausible appeal to have the 'middle classes' on its side could claim to speak for the wider community, for the 'people' rather than for a narrow factional interest.[163] While radicals painted ministers as a narrow faction, opposed by the 'people' or the 'middle and lower classes', it was no less a loyalist strategy to politicize this social middle. It was voiced effectively by Scott:

> I do not expect much from addressing the mere people on the head of their ridiculous pretensions because while the poor think it possible to get at the property of the rich by a general rising it will be difficult to offer any mere arguments which can overcome the temptation. It is the middle class which requires to be put on the guard every man who has or cultivates a furrow of land or has a guinea in the funds or vested in stock in trade or in mortgage or in any other way whatsoever.[164]

Such middle-class-based conceptions of the social order, however, did not feature in another area of loyalist endeavour, the loyal resolutions and addresses that flooded in from county and town council meetings from October.[165] These addresses, which were widely printed and reported in the press, attempted to push the vision of a loyal community. The stress, like that of radical meetings, was on unanimity, something not lost on the radical press. The *Spirit of the Union*, mindful of fissures appearing in radical ranks after Peterloo, argued that radicals might model themselves on the meetings of their opponents, where 'the half-measure men are lost in the crowd of unanimists'.[166] In one sense, of course, the communities represented in addresses were ones of rank and property, especially of the Nobleman, Gentlemen, Freeholders, Justices of the Peace, Commissioners of Supply and Heritors that constituted county meetings. County and burgh resolutions almost universally commented, however, on the peaceable and loyal disposition of the lower orders in their respective locality, while reprobating the efforts of radicals to seduce the lower orders from their religious and civil duties in the disturbed western districts.[167] In loyalist resolutions, therefore, the danger was presented as socially and geographically restricted, confined to a small, factional and unrepresentative minority. Radicalism was a localized aberration not a national movement.

Such meetings were more revealing, in fact, of party fissures than of social ones. English Whigs had attempted to launch a series of county meetings (with varying levels of success) to call for an inquiry into events in Manchester. The most notable had been the 20,000 strong Yorkshire county meeting, for which Fitzwilliam lost his Lord Lieutenancy and which loyalists saw as an opportunity: 'I hope the Whigs will contrive to identify themselves with the Radicals and Revolutionists'.[168] Such an option was not open to Scottish Whigs, who instead supported loyal resolutions but moved amendments to addresses. These tried (but universally failed) to incorporate a recognition of the distresses of the people and a call for remedies into addresses, or else reprobated some of the content of loyal resolutions. In Edinburgh, Francis Jeffrey sought to amend the address. This began with the common idea that the disaffected could not be blamed and that 'ninety-nine in a hundred were misled by lies and delusions'. He went on to push the Whig idea that the people should be 'tenderly and indulgently treated in this period of unparalleled distress' and alluded both to Peterloo and to the prospect of coercive legislation:

> That no encouragement should be given to the precipitate or unnecessary use of force ... That no restraint should be put on the great constitutional right of the people to petition for redress of grievances ... That every effort in short should be made not only to repress and intimidate the few mischievous and daring individuals who are endeavouring to seduce the people from their allegiance, but to conciliate and attach the multitudes who are exposed to their seduction.[169]

At the Fife meeting James Stuart objected that the evidence for the circulation from one location in Dunfermline of the *Black Dwarf* and a single copy of the *Age of Reason* was insufficient to pass an indictment on the whole county. Similarly, he rejected the loyalist construction put on the orderly behaviour and military organization at radical meetings: this, he argued, was simply a consequence of the near ubiquity of military training during the French Wars.[170]

These meetings and the failure of Whigs to pass any amendments to loyal resolutions demonstrate their relative weakness and their increasing participation in a broad loyalist consensus. This was underlined in their participation in the final area of loyalist activity, the efforts to raise yeomanry and volunteer corps. Cockburn looked back on his own service wryly:

> New offers of voluntary service were made, and accepted; and as the Whigs could not keep back, without seeming to encourage the enemy, once more did I prepare to gird on my sword as a captain in a thing called 'The Armed Association'; which was meant to be something more military than constables, and less military than soldiers.[171]

As in 1816–17 the preference of governing elites was for yeomanry regiments, which were less costly to government and more socially exclusive (and so ideologically sound) than armed volunteers. In the aftermath of Peterloo this species of force undoubtedly furthered polarization. Moderate reformers, such as Lord Archibald Hamilton, who supported the establishment of yeomanry corps as 'the most proper and constitutional' force, were attacked in the radical press.[172] Atrocities committed by mounted troops and especially by yeomanry were standard fare in the *Spirit of the Union*.[173] Members of the yeomanry were also responsible for some of the more vicious statements of intent that drove this polarization further.

While the government preferred yeomanry corps as the armed wing of loyalism, the events of 1819 helped to overcome some of the reservations about arming the most respectable citizens as volunteers, though government stuck to its guns on the matter of payment. The many offers to form volunteer regiments and the quick enlistment into some of these suggest that historians may have underestimated the strength and depth of loyalist sentiment that developed in 1819.[174] Such offers were tempered by locality and by events. Charles Hope thought that the embodiment of the Edinburgh volunteers would be profoundly important: 'nothing would tend so much to give spirit & confidence to the Country at large, as to see Edinburgh again arming itself'. In the same letter, however, he lamented that the armed association was filling slowly. It took the steadily increased military presence and rumours of armed rising to boost enrolment. In particular, the show of force in Glasgow in December – when the military left Edinburgh and the volunteers garrisoned the Castle – had an effect on the 'lazy and incredulous', and Hope could report that it was expected the 1,100 limit would be reached in a few days.[175] In Glasgow too, recruitment was swift. Samuel Hunter, editor of the loyalist *Glasgow Herald* and a former volunteer like Hope, led the enrolment of the Glasgow Sharpshooters and the limit of 1,000 volunteers was reached within two or three days.[176] Elsewhere, local circumstances militated against enrolment. In Kilmarnock one of the town councillors lamented that the idea of an armed association was stillborn when they had only managed to raise sixty-seven special constables from a town the size of Kilmarnock.[177]

While Cockburn was grudging in describing his own reasons for joining up there is little reason to doubt the appeal of volunteer regiments to many members of the middle classes, who had come to regard radicalism as a threat to property. Cookson has eloquently argued that during the French wars readiness to join a volunteer regiment should not be conflated with 'loyalism'. Many other factors were at work: civic pride, ideas of masculinity and manly behaviour, local connections and self-interest.[178] As one radical correspondent from Newcastle was keen to point out, however, there was a major difference between 'arming against a foreign foe and an unoffending people'.[179] The absence of the central plank of 'national defence patriotism' – the threat of invasion – undoubtedly made the armed loyalism of 1819 a different phenomenon to its predecessor and opened it to considerable criticism and resistance. A 'Quondam Volunteer' in Edinburgh objected to the reformation of the first regiment of volunteers on the basis that with no threat of invasion there was no rationale to arm to solve 'our internal dissentions and party bickerings'. The correspondent was also perceptive, though in less trenchant terms than Wooler, on the probable polarizing consequences of an armed loyalism: 'What is done by one party may be done by another. The Radical Reformers have as good a right to arm in support of their opinions as the followers of the present Ministers in support of theirs'.[180]

Scott's breathless correspondence demonstrated his own enthusiasm for embodying volunteer forces and for a robust military response to radicalism:

> After all I am sure the dogs will not fight and I am sorry for it – One day's good kemping would cure them most radically of their radical malady & if I had any thing to say in the matter they should remember the day for half a century to come. I have no pity on these scoundrel pit-men and coalliers [sic] who have more employment than they chuse [sic] to take & yet are drinking their gin to the toast of Blood and plunder.[181]

Scott did not, however, offer unqualified praise for the approach adopted in the winter of 1819–20 and he demonstrated some of the tensions within loyalism. He put what he saw as the government's possible choices in stark terms in a letter to Lord Montagu: '1st. The arming of citizens of the better classes. 2d. The embodying such of the common people as may be trusted'. His argument was that in sizeable towns and in the disturbed districts the first option was preferable on both practical and political grounds. There were enough small property owners to form a body of armed men and to reach below this level in towns 'would be an act of the greatest rashness & in fact would be in most instances raising men for the radicals'.

In the large part of the country 'happily uninfected' by the radical malady, however, different arrangements should be made. There, face-to-face relations of masters and men had been maintained while the petite-bourgeois class of shopkeepers who might form volunteer regiments was small. Behind Scott's apparently bizarre plans of arming shepherds as 'dismounted yeomen', mustering the Buccleuch tenantry and raising the Highland host was a serious point. If government persisted in arming only the propertied they played into radical rhetoric, which increasingly painted a Manichean struggle between the rich and the poor: 'It is a war between strength & weakness between riches & poverty in which our numbers are as 100 to one and in which we have every thing to gain and nothing to lose'. The wider point was an ideological one about the loyalty of the community as a whole. To arm the loyal weavers of Gala would provide not only an effective fighting force, but a rebuff to radical claims to represent the people and a means of preventing a war between the haves and the have-nots.[182]

V

1819 thus witnessed a profound process of polarization in Scotland. Both radicals and loyalists sought to make their own appeal to 'the people' and both claimed to represent the 'nation'. As the quote that opened this chapter suggests, politics were filtered through and driven by local circumstances to create both a loyalism and a radicalism that were distinctively 'Scottish'. Nevertheless, the British context provided by Parliament, by the means of political communication and by the consciousness of being part of 'national' movements was crucial. Both radicals and loyalists developed their own interpretations of the activities sanctioned by the British constitution and demanded by the rapidly shifting political situation. In this dialogue about the nature and limits of the constitution, it was loyalists who would have the last word in 1819, by passing the Six Acts at the very end of the year.[183]

Fulcher has encouraged us to see the Six Acts less as an act of flat physical repression than as a 'move' in this discursive game.[184] Their purpose was to define and police the boundaries of the constitution more effectively and they embodied an explicit attempt to render innovative radical practices 'alien'. Attempts to define in more restrictive ways what constituted a 'newspaper', for example, were aimed at the burgeoning radical press, which had played a crucial propagandizing and organizational role in 1819. The mass platform was recognized as a qualitatively new type of collective action, some of the most alarming aspects of which were its militarized ones. It did not allow MPs and loyalists to dismiss it as a 'mob' and so existing legal and political strategies for dealing with it were deemed to be insufficient. The Lord Chancellor and the Home Secretary were engaged in a lengthy correspondence after Peterloo, pondering whether declaratory acts, which clarified the existing legislation, were sufficient or whether new legislation was required. That the removal of the kind of ambiguity on which radicals thrived was a central concern was certainly clear, and was spelled out by Sidmouth: 'it is very evident that what is confessedly and most mischievously weak should be strengthened, and that all Ambiguity on material points, about which ambiguity now exists, should be removed'.[185]

In the debates surrounding the Six Acts and, indeed, in the language employed by the measures themselves, it was the military features of popular radicalism that were especially highlighted and attacked. The first measure to become law banned 'all Meetings and Assemblies of Persons for the purpose of training or drilling themselves, or of being trained or drilled to the use of Arms, or for the purpose of practising Military Exercise, Movements and Evolution'.[186] The Act restricting meetings outlawed attendance even at a legally constituted meeting 'with any Flag, Banner or Ensign, or displaying or exhibiting any Device, Badge or Emblem or with any Drum or Military or other Music, or in Military Array or Order'.[187] In moving the legislation Castlereagh dwelt on the militarized symbolic display of radicals and pursued the rhetorical strategy of the 1790s, claiming that the legislation would arrest 'a practice which had never been British, but was borrowed from the worst times of the French revolution'.[188] In one way, the months running up to the spring of 1820 and the 'Radical War' were an attempt by radicals to come to terms with and respond to this political master stroke, which pulled the rug from under their claims to be a 'constitutional' movement.

4 THE 'GENERAL RISING' OF 1820

The bubble seems to have burst and with a slighter explosion than could have been expected.[1]

[T]he bubble had burst and the radical war was at an end.[2]

Previous accounts of the 'Radical War' have been rather more concerned with gauging its size and scale than determining where it came from. Attempts to answer either of these questions are complicated by the nature of the source material on which historians must rely. This falls into four categories: first, material generated by government and local political elites, found in local archives and Home Office papers; secondly, press reports contemporaneous with the events they describe; thirdly, legal material, including precognitions of those examined for their involvement in the rising and the lengthy account of the trials of the special commission of *oyer et terminer*; and fourthly, personal accounts, frequently printed long after the events they purported to describe.

This chapter will use all of these sources to provide a brief narrative of the 'Radical War'. It will then move on to consider the genesis and resolution of what should be considered the end point of a significant crisis within Scottish society. It will offer an interpretation that lies somewhere between two existing extremes. The attempted rising did not amount to the full-scale spy-fomented separatist-nationalist insurgency of Ellis and Mac a'Ghobhainn's *Scottish Insurrection*, but nor was it quite the 'futile revolt of a tiny minority' dismissed in Thomis and Holt's account of revolutionary threats in Britain or the 'pathetic storm in a teacup' of the recent volumes of the *History of Parliament*.[3] It was a serious and profound event, taken seriously by those whose responsibility it was to maintain law and order and by those who took part.[4]

Expectations of an attempt at a 'general rising' were current among political elites from the autumn of 1819. Commentators who looked back frequently conceptualized the 'Radical War' as encompassing both 1819 and 1820, rather than simply the latter year and this is the wider framework within which historians ought to view the events of April 1820.[5] In contrast to 1816–17, the fear in 1819–20 was of a national underground, with delegates moving between the west of Scotland and disturbed areas in the north and midlands of England. There is no reason to doubt that some sort of a national underground did exist across this period. There are numerous accounts of Scottish delegates attending meetings in England from both first-hand and government sources. Brayshaw's tour of Scotland in autumn of 1819 had established those Union Societies which, as well as acting as reading clubs, were bodies well designed to answer other purposes such as clandestine drilling and, eventually, armed rising. In the aftermath of both Peterloo and the riots in Glasgow and Paisley in September, reports of nocturnal drilling and intimations of an intended general rising increased.

The government response to this increased activity was twofold. First, there was an increased military presence. This took the form of both increased regular troops and the mobilization of the yeomanry and volunteers raised across the previous year. By November, the commander in Scotland, Major-General Bradford, was convinced that a display of military strength was needed: 'it is much to be feared, the Country cannot be returned to tranquillity without a serious, and energetic action of the Military against the Mob'.[6] On the same day, Charles Hope concluded that the situation was such that it could not now be resolved without violence: 'it will come to blows, & that speedily'.[7] The first intimation that the government received of an intended rising was on 13 December 1819, a Monday that radicals intended to mark with simultaneous meetings, a strike and a mock fast.[8] Even though they had some warning that the attempt had been called off, the government response was to stage a spectacle of military strength in and around Glasgow as regular troops and the Midlothian yeomanry marched to the west. Charles Hope was gratified that this strategy of military display seemed to have paid off, but he noticed a phenomenon that in part helps to explain the outcome of the more serious attempted rising in 1820:

> The imposing appearance of the Troops – & the arrival of the distant Yeomanry, on which the Radicals had not at all calculated, disconcerted & overawed them – & the rising was countermanded. But there is intelligence from Kilsyth, that the counter orders had not reached some of the Villages in that Neighbourhood, in consequence of which between 2 & 300 men marched into Kilsyth, on their route for Glasgow, publicly & openly armed with Pikes – but on finding all quiet there, they retreated – & the Troops being all at Glasgow, there was no means of seizing them.[9]

While the community organization of radicalism was strong and could sustain the drilling and mustering of local groups, its ability to coordinate any activity beyond the purely local was extremely weak. Troops were heavily concentrated in major population centres, most notably in Glasgow and Paisley, in line with Lord Cassillis' advice to: 'Keep the Body in a due state of health and the Legs and Arms will do their Duty'.[10] Populations did not and could not mobilize effectively in these large urban centres and it was rather the villages and small towns of the central belt that saw most activity. Even so, the effect of the overawing military display was apparently short-lived, and by the end of December Sidmouth was receiving reports that the 'Effect of Intimidation' had not been achieved and radicals had regrouped, formed a new committee and continued to arm themselves.[11]

Reports of intended risings and good information as to planned dates came from the second strategy of political elites: the employment of spies and the gathering of police intelligence. Rae had written to Sidmouth in August of 1819 complaining about the 'defective system of Police' in Glasgow. The Lord Advocate, perhaps looking back to the events of 1816–17, was acutely aware of the manifold shortcomings of spies employed on an *ad hoc* basis and paid by results: 'These persons are often very ill informed themselves, and in order to make the information they give appear valuable, they are but too apt to exaggerate the danger'.[12] With that in mind Rae employed Captain Brown of the Edinburgh police, who claimed for seventy-one days expenses between August and the rumoured rising in mid-December. Brown successfully settled two of his men 'of Glasgow origin' on the committees of the reformers from August through to the end of January 1820 and reported orally to Rae.[13] This arrangement explains the complete confidence with which the Lord Advocate could report on and predict possible movements among the radicals from Autumn of 1819: 'I confess that for my own part I am no ways alarmed ... I am satisfied however that nothing material on the part of the Radicals can be attempted without my previous knowledge'.[14]

It was the combination of Brown's intelligence and the measures pursued by the Glasgow authorities that led to the arrest of twenty-seven delegates of the 'Central Committee' in Glasgow on 22 February, including delegates from Ecclefechan, Strathaven, Airdrie, Kirkintilloch, Paisley, Elderslie and Ayr.[15] Much remains mysterious about this committee of delegates, who were still in confinement in November of 1820.[16] The Sheriff of Lanarkshire was responsible for taking the declarations of prisoners and was confident that 'the whole system of the Combination of the disaffected people here will be fully disclosed'.[17] From all of these examinations, Hamilton transmitted one to Sidmouth, which he believed best outlined the system of the radicals. It was based on a cellular organization with the foundations provided by those Union Societies which had been spreading since the previous year. The class leader of each Society combined to form a district committee which in turn selected delegates for the Central Committee, which met weekly in Glasgow. It was this latter committee that had been arrested on 22 February, though general superintendence of the radical movement was invested in a Select Committee of six or seven men, whose members remained at large. The declarant confirmed that, while the initial goal of the Union Societies had simply been the pursuit of political knowledge, in accordance with Brayshaw's model:

> as they afterwards advanced in numbers and gained strength, the Reformers as well in this City as throughout the five counties became more confident & the Sentiment among them was that they could obtain their object of Radical Reform only by force. That towards the end of last year this opinion was fully prevalent.[18]

This detailed statement, which has the ring of truth about it, provides considerable information on the tactics and strategies of radicalism. Sidmouth was confident that the examinations ensured that: 'The Plans and Views of the Scotch Radicals are very clearly and fully developed'.[19] It also demonstrated what remained ministers' principal fear: connections between radicals across the United Kingdom. 'A.B.' outlined some of these connections and the movement of delegates between Glasgow and Manchester. The planned rising on the 13 December 1819 had, according to this source, been premised on English radicals moving first. In the context of February of 1820, however, ministers in London were most interested in any possible links between radicalism in the provinces and the Cato Street conspiracy. These conspirators were arrested on the following day – Wednesday 23 February – making preparations to assassinate the cabinet at a dinner supposedly to be held at Lord Harrowby's (in fact ministers had placed a false notice in the press, and the spy, George Edwards, colluded in this fiction).[20] The examinations suggested that the direct contacts of Scottish radicals were restricted to the industrial communities of the north of England, reaching only as far south as Nottingham. This information was tempered by a belief that radicals in the north of England provided the epicentre of the movement and were in direct contact with both Thistlewood in London and their Scottish counterparts.[21] Joseph Brayshaw later explained that, while he had been responsible for missions to Scotland and the north to ascertain the state of preparations, another Leeds radical, James Mann, had been sent south to London, via Birmingham, Coventry and Nottingham, to gather intelligence from Hunt, Wooler, Cartwright, Cobbett *and* Thistlewood.[22] Such suspicions were given further ammunition by the numerous reports that, according to an informant from Paisley, 'the Radicals expected news with great anxiety, every day about the end of last week; either of some great event in their favour, or of the intended assassination in London'.[23] Sidmouth heard on the same day from Maybole that expectations had been raised by the assassination of the Duc de Berri in France and some great event was keenly awaited.[24] Once he had digested all of these reports from around the country, Sidmouth could conclude: 'It is certain that the Committees of the Disaffected in Leeds, Manchester, Carlilse and Glasgow expected to hear of a Blow having been struck last week in London'.[25]

Ministers and elites in Scotland were not again to be in possession of the same quality and scale of information that had allowed them to make the arrests in February. From that point onwards, correspondence about the state of Scotland was far more sketchy than it had been. Monteith lamented to Sidmouth that the arrest of the committee had ensured 'we are not enabled now to procure that clear and satisfactory information that we have all along had' partly because they had arrested their informants among the committee, but also because the Glasgow authorities were denuded of sufficient funds. The £200 released by Sidmouth in response to this request clearly came too late to achieve significant results.[26] Assessments of radical intentions remained indistinct, though the authorities were aware that the movement of delegates and communications both within Scotland and between Scotland and England had continued after the arrest of the committee.[27]

I

The immediate political context in which the attempted rising of April emerged deserves some serious consideration. Radicals in Scotland were clearly interested in both British and European events and existing accounts of the rising have ignored some crucial aspects of this wider context that might help to explain its timing and outcome. First, the death of George III on 29 January and the formal accession of the Prince Regent as George IV raised the political temperature and provided opportunities for radical opposition. In Ayr, for example:

> when his present Majesty was proclaimed, a mob collected, and when & wherever the Magistrates prayed God to save the King, a vagabond fellow, dressed out in all the insignia of radical reform followed in the train of the procession & used the most insulting & abusive language.[28]

In Cupar, radicals ostentatiously eschewed the hogsheads of ale and porter that had been laid on for the poor to celebrate the accession.[29] In Lanark a large crowd attacked the Lanarkshire yeomanry, who had assembled for the proclamation.[30]

The death of the King also necessitated a general election which took place between 6 March and 13 April. In England this provided an opportunity for a classic statement of anti-radicalism by George Canning, which was reproduced in full in *Blackwood's*.[31] Some of the contests in Scotland were marked by riot and considerable tension, with flashpoints in the Aberdeen Burghs (where ministers failed in an attempt to oust Joseph Hume), the Elgin Burghs and Renfrewshire.[32] At the election of the delegate for Selkirk (part of Lanark burghs) the chief magistrate, constables and the sheriff were stoned and some were knocked down.[33] The election for the royal burghs of Scotland occurred on Friday 31 March and the Lord Provost of Glasgow, as a candidate for the turbulent Lanark burghs, had to be absent from his post in the week leading up to the outbreak of the 'Radical War'.[34] The accession of George IV and a protracted general election could not but encourage an atmosphere of political movement in lowland Scotland.

Secondly, European events were creating an atmosphere of expectation. In January 1820 Ferdinand VII of Spain faced a mutiny, sparked by a Lieutenant-Colonel's proclamation of the liberal constitution of 1812. The mutiny snowballed and by March a series of revolts had forced Ferdinand to accept the constitution and shelve his project to reassert absolutist rule in Spain.[35] As was clear from the petitions of 1816–17 radicals were keenly aware of European events and the post-war restoration of Catholic absolutist rule to Spain and elsewhere was a prominent part of radical demonology. Sidmouth received a stream of letters from an ex-army officer, with Peninsular experience, warning him about the domestic ramifications of events in Spain. While the constitution adopted was 'nominally monarchical' it was 'in reality almost purely republican', embracing universal suffrage and biennial parliaments.[36] Its misrepresentation in the British, and especially the Whig press was a dangerous encouragement to radicals with similar goals: 'any man who does not wish to see universal suffrage, annual or biennial parliaments, and inevitable ruin brought upon this glorious, venerable happy country must raise his voice, and proclaim his detestation of the basis of the Spanish constitution'.[37]

Alexander Boswell was certain that events in Spain had an impact on the radicals of the west of Scotland:

> There has been a good deal of agitation among the Radicals during the last fortnight – some ascribe it to the News from Spain, which in their wisdom they have discovered to be a parallel case and look for a similar result by a demonstration.[38]

The revolution was widely reported in the radical and liberal press and an appeal to soldiers to emulate events in Spain formed part of the proclamation intended to spark an uprising in April and transcribed below.[39] Events in Spain and in Europe were also a prominent part of that prophetic and millenarian literature, which, following E. P. Thompson's lead, has been examined so fruitfully as one of the languages that underwrote popular radicalism in England.[40] Archibald Mason, a widely circulated millenarian writer, was scanning the European scene for signs of the 'tottering state of throne of Antichrist, and of the thrones of some of the Antichristian princes' throughout this period.[41] More pointedly, John Scott of Old Monkland in Lanarkshire published a pamphlet in 1820, which went to four editions within the year, and looked for signs from the books of Daniel and Revelation in domestic and foreign politics.[42] The pamphlet was issued by the radical publisher, William Lang, and a short follow-up clarifying some of Scott's positions demonstrated the links that might be made between prophecy and international and domestic politics:

We saw the witnesses again standing upon their feet, and great fear fell upon them who saw them, in the meetings for reformation that were held in sundry places in the year 1819.

We have the great voice from heaven calling upon the witness to ascend, in the Spanish revolution, January 1820.

We have the ascension of part of the witnesses in the revolutions of Naples and Portugal.

We do not know which of the ten kingdoms may next undergo a revolution; but if these inferences be correct, we are certain, that before the whole of them be revolutionized, one of them will undergo a more perfect reformation than the others who have gone before it.[43]

Thirdly, domestic events were raising the political temperature in Scotland and England. In the county of Ross, on the estates of Hugh Munro of Novar, an attempt to clear tenants from Culrain met with stiff resistance from women and men dressed as women. The military escort of the civil officers were attacked; and fired in self-defence, but eventually surrendered the field.[44] While correspondents in the press and the civil authorities were convinced that the discontent in the Highlands contained 'no political Feelings' and that 'no such principles as those of radicalism are known here' they did not completely ignore the occurrence.[45] If the disturbance itself was not political it was susceptible to politicization and Monteith suggested that radicals had been sent to Ross to increase the mischief there, while the Home Office was wary of any disturbance 'capable of being peverted to political Mischief when the public mind is in so feverish a state'.[46] The disturbances in Ross were widely reported, coming to the attention of Monteith's correspondent in Manchester. One of Sidmouth's informants warned about the propaganda potential of the disturbances, coming hot on the heels of images of women confronting bayonets at Peterloo:

> The unhappy affair in Rosshire is made a great handle of by the Radicals, and published accounts of it, called up and down in the streets, to inflame the People ... The Radicals hold up the women in that part of Rosshire [sic], as an example of fortitude, not fearing to advance on the very bayonets of the Soldiers.[47]

There were signs of resistance elsewhere in Scotland. The excise, for example, compiled various reports pointing to the political complexion assumed by those engaged in illicit distillation, an interesting reprise of the links between oppositional politics and the black economy that had characterized the first half of the eighteenth century.[48] In Lochaw this was carried on 'by a desperate Banditti who style[d] themselves Radicals'. When an excise officer tried to seize ten gallons of whisky he was knocked down by the offender 'saying damn you and the King both'. Two excisemen were attacked by five women, a man and a boy 'declaring that there was no King and that [they] had nothing to do with them', while they searched for illicit stills.[49]

Of considerably more interest to civil authorities in the north of England and to radicals in Scotland was the outcome of the trials of Henry Hunt and others on charges of conspiracy for their part in Peterloo. The tenth and final day of the trial at the York assizes occurred on Monday 27 March, when Hunt (along with Joseph Johnson, John Knight, Joseph Healy and Samuel Bamford) was found guilty of 'assembling with unlawful banners an unlawful assembly'.[50] Ministers and their informants among the civil and military authorities in the north of England watched the trials anxiously and there was widespread expectation that their outcome would have an impact on the disturbed districts. Indeed, the stakes were high both for loyalists and radicals. Sidmouth interpreted the trials as a foundational test of the legitimacy of radicalism and its principles 'upon the discomfiture of which the Existence of the Monarchy and the Tranquillity of the Country depend'.[51] From Manchester the Boroughreeve wrote of the 'ferment' and 'influx of strangers' encouraged by the trials, while from Oldham an informant believed that in that town as well as Manchester and Huddersfield, 'the Design of an immediate Commotion ... has originated with a strong Feeling of Exasperation and disappointment at the Result of the Trials at York'.[52]

Once the attempted rising had broken out Sidmouth was left in no doubt that the radicals had been firmly fixed on the trials and that, had an acquittal been achieved, the defenders 'would have entered Manchester in Triumph, and it is difficult to calculate what might have been the consequence'.[53] In view of the close links between radicals in Scotland and the north of England and the English-oriented nature of Scottish radicals' sources of information, the context provided by these trials becomes important. Scottish radicals were looking to their outcome and were informed of it by a single broadside as well as in the press more generally.[54] The *Manchester Observer*, which was widely circulated in Scotland, was nearly completely thrown over to accounts of the trial.[55] It was clear that across Britain concentration was heaped on these trials as a kind of litmus test of the ministry's intentions.

II

This was the immediate context for radical attempts to spark a general rising from the weekend of 31 March to 2 April. Given the level of contact between radicals in Scotland and the north of England it is important to keep events in both countries in mind when devising a narrative. In fact, the first clear intimation of what was planned came in Huddersfield, on the evening of Friday 31 March. Though it took the authorities in Manchester some time to receive a satisfactory account, 'from the most cautious inquiry, it is supposed 1500 to 2000 persons were actually assembled at midnight (mostly armed) on various sides of the Town'. The signal for attack was made, but panic led to the dispersal of the radicals.[56] The authorities in Scotland and England had been in expectation of *some* event occurring over the weekend and in Scotland it came over the evening of 1–2 April. The Glasgow magistrates had more than an inkling of what was to happen. In explaining their conduct after the rising, they claimed that 'special orders issued by them on the night of the 31st March for the apprehension of the persons, who should be found putting up a Treasonable address' were not acted upon.[57] On the morning of Sunday, 2 April, populations across the west of Scotland awoke to a placard posted in prominent places across the region:

ADDRESS TO THE INHABITANTS OF GREAT BRITAIN & IRELAND;

FRIENDS AND COUNTRYMEN,
ROUSED from that torpid state in which WE have been sunk for so many years, We are at length compelled, from the extremity of our sufferings, and the contempt heaped upon our Petitions for redress to assert our RIGHTS, at the hazard of our lives; and proclaim to the world the real motives, which (if not misrepresented by designing men, would have United all ranks), have reduced us to take up ARMS for the redress of our *Common Grievances.*

The numerous public meetings held throughout the Country has [*sic*] demonstrated to you, that the interests of all Classes are the same. That the protection of the Life and Property of the *Rich Man,* is the interest of the *Poor Man,* and in return, it is the interest of the Rich, to protect the poor from the iron grasp of DESPOTISM; for, when its victims are exhausted in the lower circles, there is no assurance but that its ravages will be continued in the upper; For once set in motion, it will continue to move till a succession of Victims fall.

Our principles are few, and founded on the basis of our CONSTITUTION, which were purchased with the DEAREST BLOOD of our ANCESTORS, and which we swear to transmit to posterity unsullied, or PERISH in the Attempt – Equality of Rights (not of Property,) is the object for which we contend, and which we consider as the only security for our LIBERTIES and LIVES.

Let us show the world that We are not that Lawless, Sanguinary Rabble, which our Oppressors would persuade the higher circles we are – but a BRAVE and GENEROUS PEOPLE, determined to be FREE, LIBERTY or DEATH is our *Motto,* and We have sworn to return home in *triumph* – or return *no more!*

SOLDIERS,
Shall YOU, Countrymen, bound by the sacred obligation of an Oath, to defend our Country and your King from enemies, whether foreign or domestic,

plunge your BAYONETS into the bosoms of Fathers and Brothers, and at once sacrifice at the *Shrine of Military Despotism*, to the unrelenting Orders of a cruel Faction, those feelings which you hold in common with the rest of mankind? SOLDIERS, Turn your eyes toward SPAIN, and there behold the happy effects resulting from the UNION of Soldiers and Citizens. Look to that quarter, and there behold the yoke of hated Despotism, broke by the Unanimous wish of the People and the Soldiery, happily accomplished without Bloodshed. And, shall YOU, who taught those Soldiers to fight the battles of LIBERTY, refuse to fight those of your own Country? Forbid it Heaven! Come, forward then at once, and Free your Country and your King, from the power of those that have held them *too, too* long in thraldom.

FRIENDS AND COUNTRYMEN, The eventful period has now arrived, where the Services of all will be required, for the forwarding of an object so universally wished, and so absolutely necessary. Come forward then, and assist those who have begun in the completion of so arduous a task, and support the laudable efforts, which we are about to make, to replace to BRITONS, those rights consecrated to them, by MAGNA CHARTA, and the BILL OF RIGHTS, and Sweep from our Shores, that Corruption which has degraded us below the dignity of Man.

Owing to the misrepresentations which have gone abroad with regard to our intentions, we think it indispensably necessary to DECLARE inviolable, all Public and Private Property. And, We hereby call upon all JUSTICES of the PEACE, and all others to suppress PILLAGE and PLUNDER, of every description; and to endeavour to secure those Guilty of such offences, that they might receive that Punishment, which such violation of justice demand [*sic*].

In the present state of affairs, and during the continuation of so momentous a struggle, we earnestly request of all to desist from their Labour, from and after this day, the FIRST OF APRIL; and attend wholly to the recovery of their Rights, and consider it as the duty of every man not to recommence until he is in possession of those Rights which distinguishes the FREEMAN from the SLAVE; viz; That of giving consent to the laws by which he is to be governed. We, therefore, recommend to the Proprietors of Public Works, and all others, to Stop the one, and Shut up the other, until order is restored, as we will be accountable for no damages which may be sustained; and which after this Public Intimation, they can have no claim to.

AND We hereby give notice to all those who shall be found carrying arms against those who intend to regenerate their Country, and restore its INHABITANTS to their NATIVE DIGNITY, We shall consider them as TRAITORS to their Country, and ENEMIES to their King, and treat them as such.

By order of the Committee of Organization for forming a PROVISIONAL GOVERNMENT.

GLASGOW, 1st April, 1820

Britons. – God. – Justice. – The wishes of all good Men are with us. – Join together and make it one CAUSE, and the Nations of the Earth shall hail the day, when the Standard of LIBERTY shall be raised on its *Native Soil*.[58]

Even the ability to distribute this proclamation over so wide an area demonstrates some considerable level of organization. The emphasis was on posting the address in public places. On a Sunday this made churches a natural choice and in Kilsyth the proclamation was posted on the kirk and the Relief meeting house and in Johnstone a copy was placed on the pillar of the chapel gate.[59] Other copies were seen on the ends of people's houses, on shop windows, on toll bars and in other prominent or public places.[60] In Glasgow, Andrew Hardie, who was later executed, was one of a crowd who prevented a Lanarkshire JP, James Hardie, from taking down a copy being read aloud to a crowd from a watch box. James Hardie later found a copy on a pump well.[61]

Reports quickly reached government that there had been widespread stoppage of work in the west of Scotland and the authorities rallied to meet the apparent threat of armed rising. Correspondents hint at the scale of the stoppage. From Glasgow, the postmaster reported on Monday that 'the whole working class' had refrained from working and the Lord Provost reported a similar scale of strike: 'Over the whole Country, so far as we have heard, the order contained in the treasonable address, to strike work, has been obeyed with a very few exceptions'.[62] At Duntocher, a centre for cotton-spinning 'all the public works' stopped on the Monday.[63] In the area around Paisley there was large-scale stoppage of work and considerable evidence emerged at the subsequent trials of groups forcing stoppages in line with the proclamation. All thirteen or fourteen cotton mills in Johnstone stopped work on the Monday.[64] All told there is considerable evidence that the working population of the west of Scotland responded to the proclamation, by assent, fear or intimidation on the Monday.

There were clear signs that other more active preparations were being made as well. A forge in Duntocher, for example, was co-opted for the conversion of old files into pike heads. The sheriff-depute estimated some thousand were produced from Monday to Wednesday.[65] Reports of open drilling and men moving in military formation in towns increased; yeomanry were stoned and some injured in Kilsyth; and there were reports of arms raids as far north as Craigend near Perth.[66] On one of these occasions, a raid on a farm at Foxbar near Paisley, a radical, Adam Cochran, was shot and killed by the occupant.[67] The authorities responded to this escalating threat with proclamations and curfews. In Glasgow, so great was the fear of an attack that 'many of the principal people sent their wives and families out of the town, several went to Gourock some to Largs and others to Greenock'.[68] In Airdrie, loyal men spent the night in the forest at Drumpellier.[69]

The signal to Scottish radicals that a rising was to commence was widely believed to be the stopping of the mail coaches by their English co-conspirators. This was based on the premise that radicals in England were to strike first and provide a signal to Scotland. From the Monday, this was the principal concern of the civil and military authorities in Scotland, who watched anxiously for the arrival of the English mail.[70] Its safe arrival in Glasgow on Tuesday morning was met with relief and on Wednesday 'the day to which we had all looked forward with anxiety' the Glasgow Sharpshooters were mustered at half past four in the morning and disbanded on the arrival of news that the mail had arrived safely at Hamilton.[71] The appearance of the mail is strong evidence that the rising was, in fact, abortive. Receiving no clear sign that movements had been made elsewhere, only small and uncoordinated groups of radicals turned out in both Scotland and the north of England.[72]

On 4 April, a group of some sixty men led by Andrew Hardie, an unemployed weaver, set off from Glasgow to meet another group from Anderston. Their plan appears to have been to move from there to seize the Carron Iron Works in Falkirk. When there was no one to meet them at Anderston, however, the original group dwindled to some twenty-five in number, who arrived at the village of Condorrat early on 5 April and were met by another fifteen men led by John Baird, a veteran of the Peninsular campaign. The group stopped at Castlecary Bridge, and attempted to pay for their breakfast with a note for payment in six months time. When the innkeeper refused this dubious form of currency Baird was scrupulous in receiving a receipt for his expenditures, evidence that would later be used against him.[73]

The group apparently split into two, with Baird's contingent following the canal and Hardie's the road. The latter group came into contact with first, a member of the Kilsyth yeomanry, whose arms they tried to take, and secondly, a private in the 10th Hussars, who was returning from Stirling with dispatches. He was given a copy of the treasonable address and on telling the party that he was a weaver and 'a friend to their cause' he was allowed to pass.[74] The group rejoined at Camelon and, finding little further support, rested on Bonnymuir. By their own account they had decided to lie low and then return home when thirty-two cavalry, composed of equal numbers of the Kilsyth yeomanry and the 10th Hussars, arrived. Called upon to surrender, the radicals engaged the troops, there were some casualties on both sides, and eighteen radicals were ultimately taken prisoner to Stirling Castle after what Richard Carlile hailed as 'the first battle between British soldiers and British subjects in the present age'.[75] The military nature or otherwise of the engagement became a key area of political and legal debate, whose significance needs to be seen in the longer context provided by Peterloo and the militarized nature of the mass platform after August 1819. Those involved were keen to demonstrate that they had been 'in no order, but like a mob' and had been attacked by the military. Baird's declaration was emphatic: 'they were attacked by a party of the Hussars and Yeomanry cavalry, and they resisted accordingly'.[76] Such a plea argued for a constitutional understanding of their actions and furnished them with some kind of legal defence.

On the other hand, the authorities at the time and during the subsequent trials were keen to emphasise, as was Rae, that Bonnymuir was 'a skirmish commenced by the Radicals'.[77]

On 5 April, another group of radicals in Strathaven took over their village and seized arms from other inhabitants throughout the evening. Apparently operating on intelligence that Glasgow was in arms and that an attack was to be launched the following day, their base of operations was the house of James Wilson, a veteran radical weaver who had been a delegate at radical conventions in the 1790s. At one point mustering around a hundred in number, this group was diminished over the course of the night. The following day, some twenty-four set off to meet the non-existent radical army, gathered round a banner reading 'Strathaven Union Society, 1819' on one side and 'Scotland Free or a Desert' on the other. Camping on a hill near Rutherglen, they were informed of their predicament by local radicals and dispersed. Most returned to their homes safely and unmolested by the authorities, but Wilson was arrested.[78]

By Thursday, when the Strathaven radicals marched out, ministers and their informants were convinced that the worst of the danger was over and most of the local population was returning to work.[79] This was a cause of some disappointment to those who believed, like Rae, that a larger armed confrontation would serve salutary purposes: 'we shall have no opportunity of bestowing upon them any of that discipline of Chastisement which I came here in the wish of being inflicted'.[80] Such opportunities for chastisement were provided by searches for arms that commenced on Friday 7 April and were designed to 'spread such an alarm as will not induce the radicals to keep arms in their houses in future'.[81] The continuing efforts to apprehend leading radicals offered truculent loyalists such as Boswell another means of engaging in what they saw as part of an ongoing campaign of pacification: 'I trust that we shall soon intimidate these rebels, & that we may then hope for a peaceable season'.[82]

The fruit of such loyalist posturing and attempts at pacification was a final serious and bloody incident at Greenock on 8 April. A large crowd successfully released five radical prisoners from the burgh gaol, to where they had been transported by the Port Glasgow volunteers. The rescue was only effected, however, at the expense of eight fatalities and ten wounded. On investigation, the authorities were satisfied that the violence had no ostensibly political complexion and 'no connection with radicalism', but was an expression of purely local quarrels. This does not quite tally with the intelligence that many radicals had fled to Greenock and that the offensively militaristic behaviour of the out-of-town volunteers, who had arrived with a band playing, had helped to spark the trouble. It is more likely that in part the rescue and the sustained assault on the volunteers was an eruption of those tensions between radicals and loyalists that had developed over the winter.[83]

III

Existing interpretations of the 'Radical War' of 1819–20 have emphasized a number of different points. In its immediate and medium-term aftermath, Whig and liberal commentators were keen to underline the role of spies and, in particular, *agents provocateurs*. This contributed to an interpretation viewing violent insurrection as a government-inspired aberration from normal constitutional politics. This was especially effective in the aftermath of the trials of 1817 and of Cato Street, when in both Scotland and England the perception of government *agents provocateurs* goading the people to acts of violence was widely held. Ministers and elites too were conscious that their recent history made such accusations all-too-believable. General Byng, for example, made immediate efforts to stymie the possibility of such an interpretation: 'I have been hard at work to stop if I can at the commencement insinuations that the late commotions were instigated by spies'. He took the *Leeds Mercury* to task for suggesting that 'a well dressed' man had acted as commandant to the Yorkshire radicals at Grange moor.[84] In Scotland, this interpretation was developed to its greatest extent over the following decade by Peter Mackenzie. Mackenzie had been a member of the Glasgow volunteers who mobilized against the radicals, but he made his journalistic reputation in uncovering and vilifying the 'spy system' that operated in Scotland between 1816 and 1820. By this interpretation, in 1820 small numbers of deluded men had become dupes to 'Richmond and his tribe of villains'.[85]

The instrumental role of spies is also central to the modern Scottish nationalist interpretation of the rising, as represented by Ellis and Mac a'Ghobhainn's *Scottish Insurrection*. Their evidence for the role of *agents provocateurs* was largely taken from Mackenzie, but it is put to different interpretative ends. Rather than an aberration from constitutional politics, they argued that many Scots in 1820 *were* genuinely revolutionized. This, however, made them easy prey for essentially English spies operating on the instructions of an alien government. The spectre of English agents lies at the heart of their subsequent arguments. The proclamation, for example, in its appeal to rights conferred by Magna Carta and the Glorious Revolution must have been the production of an English *agent provocateur*. No self-respecting Scottish insurgent would appeal to these essentially foreign texts and 'a Scot would naturally refer to the Declaration of Arbroath in place of the English Magna Carta'.[86] Such conclusions ignore the frequency with which Scottish radicals *did* appeal to an essentially English narrative of liberty, even if they did sometimes combine it with episodes from Scottish history.

Such a reliance on spies as a key explanatory factor is problematic even when the evidence is not shoehorned into a nationalist framework. Such interpretations ascribe to these *agents provocateurs* an almost superhuman ability to plan and effect the downfall of those men who marched to Bonnymuir and from Strathaven. They also managed to do so without leaving any trace in the Home Office records or in Sidmouth's papers. Other spies – Oliver, Castle, Edwards – did leave documentation, which the government made a point of preserving.[87] To suggest that the absence of these traces represents some kind of cover-up would entail demonstrating that the voluminous correspondence expressing surprise and uncertainty at the likely course of events at the very highest levels of civic and national government is also contrived.

There is no doubt, however, that there were mysterious individuals in the west of Scotland whose roles in the rising it is difficult or impossible to reconstruct. Strangers or suspect men were mentioned as being present at all of the major flashpoints of the rising: for example, the man James Shields, who told the Strathaven radicals that Glasgow was in flames and that thousands of radicals were marching on the city from both the north and the south; or the man variously called 'English Laing' or 'daft Laing of Kilbarton', who it was claimed brought news from Glasgow to Paisley and encouraged the stopping of the works.[88] It is not necessary, however, to leap to the conclusion that these men were operating as *agents provocateurs*. Within the context of a radical movement which, since 1817, had been paranoid about the infiltration of spies into their numbers, every stranger was apt to be seen as a spy.[89] Moreover, in both political and legal contexts, the identification of spies was both a powerful rhetorical strategy to employ against government and one of the only available defence strategies in the light of previous state trials.

In fact, what the correspondence of the authorities reveals is not some all-powerful espionage network, but deep concern about the lack of adequate police intelligence on the likely movements of radicals. After the arrest of the radical committee in February, it is clear that the Lord Advocate and the local authorities had only patchy and incomplete information. When it came to apprehending active insurgents, only the unlucky, the careless or, possibly, the innocent seem to have been caught. The Bonnymuir radicals were intercepted because they had the misfortune to stop both a yeoman and a hussar on the road; most of those who had marched from Strathaven were not apprehended at all. The trials, which secured convictions, but which were far from a complete success for government in many respects, provided an opportunity for the Lord Advocate to bemoan the defective state of the police, especially in the storm-centre of radicalism around Glasgow:

> I cannot pass over this opportunity without saying, that the state of the Police of this county and city is not such as could have been desired and wished. Had that Police been well organized, I am confident that the number of persons who escaped on occasion of the late commotions would have been much less, and we should have

had many stronger examples of guilt from this city, (which was the focus of the whole conspiracy).[90]

In fact, it was a matter of self-congratulation for the Lord Advocate that convictions had been secured without tainted evidence:

> I must notice it as an occurrence almost unprecedented in the State Trials that in the course of those now concluded ... not a single person offered as a witness who was either a Spy, a Socius Criminis, or liable to the most remote suspicion in any point of view.[91]

If an instrumental role for spies is ruled out of the equation, we are left with two principal explanations as to why a general rising was planned and why it turned out in the way that it did. First, that the numbers of those prepared to play the role of active insurgent was tiny and the poor organization of this insurrectionary strand of radicalism meant that 'when the radicals did resort to arms their efforts were futile and pathetic'.[92] Secondly, that the rising was part of an *abortive* general rising encompassing central Scotland and the north of England, but that organizational weaknesses, the difficulties of communicating effectively, and the general political context conspired to prevent radicals ever mustering simultaneously or in full strength. Elements of both interpretations are compelling and the British context of the second interpretation is very important in explaining the outcome of events.

In explaining why physical force was resorted to by some in April 1820 a long view needs to be taken. As suggested above, from autumn of 1819 there was clearly an insurrectionary underground. Sidmouth identified a 'Schism amongst the Reformers' from the end of October, with some committed to constitutionalist action and others sympathetic to Thistlewood's plan of general meetings to inspire insurrection.[93] Physical and moral force approaches to politics were, however, part of a sliding scale rather than binary opposites. Over the winter the context in which reformers operated made appeals to physical resistance far more frequent and far more likely to gain a popular audience. It was this dynamic, which created a split among reformers who were responding to rapidly changing events. First and foremost, of course, the Six Acts redefined constitutional rights in more restrictive ways and increased the likelihood of insurrection. Shrewder commentators argued this at the time and, for example, one of Sidmouth's correspondents from Ayrshire argued:

> That the seditious meetings bill, as it is called, would give us in place of those daring and, I acknowledge, somewhat dangerously though open & public assemblages, in the open air, secret plots, cabals – combinations – conspiracies ... Public meetings on the plan formerly in repute were no longer possible. It was soon discovered, by the Radicals themselves, that their Object (which they scarcely concealed was to bring about a revolution by violence), might be carried into effect as well if not better, by means of union Societies, standing Committees, & secret meetings.[94]

The language of the proclamation itself was that of a radicalized constitutionalism, which carefully eschewed the idea of levelling principles and located a broken contract in 'the contempt heaped upon our Petitions for redress'. An armed rising was the only way to rescue the people's rights and the King from the hands of a narrow and treacherous faction. If there was a legal point to be scored in emphasizing Baird's claim that his party was attacked and 'resisted accordingly' it also demonstrates the essentially constitutional mindset in which most radicals operated. Playing the part of the 'nation' rising in arms to assert its rights against tyrants was within the bounds of constitutional discourse.

Attempts at armed rising also had their origins in the polarization described in the preceding chapter. As loyalism became ever more assertive and shrill in its denunciations and visible in its mobilization of armed force, especially from December, radicals necessarily considered an armed solution as the only possible one. Ideas of a 'general rising' gained purchase in this rapidly changing political context as radicals strove to develop a 'logic of confrontation' with an ever-changing enemy. As suggested above, such plans were encouraged by a sense of expectation provided by a new reign and election, the conclusion of an important series of political trials and the news of the success of armed risings elsewhere in Europe. All of these factors were likely to increase the support for armed resistance.

Finally, we should not ignore the personnel of radicalism as providing some explanation of the rising of 1820. Large numbers of those who turned out or who were reported to be active had military experience and this was likely to make them at least not utterly opposed to any idea of violence. John Baird was a peninsular veteran, while James Clelland, who was also condemned to execution but had his sentence commuted, had been a soldier.[95] So too was John Morrison, one of the leading figures in the Strathaven contingent, while James Speirs and John Smellie, who went around to make sure work had stopped at the cotton mills in Johnstone, had both been soldiers, Speirs a Sergeant in the 21st regiment.[96] Ex-soldiers or volunteers had been actively involved in drilling radicals and naturally came to the fore during the attempted rising. The man shot at Foxbar had been discharged from the rifle brigade, while an ex-volunteer had drilled radicals at Quarrelstone near Johnstone.[97] The declaration of one of the captured Central Committee demonstrated the confidence that radicals placed in the fact that the military training of a large part of the population would support the strategy of a general rising: 'it being moreover thought that so soon as they did rise they would get plenty of their own numbers who had been in the Army & who were acquainted with these regulations to arrange them into Companies & Regiments'.[98]

If all of this helps to explain why plans for an armed rising could attract support, it does not explain why the rising proved such a 'damp squib'. In the first instance, we should question accounts that are dismissive of the scale of the unrest in the west of Scotland. The evidence of the widespread nature of stoppage of work and open drilling during the week; the numerous reports of pikes and other weapons found abandoned; and the strong folk memory of the rising all attest to the numerical *potential* for the rising to have been a far more widespread and serious challenge to the authorities than it eventually was. As Calhoun has argued, however, radicalism was at its strongest the closer it came to its local base. As a form of community activism, it could mobilize entire locales and appeal across occupational boundaries.[99] This in part explains why insurgent radicalism appeared to be strongest in those small and medium-sized communities around large urban centres such as Paisley and Glasgow, rather than in the larger urban areas themselves. Successful mobilizations in a town like Strathaven or in the self-contained weaving suburbs of Glasgow, such as Bridgeton or Calton, or in villages such as Duntocher, demonstrated how deep the roots of radicalism were within communities. This sense of community was augmented by a sense of local history and Boswell identified 'the most contaminated villages' as the modest but growing weaving settlements of Newmilns and Galston, both of which had been 'poisoned since the year 1794 and the evil has fester'd ever since'.[100] As one participant later put it: 'In the street where I resided, the inhabitants were all radicals throughout'.[101]

An additional reason explaining why risings broke out in these places and were averted in the larger towns was that it was exactly these latter places that those in authority saw as most threatening. In England Manchester was quiet partly because of the large numbers of troops quartered there – where people did come out it was in smaller communities.[102] In Scotland, troops were quartered strategically at Glasgow, Paisley, Dumbarton, Kilmarnock, Hamilton and Airdrie in line with recommendations from local elites. It should come as no surprise that it was not at these large centres of population that radicals made a strong showing as they awaited the signal for a rising. One informant could report on a restless quiet at Paisley:

> but at Johnstone, Kilbarchan, & other villages around, where there is no Military Force, they were much more daring. In these places they were seen openly preparing their arms for service, screwing the heads of their pikes into the Shafts, cleaning their Firearms &c.[103]

Armed radicals thus appeared and waited, but any attempted rising was problematic and fraught with difficulty because this strength at a local level was matched by a crippling weakness at a national level. The postmaster at Glasgow managed to keep his cool on the fraught Tuesday and pointed this out in a letter to his superior:

When one allows oneself to think, you find it impossible to conjecture what it is the radicals can do to carry their project of a revolution into execution. How, or when they are to collect a force, so organized, as to enable them in any way to shew head. The truth is, that with ordinary vigilance on the part of Government, the thing is impossible, & we may dismiss all fears for any thing beyond a disturbance of the peace from the irritated feelings of our starving population.[104]

It was the spaces for communication between strong but more-or-less isolated local communities of radicals which had presented opportunities for spies to operate in 1817.[105] These spaces were also filled with rumours that the outlawed George Kinloch had returned from France with some of Napoleon's officers, including Marshall Macdonald, or that French vessels had landed in Ayrshire.[106] Involving anyone not known personally in treasonable projects was likely to lead, as it did, to suspicions of betrayal and the operation of *agents provocateurs*. Constant references in contemporary and near-contemporary accounts to 'strangers' in towns and to the dress of men offering commands bear testament to a society whose connections were still largely those of the face-to-face community. Joseph Brayshaw's subsequent account of his 'mission' to Scotland to check on the state of preparations gives an insight into the insecurities, paranoia and misinformation involved in attempts to knit together a national movement.[107] The evidence does not sustain an interpretation that ascribes either the genesis or the failure of the planned rising to the operations of spies, but it is more than sufficient to point to the obstacles, uncertainties and suspicions involved in trying to organize insurrection nationally as a crucial factor in its outcome.

Such uncertainty and suspicion was apparent in perhaps the most commonly-ascribed reason for failure among both those forces of law and order observing events and those radicals who participated in them: the failure of communication between radicals in Scotland and England and 'every where a disinclination to be the first to strike a blow'.[108] The magistrate in Manchester, James Norris, who was privy to the correspondence between the authorities in Manchester and Glasgow, was quick to predict the actual outcome of events: 'in Scotland they expect the movement to commence in England & I believe that here they expect the commencement in Scotland; this state of things will I hope prevent their moving in either country'.[109] This was certainly the attitude of Sidmouth, who also had oversight of communications from different parts of the kingdom and believed that comparing his English and Scottish correspondence demonstrated: 'that the Scotish [*sic*] Radicals expect the first blow to be struck in England, while the English are willing to give Precedence to their Scotish [*sic*] Confederates'.[110] Certainly the evidence from England suggests that radicals there were waiting for the stoppage of the mail as a sign and for intelligence that Scotland had risen.[111] Examinations taken of prisoners seized in arms at Grange

Moor on 11 April suggest that even then participants had been told 'there were fifty thousand in a Body armed in Scotland ready to come and join us'.[112]

As the English looked for the stoppage of the mail from Scotland, their Scottish counterparts similarly awaited word of events in England. The appearance of the mail amplified their doubts and in some later accounts participants in the rising highlighted a sense of betrayal: 'The ambassadors who had been sent by us to Nottingham stated that, by an agreement with the English, we were not to move until we heard that 200,000 had taken the field in England'.[113] This reading was partly confirmed by one of Sidmouth's most well-informed correspondents, General Byng, who relied on a trusted source who:

> accounts for the local and partial explosion in this part as follows – that the delegates from Scotland have been urgent in their demands on the disaffected in Lancashire and Yorkshire for an immediate and simultaneous insurrection. They equally desperate, but not so well prepared, promise to do so, not to discourage them – but on some pretext postpone the time, one day after another.[114]

What this suggests is that the rising in 1820 was, indeed, an abortive one. The fundamental weakness of any pre-modern social and political movement necessarily lay at the national level. While committees of radicals and delegates attempted to devise a national insurrectionary strategy and while the rapidly changing political context in which they operated made this more and more appealing, they were faced with a number of formidable obstacles: the fears and suspicions of strong local radical movements, whose personnel was by no means committed to active insurgency; the significant military presence in large industrial towns; and the impossibility of communicating let alone operating nationally in any other way than through the press. Those men that did turn out – in Strathaven, in Johnstone, in the suburbs of Glasgow – were even more isolated from those centres of population where they might have gleaned more accurate information by the arrival of the mail. Suspicion and uncertainty filled the spaces between community-based radical movements and there is no definitive evidence that this was fuelled by genuine *agents provocateurs*. In the final analysis, Monteith was probably quite accurate in ascribing the failure of the radicals to 'a sudden jealousy of each other, or from the Military preparations and attitude of resistance to their foolish and wicked attempts, or from both, and particularly from being disappointed of the expected cooperation of their friends in the South'.[115]

CONCLUSION

> [T]he Queen ... has done more to promote the Cause of the Radicals in three Months, than they could have done for themselves in a Century.[1]

Loyalists did not simply breathe a sigh of relief at the prospect of dangers averted and the attempted general rising increased the volume and stridency of loyalism. The events of April 1820 were immediately met with a number of sermons which were quickly published, and which laid out the case for political quiescence while continuing to couple this with an evangelical critique of irreligion among the higher classes of society.[2] Volunteer and yeomanry regiments maintained a conspicuous and often contentious presence within local communities. Indeed, many of them were still being filled long after the rising: Boswell only managed to review his three companies of Kilmarnock volunteers in November of 1820.[3]

Projects begun during the fraught winter of 1819–20 came to fruition after the eruption of the 'Radical War'. The *Clydesdale Journal*, proposed by the Lanark printer, William Murray Borthwick, to the Lord Advocate in November 1819, was released at the end of April 1820 and ran to December 1821. As a defiantly loyalist weekly newspaper it incorporated considerable work from the anti-radical sheriff substitute of Lanarkshire, William Aiton, and in its prospectus left no doubt as to its principal target:

> ABOVE all things the mania of Universal Suffrage, Annual Parliaments, Election by Ballot: – the dangerous and alarming spirit of insubordination and principles of disloyalty and infidelity, imbibed by some, especially in the manufacturing districts, will be exposed with freedom and every effort will be made to restrain those who have adopted such opinions, and to prevent them who are of sound principles from being contaminated.[4]

Similarly, it is not quite so easy to dismiss the abortive rising of April 1820 as the pathetic final act of the radical movement after 1816. Certainly, it demonstrated the frailties of a working-class movement that attempted to organize on a national basis; it also exposed the weakness of physical force radicals, whose ideas, as to the boundaries of constitutional action lay outside of those held by men of property and many men of no property. The disappearance of constitutional means of protest left most popular radicals both unable and unwilling to pursue an insurrectionary strategy with any national effect. Nevertheless, popular radicalism did not stop dead in April of 1820 and creep away to lick its wounds. Contests continued in the immediate aftermath of the explosion of early April. Later in the month in Kilmarnock, Alexander Boswell reported that 'the Radicals went so far ... as to fix the price of provisions in the market & enforced by intimidation persons to sell at the prices fixed'.[5]

Glasgow, in particular, remained in a delicate state of equipoise. At the end of June, drunken Irish soldiers of the 13th regiment began an affray in Saltmarket Street that spread to the Trongate. While Reddie was convinced that there was no 'predisposition or preconcerted plan, to assault or maltreat the military' among the people, the building tensions from the winter of 1819 must have played a considerable part in such explosions. Reddie advised removing the 13th from Glasgow for a time, despite the possibility that this might be seen as a popular victory: 'there is more wisdom in preventing the collision of such heated masses, & allowing them time to cool, than in keeping them in contest, when in a state of fermentation, maintaining order by mere force of arms'.[6] One informant told Captain Brown of the Edinburgh police that in Glasgow in December 'Radicals [were] still in the practice of assembling and frequently on the Green of Glasgow'.[7] One of the important prosecution witnesses from the state trials sought a government post away from Glasgow, because of his constant pursuit by angry crowds and the *Glasgow Chronicle*.[8]

These trials themselves and the cause célèbre of Queen Caroline's 'trial' provide a valuable opportunity for assessing the nature of radicalism, loyalism and Whiggism at the end of the period covered by this book. Both events contributed to the remaking of popular politics and served to bring them back within the shared framework provided by popular constitutionalism, following the dangerous rupture that had appeared between Peterloo and the attempted general rising.

I

The state trials themselves offered only limited opportunities for radical activity. The assimilation of Scottish to English laws on treason in 1708 necessitated the appointment of a special commission of *oyer et terminer* to try those accused of involvement in the rising. This toured the disturbed western counties of Scotland across the summer of 1820. True bills for high treason were found against ninety-eight individuals across the five 'disturbed' counties. Fifty-two individuals failed to appear and from the remainder the Crown lawyers managed to secure twenty-four capital convictions with only two acquittals after trial.[9] Three of these sentences were eventually carried out: James Wilson was executed at Glasgow on 30 August; and Andrew Hardie and John Baird at Stirling on 8 September.[10] Other sentences were commuted to transportation, with many of those convicted setting sail for the penal colonies.

As in 1817, none of the men who were prosecuted chose to defend themselves and instead relied upon counsel. The role of trials as venues for political theatre was further diminished by changing attitudes among ministers to the reporting of legal cases. The trials across this period formed part of a process whereby ministers sought through legislation to control the form of the press and through prosecution to police its content. Trials for seditious libel were all but abandoned in the 1820s. Historians have demonstrated that the forum they provided for radical arguments and publicity – notably Carlile's celebrated reading of Paine's *Age of Reason* in its entirety to ensure its cheap publication – meant that they were often counterproductive.[11] Ministers became increasingly sensitive not only to the publicity garnered by radical trials, but by the influence of the press on trials themselves. This had been particularly notable in the immediate aftermath of the Peterloo Massacre, when Eldon, the Lord Chancellor, became increasingly adamant about the need to communicate more effectively the government's message. Having outlined what he believed was a watertight defence of the Manchester magistrates he urged the Home Secretary: 'This should be laboured in the Press, for the contrary is inculcated with such incessant & such mischievous Industry, that the prosecutions on account of this Manchester Meeting will otherwise be completely written down long before they can be tried'.[12]

Such concerns had been compounded in Scotland by Maconochie's catastrophic use of the press in 1817 to publicize what he interpreted as a coordinated conspiracy in Scotland. His political role had thus compromised his ability to prosecute that conspiracy in his legal capacity. This in turn impacted on the treason trials held in 1820, where defence counsel did indeed try to mobilize similar arguments about the nature of evidence, in particular the distorting effect that the wide reporting of the treasonable address might have had on men's recollections. Increasing sensitivity to these problems meant that ahead of each treason trial the Lord President repeated a strict prohibition on reporting:

> no part of the proceedings on this trial, (and more especially the speeches of the counsel,) and no part of the evidence be published, till this and all the trials, in this and the other counties included in this Commission, be brought to a conclusion, otherwise, the severest penalties that this Court can inflict will be pronounced against them. It is essential to justice; for it is in vain that witnesses are shut up, if they can read, the next day in the newspaper, what has been said by others in Court.[13]

With the fiasco of 1817 at the front of their minds, the new Crown lawyers and members of the Scottish bench were concerned from the start both to ensure an 'authentic' record by the dispatch of a proper short-hand writer from London and to fix as far as possible the version of the 'Conspiracy & Rebellion' that was transmitted to posterity: 'especially as the hope of a great and formidable faction is to discredit & undervalue it as much as possible'.[14] Certainly, the aim of ministers and Crown lawyers was still to provide a salutary lesson and 'to influence not a particular county, but the whole of Scotland', but they were far more aware of the potentially counterproductive effects of over-zealous prosecution and, in particular, of unfavourable publicity.[15] This ensured that the official report of the trials did not appear until five years later, in 1825.

With this strict prohibition on the reporting of proceedings and the radicals' reliance on Whig lawyers, any legal victories were localized and short-lived. The acquittal of James Speirs and John Laing at Paisley, for example, was met with loud celebrations both inside and outside the court, while the men themselves were taken home in a coach and treated to a celebratory dinner.[16] Even had the press been able to publicize these events, however, similar opportunities were few and far between. When convictions had been secured in some counties, the Crown lawyers were quick to accept acquittal for remaining cases where the prosecution evidence was weaker. As Rae explained in consenting to a series of acquittals after the trial of James Wilson, he aimed to give 'a decided colour to the whole proceeding, as having originated in a desire on the part of the Crown to exercise leniency towards misguided individuals rather than for any apprehension of the nature of the result'.[17] The Crown thus made a virtue of necessity and added to the spectacle of effective, exemplary and impartial justice, while depriving Whig counsel and their radical clients of the possibility of achieving spectacular acquittals after trials.

In fact, the trials of 1820 provided more scope for the stars of the Whig legal firmament to develop their own critique and explore their own concerns than for radicals to dramatize their conflict with the state. For example, the unique nature of the special commission provoked considerable discussion of Scottish understandings of the Union and legal reform. There was a distinct lack of precedent for the trial of treason in Scotland – the 1794 trial of Robert Watt and David Downie for the 'Pike Plot' was the only Scottish precedent explored by the Crown lawyers – and this provided space for a wide-ranging discussion about the form and content of the treason laws.[18] In particular, the appearance of Serjeant Hullock, an English barrister who had been involved in the trial of Henry Hunt at York, provided the opportunity to push a technical legal defence couched in the language of patriotism. Jeffrey's complaint was that the assimilation of English and Scottish treason law had not turned a Scottish court into an English one. As such, he argued, only those competent to plead in a Scottish court could appear:

> This is a tribunal for the trial of Scotch crimes ... it is a tribunal to administer the Scottish law only. That it resembles the law of England is no argument at all: with respect to Scotchmen it is nothing but the Scotch law; it is as much the Scotch law, as all British statutes extending to Scotland are Scotch law ... We have nothing, in short, to do with the law of England here.[19]

This put the largely Tory bench in the somewhat uncomfortable position of repelling the objection. Toryism in Scotland has often been associated with a patriotism premised on an inflexible interpretation of the Union settlement as a guarantor of distinctive Scottish institutions, while the Whigs have been painted as dogmatic anglicizers.[20] In debates over reform of the legal system, Tories were likely to insist on the immutability of Scottish institutions. In reality, however, this patriotic appeal on the basis of the distinctiveness of Scottish institutions was not the property of any one political position and it cut across party lines.[21] This was revealed in spaces such as the courtroom. Such fissures were most dramatically apparent when, in a widely-reported incident, Hullock made one of many dismissive or insulting comments to Jeffrey. The Lord Lieutenant of Stirlingshire, Ronald McDonald of Staffa, a staunch Tory, passed a note to Jeffrey encouraging him to challenge Hullock and pledging to act as his second anywhere outside the county. The court told Hullock to apologize.[22] Similarly, one of the reasons the Tory Lord President, Charles Hope, insisted on the publication of the trials was 'to convince both the existing & future generations, that Treason can be as well tried here as in England – perhaps better'.[23]

If the trials thus allowed Whigs and Tories to raise wider questions about Scottish institutions and patriotism, Whig counsel largely stuck to the ground of arguing over the legitimate boundaries of constitutional protest. In the first cases to come to trial – those of Baird and Hardie – Francis Jeffrey made no attempt to challenge the evidence on which the Crown prosecution rested. Instead he attacked its interpretation. Jeffrey could not provide any evidence to dispute the assertion that Baird and Hardie had appeared in arms at Bonnymuir, but he could argue that an engagement with troops provided no evidence of treasonable intentions, especially as the troops had sought out the radicals rather than the radicals 'levying war' by pursuing the troops. A group of 'little beggarly half-starved creatures' had simply resisted soldiers sent to apprehend them for their previous misdemeanours.[24] Damning evidence of treasonable *intentions* could only come from connecting the men to the treasonable address, and Whig counsel did all that they could to destabilize these connections.

They were ultimately unsuccessful, but the trials did provide opportunities for the reiteration of the Whig critique that had been developing across the winter of 1819-20. Jeffrey urged the court to look to the wider context of the 'rising' and to ponder whether the accused might simply be men who engaged in 'the commission of that which hungry multitudes are so apt to run into, pillage and plunder, and indiscriminate attack on private property', rather than in an organized conspiracy against the constitution.[25] Furthermore, in inviting the jury to consider other possible interpretations of the evidence, he suggested that they locate the armed men firmly in the polarizing conflict of radicals and loyalists across the previous year, when 'a certain intimidation of a vague nature had been excited on the one hand, and certain strong preparations for resistance made by the police on the other'.[26] Baird, Hardie and their associates had clearly overstepped the boundaries of constitutionalism, but they had not approached the heinous crime of treason. Their guilt was great but was mitigated by the context of widespread distress and loyalist provocation.

The trials of the Bonnymuir radicals offered little in the way of evidence on which to build a defence case, but there was more promising material for James Wilson's defence. John Murray, his counsel and another rising star of Whiggism, brought witnesses to demonstrate that Wilson was a hapless victim, a peaceful and constitutional reformer constrained and forced to join more violent radicals on their abortive march to Glasgow. Questions surrounding the interpretation of Crown evidence and the demonstration of treasonable intentions remained paramount. Murray, like the other Whig lawyers, disputed the meaning of those 'overt acts' on which the counts of treason were based. When the Crown lawyers, for example, made frequent mention of the text on the Strathaven Union Society banner – 'Scotland Free, or a Desert' – Murray offered a Whiggish reading of this inscription, which traced progress to the free government bequeathed by revolution and union:

> Is it our soil, our climate, our rocks, our marshes, that prevents this country from being anything but a desert ...? Was it not, at the period of the Revolution, visited with famines, that swept away hundreds and thousands of the people? What, Gentlemen, can it be now, that produces the wealth, riches and improvement around you ... but the course of a free government established among you? and whenever that free government is lost, it will again become a desert;– that must be the sentiment of you all, and of every reflecting man in Scotland.[27]

Such efforts to place constitutional interpretations on radical actions ran alongside the beginning of efforts to dismiss the entire affair as the product of the fabrications of spies and *agents provocateurs*. This was most stridently done by Joseph Hume, who, in October 1820, moved for the examination of a Bow Street magistrate, who had apparently allowed a suspected author of seditious placards to escape confinement. This man – William Franklin, alias Fletcher, alias Forbes – was, according to Hume, the bottom rung of a monstrous conspiracy, where the issuing of seditious placards between 1818 and 1820 appeared to have the sanction of government. Though at that point Hume could not trace the April proclamation to Franklin, he strongly implied that was its source and made this claim openly at a later meeting in London.[28] He certainly did enough to encourage ministers both to ascertain that Franklin had not been in Scotland during the rising and to redouble their efforts to detect the author and printer of the treasonable placard.[29]

Hume's was an attempt to charge ministers with reviving the spy system of 1817 and it was left to others to fill in the gaps in his evidence. Parts of the liberal press took up the story, while Cobbett provided the most forceful statement. In a leading article he linked this 'Conspiracy against the People' with the unfolding 'Conspiracy against the Queen' and converted Hume's suspicions into certainties: 'There can be no doubt that the Placards, that recently led to the shedding of blood in Scotland, proceeded from the same source'.[30] The implication was clear: the people's political instincts were and remained constitutional unless they were misled by artful spies acting on the behalf of an alarmist government.

II

The state trials thus pre-eminently remained spaces for Whig and Tory interpretations of politics, where radical voices were silenced. However, as Cobbett's attack suggests, even as the treason trials were being conducted a new 'trial' – that of Queen Caroline – was acting as a focal point around which the political forces of loyalism, Whiggism and radicalism reoriented themselves. William Cobbett was simply the loudest, most active and most proficient in identifying the cause of 'the people' with the cause of the Queen from the summer of 1820.[31] The attempt of George IV to deprive his royal consort of her titles and ideally achieve a divorce had a long pre-history. His attempt to exclude Caroline from the prayers for the royal family was the catalyst that brought the Queen back to Britain in June 1820 after a lengthy sojourn in continental Europe. Caroline returned to the vociferous support of Whig and radical politicians, a liberal and opposition press, popular radicals and a considerable majority of British public opinion. The King's strategy was to pursue the passage of a bill of pains and penalties through Parliament, which was launched in the House of Lords in August 1820. From then until her death in August 1821, Caroline's 'cause' electrified politics and provided the rallying point for a national political mobilization in defence of her claims.[32]

The attraction of the Queen's cause to a range of different political and social groups has been anatomized by historians. The central conundrum for political historians lies in explaining the significance of a mass movement, focused on a royal figure and seemingly centred on issues of matrimony and domestic virtue or, according to one historian of Whiggism 'an apolitical discourse lamenting the plight of a woman scorned'.[33] The Queen's cause undoubtedly offered points of attraction to different groups. To Whigs it offered a superb opportunity to harass ministers and assert national leadership in a cause which steered clear of the kind of sticky ground involved in explicit support for parliamentary reform. For the press, it offered a sensational and profitable melodrama. For erstwhile radicals and for the population at large it offered a political appeal that was both oppositional and, in supporting the Queen, undeniably constitutional and loyal. Through its rich mix of spectacle and melodrama it allowed for the expansion of many of the innovative strategies of the mass platform and could domesticate the female involvement in politics which had so alarmed loyalists during 1819.

In Scotland, the Queen's cause attracted considerable and widespread support. Scottish Whigs were at the forefront. The centrepiece of their involvement came with the large meeting in the Pantheon in Edinburgh on 16 December 1820. Whigs such as Adam Black regarded it as a crucial turning point: 'I date the complete emancipation of Edinburgh from political thraldom from the Pantheon meeting'.[34] Following the Queen's 'acquittal' this meeting was part of a concerted effort to channel evident discontent in more overtly party-political directions. The resolutions embodied in an ostentatiously loyal address called for the dismissal of the King's ministers. Such a demand was premised not only on the assault on Queen Caroline, but on a long line of misdemeanours – extravagant public expenditure, the erosion of the liberties of the subject and the establishment of a 'spy system' and an illiberal foreign policy – of which this simply formed the most recent example.[35]

The Queen Caroline affair slotted very snugly into a reform critique of British and Scottish institutions and became a stalking horse for the discussion of other issues. One of the earliest controversies in the affair, for example, surrounded the King's attempt to remove the Queen from prayers for the royal family within established churches. When it was attempted to extend this Order in Council to Scotland, where the established church observed no formal liturgy, it raised the ire of Whig-leaning churchmen. There had been a precursor to these disputes in 1817, when Andrew Thomson, the pre-eminent Whig minister in the Church of Scotland, had refused to hold a service for the dead Princess Charlotte on the grounds that such an order transgressed both the laws and the independence of the Kirk. For this he was calumniated as a Whig partisan, bringing politics into the pulpit.[36]

Similar ecclesiastical, national and political issues were at stake in 1820, when once again Thomson was vilified by an increasingly vociferous loyalist press. When he opposed a loyal address to the King from the Presbytery of Edinburgh, he attracted notice in the new loyalist mouthpiece, *John Bull*, which reviewed his heinous crimes in praying for the Queen by name and acting as the head of a 'phalanx of *Kirk radicals*'.[37] The arrest of Rev. William Gillespie, a clergyman in Kirkcudbright, who had prayed for the Queen in front of the yeomanry, became a notorious cause célèbre as press and print offered a robust defence of the independence of the Kirk.[38] The issue of the rights of the Church of Scotland was pressed relentlessly in Parliament by one of the Queen's most vociferous Scottish supporters, Lord Archibald Hamilton, who argued that:

> The order had been what it ought to have been in England, mere waste paper. It might not then be too presumptuous for him to add, that as the conduct of government had been clearly illegal with regard to one part of the kingdom, it might be suspected, that it was not completely legal with regard to another.[39]

Burgh reform and parliamentary reform could also be intruded into the wide-ranging debate about the nature of 'public opinion' that was sparked by the Queen's affair. It became a political commonplace to remark on the unrepresentative nature of loyal addresses to the King that issued from town councils and from county meetings. On the Queen's acquittal there were riotous illuminations in those places where a general illumination was opposed by the civic authorities.[40] These were, for the *Scotsman* 'another illustration of the pernicious effects of the Scots burgh system, which tends so strongly to give Magistrates separate views and interests from those of the people they govern'.[41] The liberal press and the Whigs in Parliament consistently pushed the case that public meetings and addresses were openly canvassed and represented respectable, propertied and popular opinion, while county addresses in support of ministers were the work of secret cabals.[42] They contested the loyalist analysis that the agitation was a perilous Whig-led attempt to move the discussion away from its proper place within established institutions (which included, for the Queen's trial, the House of Lords) so that: 'the true judgement court was in the work-shops and alehouses, and receptacles of low debauchery and haggard disaffection'.[43] There was a similar concern to contest the idea that the established means of addressing the Crown from town councils and county meetings had any monopoly on loyalty. The Queen's affair was ideally suited to this purpose. All addresses both to the Queen and, subsequently, to the King urging him to dismiss his ministers, were ostentatiously loyal. The agitation offered Whigs and radicals an opportunity to recapture this term following the crisis of 1819–20 and to brand their opponents as 'exclusive loyalists'.

The Queen's trial thus had a signal effect in furthering the polarization apparent from the winter of 1819 and forcing developments within loyalism.[44] This was demonstrated in considerable tensions over public space and the running battles over venues for the placing of addresses and holding of meetings. In Glasgow, where the authorities and much of the populace at large were still wary of the potentially treasonable connotations of 'addressing', the contest was especially fierce. Those who sought to address the Queen and those who wanted to organize a public meeting after her acquittal were denied access to civic buildings and established churches and had to rely on venues controlled by the Relief

Church.⁴⁵ Similarly, attempts to use volunteer regiments to police Caroline protests and meetings were common, but came up against the split loyalties of volunteers themselves.⁴⁶ The use of the Edinburgh volunteers in such a capacity provided an opportunity to criticize a militaristic loyalism, stepping beyond its bounds.⁴⁷

In particular, the assault on Whig elites as the abettors of radicalism sharpened. The scale of loyalist propaganda increased and seemed to gain a considerable audience. At the heart of this critique was the idea that the Whigs were engaged in the single-minded pursuit of a 'BOLD STROKE FOR PLACE', which endangered all national institutions by trying 'to rival the radicals, and shew that whigs can go as far *ad captandum vulgus*'.⁴⁸ Once the likes of Jeffrey, Moncreiff and Grant had lowered themselves to 'hold a solemn festival of fraternization with the *elite* of the Cowgate' all social subordination and social order was at an end.⁴⁹ Such concerns drove the increasingly vitriolic tone of the loyalist press, which, through the *Clydesdale Journal* (subsequently the *Glasgow Sentinel*) and, more notoriously the *Beacon*, would result in a famous duel and a prolonged legal and parliamentary contest between Whigs and Tories.⁵⁰ Starkly polarized language spilled into loyalist addresses as well, and one clergyman felt compelled to explain to Lord Sidmouth the violent content of the address from the Presbytery of Langholm:

> the hostility of the lower orders throughout the country to the measures of Government, and especially on a recent occasion, has been owing entirely, if not to the unconstitutional speeches ... at least to the Violence and misrepresentation of the Opposition Speakers and Opposition Papers: which Papers, I am sorry to say, are generally read by the lower orders here and elsewhere.⁵¹

Despite loyalist protestations that the Queen's cause was being used by Whigs to dupe the lower orders into backing their bid for place, there is no doubt about the genuine, widespread and sustained support for the Queen in Scotland. One account counted illuminations on her 'acquittal' in over eighty places.⁵² The celebrated events of the trial and the spectacle of perjured witnesses, especially the Italian servant Majocchi, whose cross examination saw him repeat 'non mi ricordo' some eighty times, became part of the common currency of life. In the small debt court at Galston, for example, 'one vagabond struck his hand upon the table & exclaimed we'll have no Majocci-ing [*sic*] here by G[od]'.⁵³ When, during the summer of 1821, the Queen considered her next step after the fiasco of her non-admittance to George IV's coronation, she mooted a visit to Edinburgh and Glasgow to revive her cause, having been impressed with the demonstrations of support from north of the border.⁵⁴

The addresses and illuminations, which were co-ordinated with the different stages of the 'trial', reached a crescendo with ministers' decision, after a slim victory for the third reading of the bill in the House of Lords, not to pursue it any further. The response demonstrated the popular purchase of the Caroline mobilization. Addresses, illuminations and their attendant meetings and processions were extensions of the strategies of the mass platform agitation of 1819. They provided similar opportunities for popular community expression. The paraphernalia of non-verbal communication – flags, banners, effigies and the use of the colour white as a symbol of purity – were all present. This developing material culture of politics was also apparent in the numerous pieces of commemorative pottery, featuring the image of the Queen, that survive.[55] So too, the involvement of women, which had proved such a controversial feature of the agitation of 1819 was 'domesticated' within the context of the Queen Caroline agitation. Addresses from the 'Ladies of Edinburgh', for example, demonstrated the attempt to forge female involvement within public debate.[56] To some observers, such as Thomas Creevey, the banners, the music and the marching in order to present addresses provided a weekly reprise of the Manchester meeting of August 1819: 'I should like anyone to tell me what is to come next if this organized army loses its temper.'[57]

Part of the attraction of the Queen's cause was doubtless because such mobilization was fun and exciting. One of those who was examined for the riots that took place in Glasgow on the Queen's 'acquittal', and who bludgeoned someone trying to extinguish a bonfire, claimed to have attended simply from curiosity. Similarly, the attraction of the affair was boosted by its prosecution through discourses of 'domestic melodrama', which opened it to a wide potential audience.[58] There is less agreement among historians as to how far the Caroline agitation represented a politically significant moment. For E. P. Thompson, the episode was an irrelevant, even embarrassing, aberration within the development of working-class radicalism.[59] For Craig Calhoun, it provided a resounding affirmation of the essentially populist, non-class and atavistic nature of radicalism.[60] More positive assessments have tended to dwell on the form or the style of the agitation to make the case for its political significance. By such readings, the aims and claims of Caroline's supporters were less important than the manner in which these were expressed. Its significance could thus be located in a number of areas: in creating a space for popular politics within the constraints of the Six Acts; in providing an alternative style of politics autonomous from the parliamentary obsessions of Whigs and middle-class liberals; or in providing space for the involvement of plebeian women in popular politics.[61]

All of these explanations certainly help to explain support for Caroline in Scotland. Both Dror Wahrman and Catriona Macdonald, however, have attributed a more obviously political significance to the agitation by looking at it through the lens of popular constitutionalism and in the context of the prolonged dispute over the meaning and power of public opinion since 1816.[62] The

Queen Caroline agitation was not only a 'victory', but it achieved certain goals that had been at the core of radical agitation after 1816. The claim to be acting constitutionally, indeed loyally, could be plausibly and powerfully made and forced loyalism into some uncomfortable redefinitions.[63] Perhaps more importantly, the cause played very well into the rhetoric of being a 'national victory' and an extension of previous movements.[64]

The rhetoric of the agitation focused on presenting a populist vision of a nation full of the Queen's supporters and struggling against a small anti-national faction. This was done principally through the press and addresses, which provided space for the articulation of this vision. The presentation of the Paisley Address to the Queen, for example, was undertaken by Major Cartwright and John Borthwick Gilchrist, both important figures in the mobilization of Scottish reform in 1815. They travelled by barouche on the driving box of which was: 'a person bearing a large white silk banner; device, Caeldonia seated by an urn; on the pedestal of which was inscribed "Scotia, the land of Wallace, Bruce, and Knox!" and underneath, on a scroll, the national motto – "*Nemo me impune lacessit*"'.[65] After the Queen's acquittal, the radical press tried to sustain this sense of national endeavour and the *Black Dwarf*, for example, recommended that the Queen make a national progress taking in Edinburgh, Dublin, York, Manchester, Birmingham and Glasgow.[66] The tour never took place, but the Queen's cause seemed to provide a model that overcame the limitations of national organization.

A crucial but largely overlooked aspect of the Queen Caroline affair was the assiduity with which Caroline (or rather her supporters) answered these addresses.[67] In the first instance, such responses confirmed and furthered the idea of the national basis of the movement. The reply to the address of the Perth Trades, for example, could emphatically claim: 'The nation has been insulted in the person of the Queen'.[68] Within popular radicalism after 1816 and especially in 1819 a crucial issue had been the apparent breach of contract between prince, Parliament and people, exemplified in refusals to accept petitions and Sidmouth's refusal to transmit remonstrance to the Prince Regent. The Queen's detailed responses, drafted principally by Cobbett from mid-July, went some way to close this breach. The agitation thus acted as a salve for the constitutional politics which had been threatened by Peterloo and its aftermath. So powerful was this device that it pushed the King to follow suit. J. W. Croker's *Letter from the King to his People*, eschewed the constitutional norms of addressing the people through the medium of Parliament or the Privy Council, and sought to lay the King's case directly in front of the public.[69]

The Queen's responses echoed back the claims and criticisms manifest in popular opinion and drew implicit and explicit comparisons between her own situation and that of the people. In response to the address from Glasgow, for example, the claims of reformers to represent a national movement standing against a narrow faction were affirmed: 'I cannot charge any of my wrongs to the Nation – I charge them upon that selfish Junto, which, when it might have redressed them, only made them the means of gratifying their lust of domination.'[70] The answer to the Paisley address was issued as a separate broadside in which the blamelessness of 'the people' in the recent disturbances was contrasted with the nefarious 'spy system' of ministers:

> Violence there has been; but that has not originated with the People. It has been instigated by the enemies of the People. Secret agents and insidious emissaries have been busy in creating disloyalty, where it did not exist, and in producing treason where it would not otherwise have been found.[71]

It was its role as both a magnet for this language of popular constitutionalism and as a means to rehabilitate its central myths that the real political significance of the Queen Caroline affair can be found.

III

The argument at the beginning of this book suggested that to understand popular politics in Scotland they needed to be located within their proper contexts. First, it was asserted that the isolation of popular radicalism risked missing the other groups that together constitute a political culture. In turn this would ignore the extent to which politics was largely conducted within a common language and was framed as a contest over the boundaries and meanings of the British constitution. Secondly, it was argued that to look at popular politics only in Scotland and through 'Scottish' sources was misguided. The ideological, rhetorical and organizational focus of popular politics was genuinely British in scope. The aim of these concluding sections is briefly to outline how different political positions and groups met the fundamental challenges of adjusting to post-war politics. It will finish by focusing on the experiences and changes within popular radicalism.

The volatile period after 1816, marked by near permanent government instability to 1822, could not fail to have a profound impact on ministers. Liverpool considered resigning in the summer of 1821, convinced that the continuance of his government could no longer be justified given the hostility of public opinion. Its reconstitution and the change of tone and policy wrought by the so-called 'liberal Tories' who joined the government between 1820 and 1822, was a consequence of this period of instability and had profound implications for the conduct of politics.[72] While a recovering economy after 1822 was clearly an important context for this qualified Tory revival, the liberalizing elements which made themselves felt in foreign and economic policy and limited measures of economical and legal reform shifted the context of political debate. As

Fulcher has argued, one dramatic consequence of the period between 1816 and 1820 was the transition from a political culture opposed to reform to one where it was at least a possibility.[73] Crucially, the achievement of genuinely popular reforms in Scotland and a changed tone, which saw ministers more comfortable responding to and courting public opinion and explaining their actions, meant that radical arguments that economic and social ills were all attributable to a political source rang hollow for much of the 1820s.[74]

Official and active loyalism was a relatively weak presence in response to the radical movement of 1816–17 and this provided one reason for ministers' increasing sense of isolation. Certainly, the resources were apparent in terms of military spectacle, royal ritual and the readiness of local and national institutions to vote loyal resolutions and addresses. The crucial plank of a plausible claim to be the *only* patriotic language of politics, however, was removed after the cessation of hostilities. The loyalism that did emerge slowly in 1816–17 and more vigorously during the greater threats of 1819–20 only culminated in the response to the Queen's cause and 'the most significant loyal reaction in terms of the press and organization since the end of the Napoleonic Wars'.[75]

Post-war loyalism was markedly different from its wartime predecessor. Chased from the easy appeal to wartime patriotism, it had to be reconfigured around other concepts. The idea of a 'middle class', which had been mobilized to serve oppositional politics in the 1790s, now became the site of a vigorous struggle between loyalist, radical and Whig. In the aftermath of the Queen Caroline debacle, loyalists were more apt to eschew the idea of loyalty to a particular royal *person*. Instead, they stressed a more generalized loyalty to *institutions*, moved by the conviction that habits of insubordination and vulgarity would end by 'subverting the Throne and the Altar'.[76] Loyalists capitalized on the hostility to female involvement in politics both in the person of the Queen and her supporters to refurbish and refashion the concept of loyalism around a middle-class ideal of domesticity. They met with considerable success and Fulcher has noted the speed with which support for the Queen evaporated after her acquittal in November of 1820.[77] Scotland's towns furnished numerous examples of this apparent loyalist swing during the celebrations of the King's coronation in 1821. Though we should not, perhaps, overstate the depth of these sentiments, the change in tone in the reports of local elites in Glasgow was especially marked:

> every man seemed to vie with his neighbour in sentiments of loyalty; among the numerous acts of loyalty, the statue of King William III, was decorated with laurel and orange flowers, not by the constituted authorities, but by a spontaneous effusions from an assemblage of the working classes; the ladder used on this occasion was the shoulders of his Majesty's loyal subjects.[78]

We do not need to swallow whole Henry Cockburn's heroic account of a Whig millennium, the opening act of which was bracketed by the meetings of 1816 against the property tax and 1820 for addressing the King, to realize that the period had a particularly profound impact on Whigs and Whig politics. Public meetings after 1816, the pages of the *Edinburgh Review* and the *Scotsman*, parliamentary offensives over burgh reform and the role of the Lord Advocate and public defences of radicals in both 1817 and 1820 provided a wide space for the reorientation of Whiggism in Scotland during these years. In particular, the crisis of 1819 to 1820 – with the government's removal of Fitzwilliam and the threatened removal of the Duke of Hamilton – exercised an effect on the younger Whig leaders, who would form the vanguard of reform activity in the 1820s. It was this period which led many Whigs eventually to support political reform and to engage wholeheartedly in the strategy of leading the people in its pursuit.[79]

Scottish Whiggery's contribution during this period seems to have been especially important. Not only was the *Review* the principle vehicle for the discussion of the intellectual and political premises of Whiggism, but a distinctive critique of Scottish institutions and politics also became an important area of strategic and parliamentary endeavour. The issue of burgh reform had revealed some chinks in the Liverpool government's armour in 1819 and continued to be agitated to 1822. It was joined by other Scottish issues, most importantly the contested political role of the Lord Advocate and the 'special case' for the reform of Scotland's uniquely restrictive political system.[80]

IV

In terms of popular radicalism the period between 1816 and 1820 was formative. Within the Scottish context, the period has not always been seen as important for the right reasons. In particular, the pieties of the nationalist approach to popular politics, where radicals are either latent or actual republican separatists, cannot be sustained. There is certainly considerable evidence that radicals used the Scottish past and patriotic appeals extensively in articulating distinctive grievances and developing approaches to common problems. They did so, however, within a shared language of popular constitutionalism, which was, in the final analysis, unionist in its implications. They also did so within a movement whose networks of communication and methods of organization were pan-British and which retained a focus on Parliament and British figures such as Cartwright and Cobbett as much as on more specifically Scottish concerns. To have done anything else would have been to abandon the most powerful available strategy within popular politics after 1815: the claim that radicals represented 'the people' or 'the nation', both of which were conceived in British terms, struggling against an anti-national 'junto' or 'faction'.

In one sense the story of these years both north and south of the border was of one long dispute over the proper boundaries of the constitution. And this *was* a dialogue, as the languages, political strategies and activities of radicals, loyalists, Whigs and ministers all aimed at providing definition to the proper limits of freedoms of petitioning, assembly and speech and restricting or shaping the action of other groups. Radical and reform mobilization was most effective when the 'nation' and 'the people' were plausible as synonyms for the supporters of reform. In this sense, the movement of 1816–17, which could claim both a more socially and geographically diverse constituency than its successor in 1819–20, whose purchase was limited to the industrial areas of lowland Scotland, was the greater success. So too was the Queen Caroline agitation, which could also claim genuinely national support.

If the movement of 1816–17 was more successful in its claims to be 'national', the more restricted audience for radical appeals and the dynamism of events after 1819 pushed considerable innovations. Foremost among these were the sophisticated political strategies of the mass platform agitation, which had developed since 1816 but reached its apogee in 1819. Part exercise in constitutional intimidation, part community ritual, part patriotic display, the mass platform was a crucial development within extra-parliamentary politics, whose central strategies would shape much subsequent activity. It also demonstrates the importance of examining radicalism within its proper contexts. Certain aspects of the platform both in Scotland and elsewhere – its embrace, for example, of visual spectacle as a strategy for mobilization – are inexplicable without reference to the culture of loyalist display, which had developed during the French Wars, and the activities of loyalist themselves.

Constitutional instincts remained at the core of popular politics in Scotland. Understandings of the constitution armed radicals with powerful weapons and, as Wahrman has argued, had they pursued the implications of a policy of mass simultaneous meetings across the winter of 1819–20, the radicals could potentially have brought government to its knees.[81] Constitutional instincts, however, also limited and restrained radical actions. While structural weaknesses, most notably the complete inability to organize and coordinate on a national level, are crucial in explaining the 'Radical War' of 1820, ideological issues certainly played a role. There were certainly many who were happy to embrace a language of constitutional resistance after Peterloo and argue that if petitions were met with sabres and bayonets then there was a duty to resist. The appeal to active insurrection, however, could not mobilize on any kind of national level. There were clearly significant numbers of people prepared to argue that the constitution and the compact between ruler and ruled had been broken in the winter of

1819; there were far fewer who were prepared to believe that a general rising was either a constitutional or an effectual means of repairing it.[82]

Mass radicalism's end, like its beginning, was not the simple by-product of economic forces. E. P. Thompson's 'strangely quiet' 1820s were certainly partly premised on a returning prosperity. By spring of 1822 a circular sent to Glasgow and other manufacturing districts for a report on wages and unemployment received a very positive response from Kirkman Finlay.[83] There are, however, political explanations for the quieting of popular radicalism which are equally plausible. The Queen Caroline agitation and a revived Whig leadership of reform certainly had an impact. Liberal Toryism and the changed tone of government certainly removed some of the more popular targets of popular radicals and a willingness to legislate on some controversial issues – such as the Corn Laws and the Combination Laws – helped to weaken the appeals of radicals that economic woes had political causes. One response to the events of 1819–20, which met with no success in Scotland, was represented by Henry Hunt's abortive attempt to revive the mass platform agitation through his Great Northern Union.[84] Another, which seems to have had more purchase in Scotland, was to change the terms of the argument. Instead of assigning political causes to social and economic problems, followers of Carlile's revivified Paineite rationalism and of Owenism concentrated both on individual self-reform and on explanations that identified problems in sites other than the political system. We should not, however, overstate this 'search for alternatives' in the 1820s. In many ways reform was pursued through countless local campaigns and its languages mobilized and aimed at the reform of numerous institutions.[85]

Two consequences of the period 1816–20 were more long-term. The first was that it witnessed the reification of 'radicalism' and its final transformation from a language of political exclusion into an ideology. Such a process is inexplicable without tracing the manner in which the hostile critiques provided by both loyalism and Whiggism encouraged greater self-definition among radicals. 1819–20 in particular witnessed frequent denunciations not only of the programme of 'Radical Reform' but of the wider concept of the 'doctrines of Radicalism'.[86] Hostile comment was often accompanied by an attempt to define this new and disturbing force: '"radicalism", which is just a compendious method of expressing – insurrection – murder – assassination – revolution & republicanism'.[87] Such unfavourable accounts, along with the attempts of Whigs to distance themselves from the natural rights precepts of popular radicals, helped to crystallize radicalism as an ideology into the 1820s, with the paradoxical effect of lending it some kind of legitimacy.[88] Fulcher has gone as far to see the period as one in which radicalism became the 'third party' in the state. By the sustained attempt both to argue and legislate radical reform out of existence, ministers, Whigs and loyalists had only succeeded in acknowledging it: 'Reform of the franchise was firmly on the political agenda, where it could be explicitly rejected, but no longer ignored'.[89]

The second more long-lived consequence was that the period provided crucial resources for the political agitations of the future. In Scotland, the events at Thrushgrove and, in particular, those during the 'Radical War' provided heroes and villains, lessons and warnings to generations of activists, all of whom would shape them to their own uses. The Lord President had been sensitive to this possible outcome when he pronounced capital sentences on Baird and Hardie at Stirling:

> I am well aware, that, from the delusion which has been practised against you, and from the principles, perhaps, which some of you have imbibed ... you may consider yourselves, not as the victims of justice, but as martyrs for liberty.[90]

It is the contested legacy of the 'martyrs' of 1820, in particular, and the political usability of this period across the nineteenth and twentieth centuries that is considered in the epilogue.

EPILOGUE: THE LEGACIES OF 1820

On 5 September 2001, the SNP MSP for Central Scotland, Gil Paterson, moved some members' business in the Scottish Parliament:

> That the Parliament recognizes the sacrifice of the three 1820 martyrs, James Wilson from Strathaven and John Baird and Andrew Hardie from Glasgow, who were hanged and beheaded in the 1820 rising, which fought for social and economic justice, workers' rights and an independent Scottish Parliament and believes that the history of their struggle should be included in the education curriculum in order to mark the anniversaries, on 30 August and 3 [*sic*] September, of their sacrifice for Scottish rights 181 years ago.[1]

This very motion itself was a commemorative act, pointedly delivered as close as possible to the day on which Baird and Hardie had been executed in Stirling. Paterson went on to deliver his own interpretation of the rising of 1820, which stimulated contributions from other MSPs. Later in the proceedings, Paterson's SNP colleague, Linda Fabiani, a member of the 1820 Society and a resident of Strathaven, spoke of the martyrs' role in 'the cause of Scottish self-determination' and underlined the nationalist interpretation: 'The rising encouraged Scots to pursue their liberty – as individuals and as a nation'.[2]

Paterson's speech had been followed by Lloyd Quinan, a radical and former STV weatherman, who reflected on his time as a member of Glasgow Trades Council, which organized a May Day demonstration in 1987 that had linked an occupation of the Caterpillar factory at Tannochside with the shootings and transportations that had ended the combination of the Calton weavers in 1787.[3] This, he claimed, was just another aspect of 'our forgotten history' that a new parliament ought to recognize.[4] Quinan was followed by the Labour member for Dundee East, John McAllion, who supported Paterson's motion, but also placed a slightly different emphasis on the lessons to be learned from 1820. For him it was less an episode in the long campaign for Scottish independence and more proof that: 'The real heroes of Scottish history are not the kings – French, Norman or whatever – but the ordinary, working-class people who have contributed so much'. He placed 1820 in the context of a long line of 'reactionary Tory governments in Scotland' and took the opportunity to have a dig at the small Conservative rump in the Scottish Parliament.[5]

In response to the Nationalist and Labour interpretations, the Conservative member for mid-Scotland and Fife, Brian Monteith, rose to offer his reading of the 1820 rising. Progress and prosperity, he argued, had lain in another direction and had 1820 been successful it 'would have stopped the Scots from becoming full partners in the union as the Irish never did'. Soldiering on through repeated attempted interventions he reminded the Parliament that 1820 had been defeated not by any external power 'but by the Scottish people' – and he was relieved that it had, so that the road was clear for the 1832 Reform Act when 'the political life of modern Scotland was created'. In the final analysis he argued the Scots 'chose Walter Scott, not the martyrs of Bonnymuir' and, while he would support more teaching of Scottish history in schools, 'we would be wise to teach the lessons that the nation has learned from that history rather than glorifying men who betrayed it'.[6]

The attempt to commemorate the 1820 martyrs in the new Scottish Parliament demonstrates the highly contested nature of such activities. Such contests were doubtless made all the keener by the fact that the battleground was the new Parliament of a nation that had recently 'recovered' important trappings of its statehood. In this case, 1820 was used as a pivot for at least three competing narratives of the Scottish past. This epilogue will attempt to trace similar contests over the memory of 1820 – never entirely a piece of 'forgotten history' – throughout the nineteenth and twentieth centuries and suggest that such a case study can throw light on commemorative practices, radical political culture and narratives of the nation.

There is now, of course, a vast literature on memory as a subject in its own right, while commemoration figures prominently in important works on both nations and nationalism and on ritual.[7] In the British context, while there is a burgeoning literature on the commemoration of great deaths, great victories and great events, there is a curious lacuna in exploring the commemorative activities of those not involved in the attempted production of 'official' or 'national' memory.[8] Indeed, it is the focus on these attempts to forge 'national memory' which Raphael Samuel thought had inured historians to 'thinking of commemoration as a cheat, something which ruling elites impose on the subaltern classes'.[9] This lacuna is perhaps the more striking when one looks to the historiography of Ireland, where the very tangible relationship between commemoration and oppositional politics is a field of study in its own right.[10]

Some impressive recent work has, however, started to examine this relationship in the British context, with illuminating results.[11] This epilogue aims to take one event – the abortive rising of 1820 – and explore its commemoration over the *longue durée*. In so doing it will concentrate on the contexts in which commemoration occurred as part of a public sphere 'constituted from a field of conflict, contested meanings, and exclusion'.[12] 1820 survived as 'fragments of history', which allowed it to be imagined and re-imagined by different groups pursuing often divergent aims in a range of circumstances. If specific political situations gave meaning to their actions these were also provided by the particular commemorative contexts in which they operated. History is often mobilized precisely when new directions are being sought, change is being negotiated and contest is being contemplated and this provides a revealing framework within which to examine commemorative activity and the uses to which 1820 could be put from the early nineteenth century until the actions of MSPs in the new Scottish Parliament.[13]

This epilogue will examine the key phases in the commemoration of the martyrs of 1820, which do not easily fit models of commemoration which emphasize its repetitive and formalistic features.[14] Rather, the emphasis on context allows for the exploration of how the memory of 1820 impacted on both the language and practice of politics and the articulation of national narratives at certain key moments: first, the activity surrounding the passage of the Reform Act (Scotland) 1832; secondly, the establishment of monuments to the martyrs at Strathaven in 1846 and Glasgow in 1847, which once again occurred at a time of heightened political tension; thirdly, the centenary commemoration organized by the Independent Labour Party (ILP) in 1920 in the context of a volatile post-war situation, which was in some ways analogous to the period 1815 to 1820; and finally, the renewed interest in 1820 after 1945 when commemoration was enthusiastically pursued by nationalists and other groups as a highly politicized activity involving contests at local and national levels.

I

The 'Radical War' in Scotland and the conviction of both the Cato Street plotters and Hunt and others for their activities at Peterloo brought to an end a fraught period of agitation, E. P. Thompson's 'heroic age of popular radicalism'.[15] Posthumous heroic reputations can, however, be a long time in the making. There was some immediate comment on the attempted general rising, but this was quickly overshadowed by the Queen Caroline sensation. As well as extensive press coverage during the first week of April and some comment on Hume's attempt to uncover the 'Placard Conspiracy' later in the year, songs and ballads began to circulate quite quickly. Most of these struck a melancholy note, but, like Hume's speeches in Parliament and Cobbett's journalism, they began to identify the manner in which the event could be explained:

> By evil counsel nurs'd and fed,
> By traitors and deceivers led,
> They left their hamely, peaceful bed,
> N'er to return from Bonny-Muir.[16]

It would be ten years before the 'Radical War' was given sustained attention in the context of another mass agitation for parliamentary reform in 1830–2. The first interpreter of these events, who sought to commemorate the executed, was Peter Mackenzie from Glasgow, who had been a loyalist volunteer in 1820 but had turned into a radical journalist.[17] His own memoirs are a rich source for the politics and society of Glasgow in the first half of the nineteenth century and delivered a sustained narrative of his own involvement in reform politics, which revealingly began with the Glasgow petition in favour of Queen Caroline.[18] It was the agitation for parliamentary reform after 1830 that really thrust Mackenzie into the limelight, and it inspired a period of incredible productivity. His principal achievement lay in launching the radical newspaper *Loyal Reformers' Gazette*, the first number of which appeared on 7 May 1831, following the first rejection of Lord John Russell's reform bill in the House of Commons and during the hotly contested general election that followed. Mackenzie claimed a circulation of 20,000 for his newspaper, which the government took seriously enough as an opinion former for the Lord Advocate to sustain a correspondence with Mackenzie.[19]

The tone of the *Gazette* was, however, ostentatiously of a popular constitutionalist kind, offering an appeal to liberties gained in 1688 and proclaiming unbreakable attachment to the patriotic monarch William IV, who, if not a warm supporter of parliamentary reform, was at least less than a staunch opponent of it. This tone only changed during the 'Days of May' when the King accepted the resignation of Grey's reform ministry, a decision that was met with monster meetings and petitions throughout the length and breadth of the country.[20] Mackenzie's response was to drop the 'Loyal' prefix from the title of his newspaper, and the crown was removed from its masthead – a good example of the kind of iconographical threat that was everywhere apparent in May 1832.[21]

It was in this context of agitation for parliamentary reform that Mackenzie considered the events of 1820. Not only was the history of radicalism in Scotland a constant reference point in his articles, but he also produced inexpensive volumes dealing with the trials of the 1790s and Scotland's post-war experiences.[22] In these the executed radicals appeared as passive victims, gullible but desperate men led by government agents into committing acts of extreme folly. In particular, the figure of Wilson was used to evoke considerable pathos, and the account of his trial included a dying testament, which, while it urged his countrymen to continue to press for reform, also claimed that he had largely been coerced into turning out by younger and wilder spirits.[23] The interpretation he offered of 1820 has been much criticized and, indeed, was attacked in John Stevenson's account of the rising in Strathaven, which was published in 1835 in part as a conscious refutation of Mackenzie's writings.[24] In their *Scottish Insurrection*, Ellis and Mac a'Ghobhainn supported Stevenson's contention that Mackenzie was duped by a forged dying testament attributed James Wilson, and even went so far as to suggest that Mackenzie might have forged the document himself, in an effort to support his own peculiar interpretation of the event.[25]

Of course, however, no commemoration can be seen as an objective record of past lives. As will be suggested later, the approach of the authors of the *Scottish Insurrection* is no less shaped by their own commemorative agenda (that the radicals should be remembered as active revolutionary and preferably nationalist agents fired by the courage of their convictions) than Mackenzie's was. Viewed in this way, Mackenzie's account was not wilful lying, but offered a particular narrative because the political context in which he operated meant that he wanted the didactic weight of commemorations in both print and stone to convey a specific message. Mackenzie sought to integrate the events of 1820 into a narrative of the Scottish reform agitation from the 1790s through to its apotheosis in the events of 1830–2. It is this purpose that explains why Mackenzie's writings set great store by the meeting held at Thrushgrove in 1816 rather than the rising of 1820, which was invariably coupled with this earlier event. The lesson was one for putative radicals and the authorities as well – attempted risings and executions were to be expected if the opportunities to engage in constitutional activities, exemplified by the meeting at Thrushgrove and the monster meetings that were ensuring the passage of the reform bills, were shut down in favour of relying on the machinations of spies.

This approach was amply demonstrated in the first attempt physically to commemorate the martyrs of 1820 in the monument that was erected to Baird and Hardie in November 1832. The project was funded by radicals, Whigs and the profits from Mackenzie's flurry of writings, and so Mackenzie himself had a good deal of control over its details. Failing to get a site from either the Stirling or the Glasgow authorities, the monument was erected on James Turner's lands at Thrushgrove, a result which certainly helped to reinforce Mackenzie's message.[26] Furthermore, the inscription on Neilson and Galbraith's simple monument made clear where its didactic freight was intended to lie – it gave a lengthy description of the meeting at Thrushgrove, where 40,000 inhabitants of Glasgow 'first bravely met' to petition for reform. This was followed by a brief dedication of the monument as 'sacred to the memory' of Baird and Hardie, whose activities did not even rate a mention. There was little scope for ambiguity, or an interpretation that represented the pair as genuinely heroic martyrs. Instead they were stripped of their agency and appeared as victims 'betrayed by infamous spies' and sacrificed 'for the cause of Reform now triumphant'.[27] The monument had absolutely nothing to say about the Union for the simple reason that the radicals and reformers who subscribed to it had very little to say about it and framed their own activities in relation to a wider British history of liberty.

The monument to Baird and Hardie was only the beginning of Mackenzie's commemorative career. He quickly became involved in plans for raising a monument to the martyrs of the 1790s. This was in part an exercise in party political contest and the resolutions of the subscription committee made much of highlighting the men as victims of 'rancorous tory persecution', while the project's originator, Joseph Hume, thought that picking over the 1790s would allow radicals 'to keep up a running fire agt. the Tories'.[28] In being conceived as a monument both to the disappointed constitutional patriotism of reformers and to the unconstitutional actions of a Tory government, Mackenzie's involvement was absolutely consistent with his earlier activities. Both the 1790s and the period between 1815 and 1820 were woven into a narrative of peaceful constitutionalism and the progressive triumph of parliamentary reform.

II

As Stevenson's pamphlet demonstrates, Mackenzie's constitutionalist narrative was quickly challenged and divergent interpretations of the events of 1820 remained a part of radical discourse in Scotland. In particular, Chartists, who were opposed by Mackenzie's *Reformers' Gazette* and denounced him at meetings and even burned copies of his publications, were apt to draw different lessons.[29] Commemoration as part of Chartist political culture has received little attention, but it was clearly an important means of contesting public space and placing Chartists in a narrative of reform.[30] It was taken seriously by the authorities as well. For example, police raided the house of two Peterloo veterans and seized relics which they had intended to display at the event's twentieth anniversary.[31]

Small wonder, then, that Chartist orators and the Chartist press frequently looked to 1820 when they plundered the past in search of lessons or emotionally stirring episodes. The particular episode could not, however, command consensus: the memory of 1820, indeed, could have a divisive role within one of Chartism's key debates over the merits of physical versus moral force. Most often, in fact, 1820 was used to push a constitutionalist moral force position, taking the line that it was physical-force thinking that had lost the reform movement the services of men like Hardie and Baird.[32] It also proved an especially useful narrative to mobilize when moral force advocates sought to warn Chartists of one of the biggest dangers the movement faced: '"Beware of spies!" They swarm like locusts. Let every man who proposes a secret organization be at once denounced as a traitor to the people.'[33] This use of 1820 was all the more potent when it came from John Fraser, the editor of the *True Scotsman*, who had been arrested on a charge of high treason during the rising and was called as a witness during the trial of James Speirs at Paisley.[34] Fraser warned in 1844: 'The men of the West should never forget the bitter experience of 1819'.[35]

This interpretation of 1820 was, however, contested within Chartism. The idea of a clear division of the movement into two monolithic blocks has long been seen as too facile. There was a spectrum of opinion and, indeed, only those siding with Brewster's breakaway groups, which rejected all talk and bluster about physical force in any event, can be uncomplicatedly labelled 'moral force'. Most seemed to hold opinions somewhere between this and the more robustly physical force doctrines of men like Dr John Taylor. It was widely deemed to be legitimate to use physical force in resistance to attacks by soldiers or armed constables.[36] Even those who employed the most fraught language were careful not to recommend violence but to justify resistance.[37] Accordingly, a great deal of the purchase of populist political languages lay in their ability to mobilize history in support of this kind of idea.[38] An obvious source for this was the myriad precedents of the seventeenth century; the continuing cachet of Covenanting in popular politics in the nineteenth century and beyond is clear.[39] During his tour of Scotland, George Julian Harney was taken to a number of 'sites' associated with the events of 1820. He knew exactly which buttons to press: 'it was not the moral-force psalm-singing section of the Covenanters that gained religious freedom for Scotland'.[40]

More recent history, and in particular the annals of a reform struggle that stretched back to the 1790s, were also powerful motivators. This provided a narrative replete with villains and martyrs, great battles and sobering defeats. In this pantheon, Baird, Hardie and Wilson enjoyed prominent places. Chartists, in common with later generations, did much to attempt to establish a physical and inter-generational continuity with these earlier events. In Airdrie, for example, radicals organized an elaborate meeting in honour of Thomas Macfarlane, who had been transported for his involvement in Bonnymuir. It was an opportunity to identify Macfarlane's unstinting radicalism 'so far back as the years 1793–4', when he was involved with the Friends of the People, right through to his implication in the events of 1820 and his return, upon which he supported the cause of the Chartists.[41] His facial scar, the result of a sabre wound received at Bonnymuir, was highlighted as 'a convincing proof of the merciful disposition of a Tory government'.[42] If this was one example of radicals' attempts to place themselves in a narrative of continuing struggle, their use of material relics from earlier periods of agitation served similar ends. At the huge meeting held to welcome the liberated Chartist leaders John Collins and Peter Macdouall to Glasgow, the prominence of 'a small flag made of the handkerchief which poor old James Wilson dropped for the sign of his execution, which was fringed with a black border, and had the words, "the signal of James Wilson'" was noticed both by the press and by the speakers.[43] Again, context was crucial. In welcoming to Scotland Chartists who had been victims of government persecution, the events of 1820 provided useful analogies.

If these stories – of 'poor old James Wilson' and others – could be mobilized as tragedy, as three unnecessary deaths caused by a government spy system, they could be used in other ways. Chartists could suggest that 1820 had seen the people, crushed with taxes and authoritarian government, reaching for the *ultima ratio*. John Stevenson, who had kept up a fire against Mackenzie for his emasculation of Wilson's role, was a driving force behind the erection of a monument to Wilson. At its inauguration he certainly pushed a radical take on the physical resistance of 1820, outlining the battles of Drumclog and Bothwell Brig and then telling his audience: 'But, gentlemen, we stand on historic ground. Another rising for civil and religious liberty took place at Avondale in 1820'. This linkage between recent and distant past was underlined by the procession at Strathaven, which marched in military formation with bands and banners, including the 'old flag which was at the battle of Drumclog'.[44]

This interpretation became especially marked at certain points. In particular, the resurgent but embattled movement of 1848 was apt to draw analogies between its own bleak situation and that of the post-Peterloo movement and some went so far as to voice demands openly for 'a general rising'.[45] The government raid on the offices of the *North British Express* and the arrest of a number of prominent Chartists in Edinburgh and Glasgow connected with the paper elicited just such comparisons with the aftermath of Peterloo.[46] The trial of one of these Chartists, the ageing shoemaker James Cumming, suggests another way in which the legacy of 1820 could be mobilized in popular politics. In a letter intended for the Glasgow Chartist, James Smith, but which had fallen into official hands, Cumming had described the state of play in Edinburgh and given names and numbers of armed insurrectionary clubs in Edinburgh. The names demonstrated the protean influences on Scottish radicals: the Irish influence was apparent in the Mitchell and Emmet clubs; the Muir and Gerrald clubs recalled the struggles of the 1790s; the Washington Club looked even further back and further afield; and the Baird and Hardie club, with twenty members, once again invoked the memory of the men of 1820 in the cause of armed insurrection.[47]

It was against this background that the physical commemoration of 1820 was taken to a new level. In pushing for commemoration of 1820 it is clear that several contests were going on, particularly over the bodies of executed radicals and the uses of public space. The only sustained account we have of the commemoration of Baird and Hardie is John Campbell's *Recollections of Radical Times*, based on a series of interviews with Edward Freir.[48] Freir, whom Campbell described rather vaingloriously as 'the last power-loom tenter in Scotland', had been present at the executions of Baird and Hardie at Stirling.[49] Campbell's accounts of Freir's recollections originally appeared as a series of letters in the *Rutherglen Reformer*, and were part of a vogue for autobiographical reminiscences and biographies that would keep the events of 1820 in the public sphere into the second half of the nineteenth century. Over innumerable glasses of lemonade in the Royal Standard Temperance Hotel in Glasgow, Freir related to Campbell the story of his life and involvement in popular politics of various descriptions. In particular, he delivered a poignant version of the last moments of Baird and Hardie on the scaffold. It was Freir himself who played a leading role in securing the exhumation of Baird and Hardie's remains from Stirling, their reinterment in Glasgow's Sighthill cemetery, and the construction of the commemorative monument which has become an abiding *lieu de memoire* of Glasgow's and Scotland's past.

Campbell, in reporting his interview with Freir, created a powerful narrative of 1820. After relating the events of that year, in particular the tale of the young boy Andrew White, who charged the mounted troops at Bonnymuir, Campbell moved on to the idea of commemoration.[50] In the first instance, this was stripped of any obvious political content. Freir, he claimed, was a trade unionist but had not been involved in politics after 1820 until 1848, despite the testimony of Freir's son that his father had been a Chartist. His involvement in the campaign over the bodies and the monument was instead given a romantic explanation. Freir had been working near the site of the little monument that had been erected in 1832 and saw it 'falling fast into complete decay'. It was this melancholy sight, and the range of symbols and episodes it brought to mind, that inspired Freir's reengagement with radical politics. He quickly canvassed the opinions of local 'old radicals' and a meeting deputed him to correspond with the Home Secretary over the exhumation of the remains and the raising of a monument.[51]

Contemporary press reports testify that the exhumation at Stirling took place in the early hours of 20 July 1847 and was apparently 'conducted with the utmost privacy'.[52] In the hands of Campbell, however, the story was made appropriate to an age shaped by novelists such as Wilkie Collins, and was rendered as a kind of Gothic melodrama, with a night-time excursion to Stirling. The party could only identify the burial site by enrolling an old man who knew the location. Freir described being overcome with a kind of religious ecstasy on discovering the remains and related how they identified Baird's remains as those with a crushed jawbone, the legacy of the drunk or incompetent executioner. Other incidents that were reported in detail lent the story the tone of a novel, such as a stop at the village of Condorrat, where the party had a poignant meeting with Baird's sister.[53]

The style of narration, and the fact that the interviews took place in 1879, actually veiled the very real political contests that were involved in the exhumation and commemoration. In the first instance, there was no mention of the highly charged political context. Chartism was everywhere in decline in the mid-1840s and one interpretation would be to see commemorative activity as a response to the decline and abeyance of radical political activity and part of that search for new initiatives encompassing such areas as education, temperance and land reform.[54] Radicals were literally picking over the bones of the past both to see them through another dark time and to find inspiration for the future. Indeed, the exhumation itself took place during a hotly contested general election, which saw Chartist candidates take to the hustings and which one recent account has seen as a crucial and timely opportunity for the movement to reaffirm its central purposes.[55] Additionally, in spite of Frier's later claims, the close links between the commemoration and Chartism were inescapable. Not only did leading Chartists play key roles on the committee but the public meetings dealing with the commemoration took place at the Christian Chartist Church on Regent Street.[56] A faltering movement seeking to underline its core goals could fruitfully look to the past to do so.

Another context that the *Recollections* ignored was that of other commemorations. In 1846, during Freir's campaign, a monument to James Wilson was erected by public subscription near (but crucially not *in*) Strathaven churchyard. Again, this had involved a contest, this time with Rev. James Proudfoot, who had given a hostile rendering of the events of 1820 in the *New Statistical Account* and quashed moves to commemorate Wilson in the churchyard.[57] When the monument was inaugurated, on the site of Wilson's old home, it was accompanied by a radical procession and Stevenson's fiery speech, a rally on the common green and a dinner.[58] Alongside this, Peter Mackenzie and Joseph Hume (along with other parliamentary radicals) had just completed the end of their long campaign to commemorate the Scottish martyrs of the 1790s in Edinburgh's Calton Cemetery.[59] The 1840s thus saw a sustained attempt to use the radical past.

All of this radical commemorative activity took place in the context of moves by government, by local political elites and by urban middle classes to fix their own versions of national and civic pasts in stone in the centres of Scottish towns and cities. In Glasgow, for example, George Square had begun its long process of being filled with statues of the great and good, such as the peninsular commander, Sir John Moore, and James Watt.[60] The opening of Glasgow's Necropolis, modelled on Paris's Père Lachaise, provided an ideal commemorative site for the most eminent citizens and became 'the Westminster Abbey of Glasgow'.[61] Edinburgh's statues had long played a key role in the 'Toryfication' of the urban landscape. Concurrent with both Chartism and attempts to commemorate radicals, both Edinburgh and Glasgow were witness to lengthy and protracted battles over first, the celebration of the Duke of Wellington (in the 1839 testimonial) and later his commemoration in statues in Glasgow (1844) and Edinburgh (1852).[62] Chartists in Glasgow vehemently opposed the erection of a monument to Wellington and disrupted public meetings on the subject with groans and heckles.[63] Radical activity in the 1840s thus took place in a decade during which there was a marked change in the use and management of 'great deaths', a change that radicals sought to contest with their own commemorative acts.[64]

It was in these highly-charged political and commemorative contexts that 1820 had been revived as a growing concern. Sensitivity to these contexts marked the proceedings. Freir, himself, recalled that the repeated applications to the Home Secretary had to be sent 'under the pretence that it was a few old relations of the martyrs that desired to have the remains brought from Stirling to Glasgow'.[65] The government's response, through the Lord Advocate, Andrew Rutherfurd, clearly demonstrated how much importance it attached to the politics of commemoration, while the activities of radicals showed how they were prepared to view the exhumation and commemoration as a contest. First, if the Stirling authorities granted the request, then the bodies were to be exhumed 'without any public notice or intimation, and without any procession, or concourse, or attendance of people, but in the presence of a few friends only'.[66] While the exhumation took place at night, Freir recalled a funeral procession in the afternoon 'with some thousands of followers and stragglers'. Second, the inscription for any monument in Glasgow was to be sent to the authorities for editing. This certainly happened and 'a number of sentences were obliterated ... as they had considered to be rather violent, with a high radical spirit'.[67]

Nevertheless, the inscription on the monument, even after censorship, still offered a more open interpretation of 1820 than had the previous inscription at Thrushgrove. Indeed, the very fact that the initial plan of simply moving the monument from its earlier site was abandoned does suggest that new meanings were being sought.[68] Unlike the previous monument, there was no mention of spies. A short poem instead lauded the weavers as patriots and martyrs, who suffered death 'for the cause of freedom'. The monument in Sighthill thus registered the kind of openness of interpretation that had been the hallmark of radical engagement with 1820. As was made clear in the speeches at a 'numerous and highly respectable' anniversary soirée, with James Turner once again in the chair, this interpretation still carried considerable weight.[69] Unlike Mackenzie's strictly constitutionalist interpretation, however, the monuments both at Sighthill and at Strathaven left 1820 open to a range of different groups, from Whig constitutionalists to committed insurrectionaries.

Repairs to the Sighthill monument in 1865 and 1885 and the erection of another monument to Baird, Hardie and Wilson in Woodside cemetery in Paisley in 1867, do suggest that one group found 1820 especially 'usable'. After mid-century 1820 could be safely incorporated into the languages and history of popular liberalism and commemorative activity thus mirrored developments within popular and parliamentary politics.[70] At a mass reform demonstration in Glasgow in 1884, for example, the Cumbernauld contingent carried Baird's gun and the bible that had fallen from his hand on the scaffold. Employees of the publisher William Collins were on the back of a lorry running off and distributing lithographs of the Sighthill monument.[71]

This tailoring of commemoration to popular liberalism was nowhere more apparent than in the inscription added to the Wilson monument by his grandson in 1865:

> Erected by public subscription in affectionate memory of James Wilson, a patriotic Scotsman, who suffered death at Glasgow, 30 August 1820, for enunciating the principles of progress and reform, by the adoption of which Great Britain has secured domestic peace, and consolidated her power among the nations.[72]

The coincidence of these renewed commemorative efforts and renewed attempts at parliamentary reform suggest how effectively the episode could be harnessed to this agenda. In the Strathaven case it also illustrates how what had been conceived and executed as a self-consciously ultra-radical act of commemoration in 1846 could, by 1865, be reinvested with far more moderate meanings.

III

Once again this apparent consensus was challenged, when contests over the meaning of 1820 occurred in a radically altered context. The next attempt at commemoration was even more impressive and was superintended by the Independent Labour Party (ILP) and culminated in elaborate centenary commemorations in Glasgow, Stirling and Strathaven.[73] One context for the commemoration was the success of the Labour movement in the west of Scotland, especially after the First World War. The best work on this phenomenon has pointed to the central role played by the ILP in broadening socialism's appeal, organizing grass-roots support and in focusing attention on key issues such as housing. Some part of the ILP's success might also be attributed to its cultural politics, including commemoration, and one local study has shown how politics in the period were shaped by fierce contests over the past.[74] A second context was provided by the continuing debate over the Scottish nation. The Scottish Home Rule Association had been born in the political crisis caused by Irish Home Rule in 1885–6 and so Scottish self-government remained a live question into the 1920s and beyond. Home Rule was not, of course, a programme of separatist nationalism, but its emergence coincided with a growing cultural nationalism and a keen interest in the distinctiveness of Scottish history and culture. Contests over the Scottish past were both omnipresent and politically charged.[75] A final context was provided by the aftermath of the First World War, which saw not only an unprecedented level of commemorative activity, but also a post-war recession and industrial and political strife which made the period 1815–20 a fruitful one for those who sought historical comparisons.

Just as with previous commemorations, published works dealing with 1820 kept interest in the event alive. Crucially, prominent ILP supporters were at the forefront of this. Thomas Johnston, whose *History of the Working Classes in Scotland* had originally appeared as a series of articles in *Forward*, included an account of the event. This was clearly heavily indebted to the works of 'honest Peter Mackenzie' and thoroughly endorsed the idea of spies luring 'poor workmen dupes' into action.[76] Johnston did, however, restore more of a sense of agency to the men of 1820: 'It was a large-scale, though spy-fomented strike for political freedom – a strike which the bulk of the participants expected would end in a bloody but successful revolution'.[77] Significantly, Johnston's *History* was first published in a single volume in 1920.

Even more concerned with 1820 were the writings of Gavroche, the pen name of William Stewart, the first biographer of Keir Hardie (though not, it seems, responsible for the claim that Keir Hardie was a distant descendant of Andrew Hardie). Stewart's *Fighters for Freedom in Scotland*, originally published in 1908 but purposefully brought out in a new edition in 1920 to coincide with the centenary, took in Thomas Muir and the agitation of the 1790s but overwhelmingly focused on the events of 1820.[78] Again, the interpretation was of Wilson as a 'harmless' dupe and of all of the martyrs having been fooled by 'men of their own class'.[79] When it came to deriving lessons from past examples, Stewart was less ambiguous than previous accounts. He dismissed the long process of political reform in the nineteenth century, which had seen Labour remain condemned to 'gathering crumbs from the rich man's table'.[80] In the 1920 edition, he drew an even starker lesson from 1820, one that represented a significant shift from the concerns of popular liberalism and interpreted both 1820 and 1920 as episodes in the conflict of 'two great forces – Capitalism and Organized Labour'.[81] Stewart remained at the very forefront of attempts to capitalize on comparisons between the radical past and volatile post-war politics. 'Bloody Friday' offered him the opportunity to attack the language of the *Glasgow Herald* in 1919 'the mouthpiece of disordered capitalism', which advised workers to act through a parliament which was 'as perfect as it had been found possible for the wit of man to devise'.[82] This, Stewart pointed out, was a virtual paraphrase of the language of Lord Braxfield at the trial of Thomas Muir and was an inaccurate description of a system which still weighted the vote in favour of males, property and university education.[83]

The initial impetus for the commemorations came from Stirling, but the event quickly gathered momentum when calls for a separate event at Sighthill came from Springburn ILPers.[84] The commemorative events of 1920 were advertised in the *Worker* and the *Daily Herald* and Stewart announced the programme in *Forward* in August. In that month, following representations from a Strathaven socialist, there would be a separate event commemorating the execution of Wilson. Renewed interest in the Strathaven rising was similarly encouraged by publications, most notably a collection for tourists, which gave a strong narrative account of the rising and coupled this with guides to sites associated with two great interests of nineteenth-century Scots: Covenanters and geology.[85] On 4 September, the main event would see the convergence on Stirling of socialists from across Scotland, the most prominent party being the charabanc excursion organized by Councillor Regan of the Glasgow ILP.[86] To Stewart, the purpose of the event was not in doubt – it was certainly to 'keep their memory green' – but the Stirling event would provide a 'living, moving Socialist manifesto'. The following day would see a commemoration at Sighthill.[87]

If the volatile politics of 'Red Clydeside' provided some of the context for this commemorative enthusiasm, other factors should be pointed out. According to Smyth, the Glasgow municipal election of 1920, a 'general' municipal election that had been postponed during wartime, was a crucial test of Labour strength in Glasgow.[88] The centenary events occurred just before the elections, and the platform speakers, Stewart, Maxton and Johnston, were joined by prominent councillors such as Patrick Dollan.[89] It would be difficult not to assign the much-publicized events of September some role in Labour's 'quantum leap forward' at this election.[90] While the clear impetus for ILP electoral triumphs after 1918 was their monopoly over questions like housing, changes in the representative system and their harvesting of the erstwhile Liberal Catholic vote, the success of what we might call their cultural politics has remained largely unexplored. Ian Wood, however, has tentatively argued that the ILP's continuing commitment to Home Rule was a factor in its post-war successes.[91] Certainly, *Forward* gave generous coverage to the Home Rule debate. Indeed, Thomas Johnston himself was a prominent platform speaker at the Scottish Home Rule Conference in 1919:

> These were the days of Internationalism; but before they could have the International, they must have the nations, and Scotland, with traditions, folk-lore, songs, laws, and culture distinctively her own, had something to contribute to the common pool of the nations.[92]

Renewed interest in 1820 should be interpreted within the ILP's sustained engagement with the political usability of the Scottish past. Throughout the 1920s this was apparent in the ILP and *Forward*'s involvement with events such as the rally at Bannockburn in 1923 or the anniversary in 1926 of William Wallace's execution.[93] In repairing the monument in Sighthill cemetery and adding an inscription describing the great crowd, which gathered at the behest of the ILP to honour 'two working class martyrs in the cause of liberty', ILP organizers again very physically staked their claim to ownership of the radical past.[94] This idea of establishing ownership was underscored by James Maxton at Stirling. He argued that radical Liberals rather than the ILP were the 'direct political descendants' of the martyrs. These radicals had, however, 'sold their rights and had lost the spirit in which Baird and Hardie died' and so the ILP as 'spiritual descendants' should assume the responsibility of preserving their memory.[95]

There also seems to have been contrasting tones at the Stirling and Glasgow events. Stewart claimed that the procession in Stirling was not 'to mourn our dead' but was more of a celebration of Socialist strength. The day clearly demonstrated some degree of physical strength (press reports put the numbers between 2,000 and 5,000) but also the strength the ILP had in sponsoring a wide range of cultural endeavours.[96] The tone was more sombre at the Glasgow commemoration, and there was certainly another level of contest going on. The numerous acts of commemoration were anything but neutral in the aftermath of the First World War. The widely publicized burial of the unknown soldier at Westminster Abbey was due to take place on Armistice Day in 1920, accompanied by an elaborate ritual involving George V and ministers of state, while July of the previous year had seen the march past Lutyens's Cenotaph and the inauguration of a committee to erect a Scottish National Memorial.[97] In addition, local committees throughout Scotland were engaged in erecting war memorials and organizing commemorations.[98] The ILP, which had taken a pacifist stance during the war, aped to a remarkable extent the commemorations of fallen soldiers in its activities at Sighthill. 'Flowers o' the Forest' and the 'Lament' were piped as ILPers filed slowly past the monument, which had been dressed with 'one laurel wreath trimmed with red ribbon', and demonstrated their 'solemn respect for the dead fighters for freedom'.[99] This was a counter-theatre of commemoration at its most politically charged.

In 1920 the legacy of 1820 was once again recovered, revised and re-invested with a new range of meanings. As the writings of Stewart and Johnston demonstrate, aspects of previous interpretations still carried some authority, but the changed context, provided by volatile local labour politics, the peculiar postwar situation, and a continuing debate about Scottish nationhood, gave even old interpretations new meanings. The centenary celebrations were also different in scale, rendering many more people aware of the events of 1820 both through writings and through carefully constructed commemorative events, which mirrored the increased efficiency and organization with which state institutions were marking their ritual displays. 1920 saw 1820 secure a revised position within both the political culture and, ultimately, the iconography of the Labour movement in Scotland. A socialist party banner from 1938, urging Scottish workers to join the struggle against fascism in Spain, delivered the message: 'Thomas Muir Baird and Hardie died that you should be free to choose your government. Workers in Spain are dying because they dared to choose their own government'.[100]

IV

If the ILP demonstrated a sustained engagement with both Home Rule and the distinctiveness of Scotland's past, it fell far short of advocating a separate Scottish state. The centenary, however, also provided some evidence of another reshaping of the events of 1820, this time by members of the small coterie of separatist nationalists grouped around the Scottish National League (SNL). The efforts of this body in the early 1920s were directed at providing 'a "corrective" analysis of Scottish history' and in their journal *Liberty*, a leader of the SNL could claim 1820 as a rising both fomented and repressed 'with the usual English – and shall I say Anglo-Scottish? hypocrisy'.[101] In spite of its significant role in the founding of the National Party of Scotland in 1928, the SNL was a small body that lacked a wide membership or any real degree of public sympathy and there seems to have been little sustained engagement with 1820 by interwar nationalists. The SNL version of a Scottish past characterized by English colonization of a somehow more naturally democratic Celtic race and culture certainly could deal with 'modern' history – in particular, the Treaty of Union. Commemorative activity, however, tended to focus on the more distant past and, for example, the SNL organized a public demonstration at Arbroath Abbey in 1920 to mark the six-hundredth anniversary of the Declaration of Arbroath.[102]

It was only after 1945 that a distinctively nationalist interpretation of 1820 was really developed and became a significant and consistent feature of Scottish radical politics. Once again, commemorative activity was underscored by a range of published works offering interpretations of the central event.[103] The most important of these were those associated with a growing separatist nationalism from the 1960s. *The Rising of 1820* was the work of Frank Sherry, a lawyer and Scottish National Party member with a foreword by Winifred Ewing, who had been elected to Parliament in the watershed Hamilton by-election of 1967. She painted the rising as 'both radical and nationalist, for the misery brought to Scotland by the Union of Parliaments was by now all too apparent' and linked it to what she saw as 'mortal combat' of 'forces of progress and national independence ... with the forces of unionism and political patronage'.[104] Sherry's text was an exercise in the creation of myth-history and lamented that: 'If her martyrs remain unhonoured and unsung it can only be concluded that Scotland is no more than a geographical term'. Selective editing of the original proclamation left out words such as 'Britons' and references to the Bill of Rights to make the case that: 'The rising in Scotland as far as the Scottish radicals were concerned was very much about the political and national identity of the Scottish nation'.[105]

Both more scholarly and more influential has been the work already referred to, by Ellis and Mac a'Ghobhainn, which remains the only book-length study of 1820. Both authors were involved in leftist, nationalist and Gaelic language politics from the 1960s, and a number of reviews have pointed out how this is reflected in their work.[106] *The Scottish Insurrection* offered a significant reinterpretation of 1820 and was firmly linked to the first attempts at the systematic and annual commemoration of the martyrs, under the auspices of the 1820 Commemoration Committee, founded in 1969.[107] This group operated in a context in which there was an increasing interest in the idea of public history and in the recovery of 'hidden histories'; it carried out its commemorative functions with annual rallies at the monuments, in Glasgow, Stirling and Paisley. It was also keen to expand the recovery of Scotland's radical past, one of its newsletters proclaiming that 'the list of the forgotten is long' and suggesting Thomas Muir, the Cotton-spinners of 1838, the Galloway Levellers and others as obvious candidates for resurrection.[108] In this goal the society was successful, encouraging further published work on these themes and on 1820 itself. Perhaps the most well-known activity of the 1820 Society was the campaign, along with Labour and Nationalist councillors and MPs, for the exhumation of the bodies at Sighthill and extensive renovation to the monument itself, which was completed in 1986.[109]

Several aspects of these activities bear brief comparison with earlier commemorations. There were similar attempts to draw links between the past and the present. Descendants of the men of 1820, for example, were fêted at commemorative gatherings.[110] Similarly, and poignantly, another level of commemoration was added to the Sighthill site, when the ashes of Mac a'Ghobhainn, a long-serving honorary secretary of the 1820 Society, were scattered next to the monument in 1987: a subsequent memorial to him was unveiled in 2000.[111] Finally, commemorative activity ensured that 1820 remained a reference point in both political and cultural terms. In political terms, 1820 could and, as the debate in the Scottish Parliament demonstrates, still can be used to support a number of positions. In the early 1980s, the 1820 slogan 'Scotland Free or a Desert' was adopted for use by the 'SNPs Scottish Resistance campaign of civil disobedience and direct action'.[112] In the 1996 commemoration it was the martyrs' role not as nationalists but as 'pioneers in the struggle for workers' social and economic as well as political rights' and as unwitting contributors to 'the recognition of trade union rights and the establishment of the Welfare State', which formed the basis of veteran Labour activist Jimmy Reid's address.[113]

This political usability, however, is reinforced by, and strongly linked to, the role of 1820 in Scottish culture and cultural politics. The production of histories, novels, poems and plays is well calculated 'to encourage teachers to include the story of the rising in their syllabuses'.[114] Indeed, the magnificent series of history paintings by Ken Currie in Glasgow's People's Palace Museum have, as the theme for the second panel, 'Radical Wars', with Baird and Hardie grimly swinging from a gibbet in the background. These paintings too were commissioned as commemoration, for the bicentennial of the massacre of the Calton Weavers, and their creator intended them to 'fulfill a socio-educational function' and to 'represent a suppressed and largely forgotten people's history of Scotland'.[115]

It should be clear that, while interest in the 'Radical War' has come overwhelmingly from the political left and nationalists, post-war commemoration does not mark any kind of interpretational closure on the events of 1820. Nor should we characterize it as any kind of objective exercise in the uncovering of 'hidden history'. Of course, the claim to be recovering something 'hidden' or 'forgotten' was and is central to the rhetoric of commemoration. Freir's tale of seeing an earlier monument fallen into disrepair has been repeated in some form by all subsequent commemorators. This was partly so because claims that 1820 had been 'forgotten' or 'hidden' encompassed a call for activism, in particular, to dispute those versions of the national or civic past which were being monumentalized. In one sense, these were contests over the very activity of commemoration itself. Those who looked to 1820 were keenly aware of and responded to commemorative activities on the part of the state or local elites: from shaping their own version of the 'monument mania' of mid-nineteenth-century Britain to their attempts to match the increasing scale and elaboration of state ceremonies in the early twentieth century.[116]

More importantly, commemoration was a contest over how the national past was put to political use. The usability of 1820 was enhanced by its leaving, like William Wallace, precious little in the way of documentary information on actions and intentions.[117] This has allowed for the martyrs to be imagined and re-imagined in a number of different ways and recruited to a range of political narratives: as the innocent victims of rancorous Tory persecution and an object lesson in the strengths of British popular constitutionalism; as heirs to the Covenanters and exemplars of the continuing constitutional duty to resist tyranny; as prototype proletarian revolutionaries; and, latterly, as insurrectionary republican nationalists. Historically, it has been this last interpretation which has been the most marginal and previous commemorations have instead been used to lend a peculiar Scottish inflexion to pan-British political languages and to integrate a distinctive Scottish episode into a British history of liberty. When politicians reopened the debate in the Scottish Parliament, they simply opened a new chapter in commemorative contests that have been going on for nearly two centuries.

NOTES

The following abbreviations are used throughout the notes:

BL	British Library.
DRO	Devon Record Office.
HO	Home Office Papers (in the National Archives, Kew).
Journals	*Journals of the House of Commons*, 119 vols (London, 1628–).
ML	Mitchell Library, Glasgow.
NA	National Archives, Kew.
NAS	National Archives of Scotland.
NLS	National Library of Scotland.
ODNB	*Oxford Dictionary of National Biography.*
Parl. Debs.	Hansard, T. C. (ed.), *The Parliamentary Debates from the Year 1803 to the Present Time* (London, 1812–).
Pol. Reg.	*Cobbett's Weekly Political Register.*
State Trials	Howell, T. J. (ed.), *Complete Collection of State Trials and Proceedings for High Treason and other Crimes and Misdemeanours*, 33 vols (London, 1809–28).

The notes and the bibliography identify those works printed but not necessarily published by the radical printers W. Lang of Glasgow and J. Marshall of Newcastle-upon-Tyne.

Introduction

1. P. B. Ellis and S. Mac a'Ghobhainn, *The Scottish Insurrection of 1820* (London: Victor Gollancz, 1970).
2. M. I. Thomis and P. Holt, *Threats of Revolution in Britain 1789–1848* (London: Macmillan, 1977), p. 8.
3. C. A. Whatley, *Scottish Society 1707–1830: Beyond Jacobitism, Towards Industrialisation* (Manchester: Manchester University Press, 2000), pp. 307–27.
4. P. B. Ellis and S. Mac a'Ghobhainn, *The Scottish Insurrection of 1820*, new edn (1970; Edinburgh: John Donald, 2001), p. xi. [Henceforth all references will relate to the 1970 edition unless otherwise stated.]

5. E. P. Thompson, *The Making of the English Working Class*, rev. edn (1963; London: Penguin, 1991), p. 660.
6. W. M. Roach, 'Radical Reform Movements in Scotland from 1815 to 1822 with Particular Reference to Events in the West of Scotland' (PhD dissertation, University of Glasgow, 1970).
7. F. K. Donnelly, 'The General Rising of 1820: A Study of Social Conflict in the Industrial Revolution' (PhD dissertation, University of Sheffield, 1975).
8. A notable exception is B. Harris, *The Scottish People and the French Revolution* (London: Pickering & Chatto, 2008).
9. Good discussions of developments in political history can be found in M. Roberts, *Political Movements in Urban England, 1832–1914* (Basingstoke: Palgrave Macmillan, 2009), pp. 1–9; J. Lawrence, 'Political History', in S. Berger, H. Feldner, K. Passmore (eds), *Writing History: Theory and Practice* (London: Arnold, 2003), pp. 183–202.
10. G. S. Jones, 'Rethinking Chartism', in his *Languages of Class: Studies in English Working Class History, 1832–1982* (Cambridge: Cambridge University Press, 1982), pp. 90–178.
11. J. C. S. J. Fulcher, 'Contests Over Constitutionalism: The Faltering of Reform in England, 1816–1824' (PhD dissertation, University of Cambridge, 1993), p. 3.
12. B. Harris, 'Scottish-English Connections in British Radicalism in the 1790s', in T. C. Smout (ed.), *Anglo-Scottish relations from 1603 to 1900*, Proceedings of the British Academy, 127 (Oxford: Oxford University Press, 2005), pp. 189–212.
13. Ellis and Mac a'Ghobhainn, *The Scottish Insurrection*, pp. 139–40.
14. Similar points are made in N. Davidson, 'Class Consciousness and National Consciousness in the Scottish General Strike of 1820', in K. Flett and D. Renton (eds), *New Approaches to Socialist History* (London: New Clarion Press, 2003), pp. 133–48; and F. K. Donnelly, 'The Scottish Rising of 1820: A Re-interpretation', *Scottish Tradition*, 6 (1976), pp. 27–37. For the issue of nationalism and 'popular constitutionalism' see G. Pentland, 'Scotland and the Creation of a National Reform Movement, 1830–1832', *Historical Journal*, 48 (2005), pp. 999–1023.
15. D. Wahrman, 'Public Opinion, Violence and the Limits of Constitutional Politics', in J. Vernon (ed.), *Re-reading the Constitution: New Narratives in the Political History of England's Long Nineteenth Century* (Cambridge: Cambridge University Press, 1996), pp. 83–122.
16. G. Eley, 'Nations, Publics, and Political Cultures: Placing Habermas in the Nineteenth Century', in C. Calhoun (ed.), *Habermas and the Public Sphere* (Cambridge, MA: MIT Press, 1992), pp. 289–339.

1 The Forging of Post-War Politics

1. H. V. Bowen, *War and British Society 1688–1815* (Cambridge: Cambridge University Press, 1998), p. 14; J. E. Cookson, *The British Armed Nation, 1793–1815* (Oxford: Clarendon Press, 1997), pp. 95–100.
2. M. Philp (ed.), *Resisting Napoleon: The British Response to the Threat of Invasion, 1797–1815* (Aldershot: Ashgate, 2006); L. Colley, 'The Reach of the State, the Appeal of the Nation: Mass Arming and Political Culture in the Napoleonic Wars', in L. Stone (ed.), *Imperial State at War: Britain from 1689 to 1815* (London: Routledge, 1994), pp. 165–84.
3. Cookson, *The British Armed Nation*, pp. 126–8. Cookson calculates that Scotland, which contained 15 per cent of the UK's population, provided 36.4 per cent of volunteers in 1797, 21.9 per cent in 1801 and 16.7 per cent in 1804.

4. M. Daunton, *Trusting Leviathan: The Politics of Taxation in Britain, 1799–1914* (Cambridge: Cambridge University Press, 2001), chs 1–2; M. Daunton, 'The Fiscal-Military State and the Napoleonic Wars: Britain and France Compared', in D. Cannadine (ed.), *Trafalgar in History: A Battle and its Afterlife* (Basingstoke: Palgrave Macmillan, 2006), pp. 18–43; P. K. O'Brien, 'Public Finance in the Wars with France, 1793–1815', in H. T. Dickinson (ed.), *Britain and the French Revolution, 1789–1815* (New York: St Martin's Press: 1989), pp. 165–87.
5. See the introduction to A. Marwick (ed.), *Total War and Social Change* (Basingstoke: Macmillan, 1988), pp. x–xxi.
6. C. Emsley, *British Society and the French Wars, 1793–1815* (London: Macmillan, 1979), pp. 169–82.
7. F. C. Mather, 'Army Pensioners and the Maintenance of Civil Order in Early Nineteenth Century England', *Journal of the Society of Army Historical Research*, 36 (1958), pp. 110–24, on p. 110.
8. C. Tilly, *Popular Contention in Great Britain, 1758–1834* (Cambridge, MA.: Harvard University Press, 1995), pp. 249–54; N. Gash, 'After Waterloo: British Society and the Legacy of the Napoleonic Wars', *Transactions of the Royal Historical Society*, 5th series, 28 (1978), pp. 152–7.
9. Mather, 'Army Pensioners', pp. 111–24; Emsley, *British Society*, pp. 176–7; Cookson, *The British Armed Nation*, p. 207.
10. P. Spence, *The Birth of Romantic Radicalism: War, Popular Politics and English Radical Reformism, 1800–1815* (Aldershot: Ashgate, 1996).
11. Developed most famously in Jones, 'Rethinking Chartism', pp. 90–178.
12. E. V. Macleod, 'The Scottish Opposition Whigs and the French Revolution', in B. Harris (ed.), *Scotland in the Age of the French Revolution* (Edinburgh: John Donald, 2005), pp. 79–98.
13. J. Clive, *Scotch Reviewers: The 'Edinburgh Review' 1802–1815* (London: Faber & Faber, 1957), pp. 110–13; W. A. Hay, *The Whig Revival, 1808–1830* (Basingstoke: Palgrave Macmillan, 2005), pp. 49–51.
14. B. Fontana, *Rethinking the Politics of Commercial Society: The 'Edinburgh Review' 1802–32* (Cambridge: Cambridge University Press, 1985).
15. For the press in the 1790s see B. Harris, 'Print and Politics', in Harris (ed.), *Scotland in the Age of the French Revolution*, pp. 164–95; B. Harris, 'Scotland's Newspapers, the French Revolution and Domestic Radicalism (*c.* 1789–1794)', *Scottish Historical Review*, 84 (2005), pp. 38–62.
16. R. M. W. Cowan, *The Newspaper in Scotland: A Study of its First Expansion* (Glasgow: George Outram & Co. Ltd, 1946), pp. 14–18.
17. P. Harling, 'The Duke of York Affair (1809) and the Complexities of Wartime Patriotism', *Historical Journal*, 39 (1996), pp. 963–84; Spence, *The Birth of Romantic Radicalism*, ch. 6.
18. W. H. Reid, *Memoirs of the Life of Colonel Wardle* (London: T. Kelly, 1809), pp. 206–7; Spence, *The Birth of Romantic Radicalism*, p. 124; J. Turner, *Recollections of James Turner, Esq., of Thrushgrove*, ed. J. Smith (Glasgow, 1858), p. 82.
19. *Journals*, 67, 24 April and 15, 20, 21 May 1812; A. B. Richmond, *Narrative of the Condition of the Manufacturing Population; and the Proceedings of Government which led to the State Trials in Scotland* (London: J. Miller, 1824), pp. 20–2n.
20. Though see Hay, *The Whig Revival*, ch. 2.

21. J. E. Cookson, *Lord Liverpool's Administration, 1815–1822* (Edinburgh and London: Scottish Academic Press, 1975), ch. 1.
22. A. Mitchell, *The Whigs in Opposition 1815–1830* (Oxford: Clarendon Press, 1967), ch. 4; Hay, *The Whig Revival*, p. 54.
23. *Journals*, vol. 71, 1 February 1816–25 April 1816.
24. *Dundee, Perth and Cupar Advertiser*, 1 March 1816.
25. H. Cockburn, *Memorials of his Time* (Edinburgh: Adam & Charles Black, 1856), pp. 301–2.
26. *Journals*, vol. 71, 5 March 1816, p. 135.
27. Ibid., 6 March 1816, p. 146.
28. Ibid., p. 148.
29. For examples see, J. A. Hone, *For the Cause of Truth: Radicalism in London, 1796–1821* (Oxford: Clarendon Press, 1982); K. Navickas, *Loyalism and Radicalism in Lancashire, 1798–1815* (Oxford: Oxford University Press, 2009).
30. Spence, *The Birth of Romantic Radicalism*, pp. 123–4.
31. Though see N. Murray, *The Scottish Handloom Weavers, 1790–1850: A Social History* (Edinburgh: John Donald, 1978), chs 8–9.
32. J. R. Dinwiddy, 'Luddism and Politics in the Northern Counties', *Social History*, 4 (1979), pp. 33–63.
33. Roach, 'Radical Reform Movements', pp. 15–16.
34. For Richmond's account of the campaign and of relations with England see Richmond, *Narrative*, pp. 10–34.
35. Archibald Colquhoun to Lord Sidmouth, 4 July, 17 November, 1 December 1812, NA, HO 102/22, ff. 330–2, 515–6, 554; Major Seale to Lord Sidmouth, 30 June 1812, DRO, 152M/C1812/OH4; William Fish to Keeper of Chester Gaol, 22 June 1812, NA, HO 40/1, f. 38.
36. R. Eckersley, 'The Drum Major of Sedition: The Political Life and Career of John Cartwright (PhD dissertation, University of Manchester, 1999). See also N. C. Miller, 'John Cartwright and Radical Parliamentary Reform, 1808–1819', *English Historical Review*, 83 (1968), pp. 705–28.
37. R. Eckersley, 'Of Radical Design: John Cartwright and the Redesign of the Reform Campaign, *c.*1800–1811', *History*, 89 (2004), pp. 560–80.
38. Eckersley, 'The Drum Major', pp. 200–4.
39. M. Margarot, *Proposal for a Grand National Jubilee; Restoring to Every Man his own, and thereby Extinguishing both Want and War* (Sheffield, 1812); M. Margarot, *Thoughts on Revolution* (Harlow, 1812). See also M. Roe, 'Maurice Margarot: A Radical in Two Hemispheres, 1792–1815', *Bulletin of the Institute of Historical Research*, 31 (1958), pp. 68–78.
40. M. Chase, 'From Millennium to Anniversary: The Concept of Jubilee in Late Eighteenth- and Nineteenth-Century England', *Past and Present*, 129 (1990), pp. 132–47.
41. John Connell to Lord Sidmouth, 22 December 1812, NA, HO 102/22, f. 629. For Archibald Hastie see *Black Dwarf*, 3 February 1819; [John Parkhill], *The Life and Opinions of Arthur Sneddon* (Paisley: J. Cook, 1860), p. 67.
42. Archibald Colquhoun to Lord Sidmouth, 2 December 1812, NA, HO 102/22, f. 556. Moffat was later in charge of collecting and conveying Hampden club reform petitions from Scotland to London, Roach, 'Radical Reform Movements', pp. 386–7.
43. Lord Sidmouth to Archibald Colquhoun, 27 November 1812, NA, HO 102/22, f. 537.

44. John Connell to Lord Sidmouth, 22 December 1812, NA, HO 102/22, ff. 629–30; Lord Sidmouth to Archibald Colquhoun, 29 December 1812, NA, HO 103/5, ff. 69–70.
45. For some of these contacts, see the transcriptions of letters from Cartwright to George Kinloch in 1815–16, in Roach, 'Radical Reform Movements', pp. 383–90; J. Cartwright, *Life and Correspondence of Major Cartwright*, ed. F. D. Cartwright, 2 vols (London, 1826), vol. 2, pp. 110–19.
46. J. Cartwright, *Letter, &c.* (London, 1815), p. 5.
47. *Life and Correspondence of Major Cartwright*, vol. 2, pp. 113–14.
48. *Parl. Debs.*, vol. 30, cols 256–7.
49. W. L. Mathieson, *Church and Reform in Scotland 1797–1843* (Glasgow: James Maclehose & Sons, 1916), pp. 141–2; *Chronicles of the Isles* (Glasgow: W. Duncan, n.d.).
50. *Dundee, Perth and Cupar Advertiser*, 26 May 1815.
51. Duke of Atholl to Lord Sidmouth, 21 Aprrl 1815, NA, HO 102/25, ff. 155–62. For other riots in Scotland see Archibald Colquhoun to Lord Sidmouth, 8 and 31 March 1815 and David Boyle to Archibald Colquhoun, 1 May 1815, NA, HO 102/25, ff. 78, 125, 184–6.
52. H. Southall, 'Agitate! Agitate! Organize! Political Travellers and the Construction of a National Politics 1839–1880', *Transactions of the Institute of British Geogrraphers*, 21 (1996), pp. 177–93.
53. C. Calhoun, *The Question of Class Struggle: Social Foundations of Popular Radicalism during the Industrial Revolution* (Oxford: Blackwell, 1982), ch. 3.
54. Cartwright, *Letter, &c.*, pp. 6–7.
55. Ibid., p. 10. Though see *Dundee, Perth and Cupar Advertiser*, 13 and 20 October 1815.
56. Cartwright, *Letter, &c.*, p. 5; Miller, 'John Cartwright', pp. 720–1; P. Fraser, 'Public Petitioning and Parliament before 1832', *History*, 46 (1961), pp. 195–211.
57. Cartwright, *Letter, &c.*, pp. 11–12.
58. Cockburn, *Memorials*, p. 309.
59. John Cartwright to George Kinloch, 22 November 1815 in Roach, 'Radical Reform Movements', p. 388; Cartwright, *Letter, &c.*, p. 7.
60. *Dundee, Perth and Cupar Advertiser*, 13 and 20 October 1815.
61. 'Edinburgh Politics', *Pol. Reg.*, 7 October 1815.
62. K. Prior, 'Gilchrist, John Borthwick (1759–1841)', *ODNB* (Oxford: Oxford University Press, 2004); online edn, May 2007, http://www.oxforddnb.com/view/article/10716, [accessed 29/09/2010].
63. J. B. Gilchrist, *Parliamentary Reform, on Constitutional Principles; or, British Loyalty against Continental Royalty, the Whole Host of Sacerdotal Inquisitors in Europe, and every Iniquitous Judge, Corrupt Ruler, Venal Corporation, Rotten Borough, Slavish Editor, or Jacobitical Toad-Eater within the British Empire* (Glasgow: W. Lang, 1815), pp. 68–9, 86; John Cartwright to George Kinloch, 15 September 1815 in Roach, 'Radical Reform Movements', p. 386.
64. Gilchrist, *Parliamentary Reform*, pp. 92–130. O. D. Edwards, *Burke and Hare*, 2nd edn (Edinburgh: Mercat Press, 1993), pp. 43–4.
65. Harris, *The Scottish People*, pp. 65–7.
66. Gilchrist, *Parliamentary Reform*, pp. 19–20.
67. Ibid., p. 24.
68. Ibid., p. 15.
69. Ibid., pp. 27–9.

70. Ibid., p. 170; John Cartwright to George Kinloch, 1 December 1815 in Roach, 'Radical Reform Movements', p. 389.
71. Robert Hamilton to Archibald Colquhoun, 1 April 1816, NA, HO 102/26, ff. 182–5.
72. *Morning Chronicle*, 6 August 1816; Alexander Maconochie to Lord Sidmouth, 31 August 1816, NA, HO 102/26, ff. 453–5. For similar riots at soup kitchens see Duke of Northumberland to Lord Sidmouth, 22 January 1817, DRO, 152M/C1817/OH34.
73. J. Howie, *Historical Account of the Town of Ayr for the Last Fifty Years* (Kilmarnock: J. McKie, 1861), pp. 57–62; W. S. Cooper, *A History of the Ayrshire Yeomanry Cavalry* (Edinburgh: David Douglas, 1881), p. 9.
74. Laurence Roberston, Charles Hope and Alexander Riddoch to Alexander Maconochie, 5 December, 25 November and 30 November 1816, NA, HO 102/26, ff. 579–81, 595; *Dundee, Perth and Cupar Advertiser*, 6 December 1816.
75. 'A True and Loyal Subject' to Lord Sidmouth, 12 October 1816, NA, HO 102/26, f. 483.
76. *An Address to the Public in Behalf of the Operative Weavers* (Kilmarnock: H. Crawford, 1816), p. 8.
77. G. Spater, *William Cobbett: The Poor Man's Friend*, 2 vols (Cambridge: Cambridge University Press, 1982), vol. 2, pp. 347–9; K. Gilmartin, *Print Politics: The Press and Radical Opposition in Early Nineteenth-Century England* (Cambridge: Cambridge University Press, 1996), pp. 99–101.
78. James Reddie to Lord Sidmouth, 8 November 1816, NA, HO 102/26, f. 552.
79. 'To the Journeymen and Labourers of England, Scotland and Ireland', *Pol. Reg.*, 2 November 1816.
80. The radical critique was developed at length in the three-part *Thaumaturgus; or, the Wonders of the Magic Lantern; Exhibiting at one View the Distresses of the Country, and some of the Consqeuences of the Late Just and Necessary War; in which some Living Characters are set off in a Stile Entirely New* (Edinburgh, 1816). [Editions of this work were also published at Glasgow and Paisley.]
81. *Parl. Debs.*, vol. 26, cols 993–7; Miller, 'John Cartwright', pp. 720–1.
82. For example the petition of the inhabitants of Kirkintilloch, *Journals*, vol. 72, 3 February 1817, p. 19.
83. *Report of the Proceedings of the Crawfordsdyke Meeting Convened for the Purpose of Taking into Consideration the Propriety of Petitioning the Prince Regent on the Distresses of the Country* (Greenock: Donaldson & Macfarlan, 1817), p. 15.
84. 'To the Journeymen and Labourers of England, Scotland and Ireland', *Pol. Reg.*, 2 November 1816. See for example the first resolution at Renfrew which bemoaned distress falling on the 'Agricultural, Commercial and Manufacturing interests' but which 'is felt most severely by the labouring classes', *Account of the Proceedings of the Public Meeting of the Burgesses, Householders, and Inhabitants of the Royal Burgh of Renfrew, held on the 23d November, 1816, Respecting the Distresses of the Country with a Full Report of the Speeches Delivered on that Occasion* (Glasgow: W. Lang, 1816), p. 15.
85. For social perceptions during this period see D. Wahrman, *Imagining the Middle Class: The Political Representation of Class in Britain, c. 1780–1840* (Cambridge: Cambridge University Press, 1995), ch. 6.
86. *Parl. Debs.*, vol. 32, cols 34–42, 47–53.
87. *Morning Chronicle*, 30 July 1816.
88. A. Populis, *Letter Addressed to Sir Thomas Cochrane, Commonly Called Lord Cochrane, on his Conduct in the Meeting at the London Tavern, on the 29th July 1816, met for the*

Purpose of Taking into Consideration the Distress of the Country, and the Means of Relief (Paisley: R. Smith, 1816).

89. See for examples petitions from Kilmarnock, Elderslie and Perth, *Journals*, vol. 72, 10, 24 and 27 February1817, pp. 42, 99, 116; *Report of the Meeting held in the Relief Church, Kilbarchan on 21st December 1816, to Consider the Distresses of the Country, and the Propriety of Petitioning the Prince Regent and the Legislature for Reform* (Paisley, 1817), pp. 15–16; *Account of the Proceedings of the Public Meeting ... of Renfrew*, p. 8; *Thaumaturgus*, pp. 18–19.

90. M. Brock, *The Great Reform Act* (London: Hutchinson & Co, 1973), pp. 117–21.

91. Petitions of burgesses and inhabitants of Glasgow and inhabitants of Dysart, *Journals*, vol. 72, 10 and 12 February 1817, pp. 41, 55.

92. *Report of the Meeting Held in the Relief Church, Paisley, On Saturday the 5th October, 1816, to Consider the Present Distresses of the Country, their Causes, and Probable Remedies* (Paisley: R. Smith, 1816), p. 21.

93. Petition of burgesses and inhabitants of Hamilton, *Journals*, vol. 72, 4 February 1817, p. 24.

94. *Morning Chronicle*, 9 January 1816

95. *Journals*, vol. 72, 10 February 1817, p. 42.

96. Petition of burgesses, householders and inhabitants of Renfrew, *Journals*, vol. 72, 25 February 1817, p. 108.

97. For an excellent and broadly-conceived exploration of the religious and ecclesiological issues underpinning radical and reform politics see V. Wallace, 'Exporting Radicalism within the Empire: Scots Presbyterian Political Values in Scotland and British North America, *c.*1815–*c.*1850' (PhD dissertation, University of Glasgow, 2009).

98. *Affairs being now settled ABROAD, 'tis high time to look at HOME* (Glasgow: W. Lang, 1815).

99. See, for example, the resolutions and petition from Dundee, *Dundee, Perth and Cupar Advertiser*, 28 February 1817.

100. See, for examples petitions from inhabitants of Kirkintilloch and magistrates of Brechin, *Journals*, vol. 72, 3 February and 10 March 1817, pp. 19, 149.

101. Petition of the magistrates and town council of South Queensferry, *Journals*, vol. 72, 27 March 1817, p. 190.

102. Fulcher, 'Contests', pp. 52–61.

103. *Journals*, vol. 72, 24 February 1817, p. 100.

104. For this see G. Pentland, *Radicalism, Reform and National Identity in Scotland, 1820–1833* (Woodbridge: Boydell & Brewer, 2008), ch. 1.

105. Petition of provost, magistrates, town council, burgesses and inhabitants of Linlithgow, *Journals*, vol. 72, 25 April 1817, p. 209.

106. *Parl. Debs.*, vol. 35, col. 177.

107. For example, petition of members of guild, burgesses, trades and inhabitants of Montrose, *Journals*, vol. 72, 10 March 1817, p. 149.

108. *Morning Chronicle*, 5 November 1816; *Dundee, Perth and Cupar Advertiser*, 8 November 1816.

109. *Thaumaturgus*, pp. 62–3; Pentland, 'Scotland and the Creation of a National Reform Movement', pp. 999–1023.

110. Petition of inhabitants of Kirkintilloch, *Journals*, vol. 72, 10 February 1817, p. 19; *Report of the Meeting held in the Relief Church Paisley*, p. 17.

111. 'To the Journeymen and Labourers of England, Scotland and Ireland', *Pol. Reg.*, 2 November 1816.
112. Petition of burgesses and inhabitants of Glasgow, *Journals*, vol. 72, 12 February 1817, p. 55.
113. *Report of the Proceedings of the Crawfordsdyke Meeting*, pp. 13–14.
114. *Affairs being now settled*, p. 5.
115. Gilmartin, *Print Politics*, ch. 1.
116. The best expositions of this language are J. Belchem, 'Republicanism, Popular Constitutionalism and the Radical Platform in Early Nineteenth-Century England', *Social History*, 6 (1981), pp. 1–32 and J. Epstein, 'The Constitutional Idiom: Radical Reasoning, Rhetoric and Action in Early Nineteenth-Century England', *Journal of Social History*, 23 (1990), pp. 553–74.
117. *Report of the Proceedings of the Crawfordsdyke Meeting*, p. 4.
118. *Morning Chronicle*, 5 November 1816; *Journals*, vol. 72, 30 April 1817, pp. 223–4.
119. J. Belchem, *'Orator' Hunt: Henry Hunt and English Working-Class Radicalism* (Oxford: Clarendon Press, 1985), ch. 2.
120. D. Worrall, *Radical Culture: Discourse, Resistance and Survelliance, 1790–1820* (Detroit, MI: Wayne State University Press, 1992), ch. 4; I. McCalman, *Radical Underworld: Prophets, Revolutionaries, and Pornographers in London, 1795–1840* (Cambridge: Cambridge University Press, 1988), pp. 106–12; M. Chase, *The People's Farm: English Radical Agrarianism 1775–1840* (Oxford: Clarendon Press, 1988), ch. 4.
121. *Observer*, 8 December 1816; S. Poole, *The Politics of Regicide in England, 1760–1850* (Manchester: Manchester University Pres, 2000), pp. 151–2; Worrall, *Radical Culture*, pp. 98–103.
122. James Reddie to Alexander Maconochie, 11 December 1816, NA, HO 102/26, ff. 633–4.
123. James Reddie to Alexander Maconochie, 14 December 1816, NA, HO 102/26, f. 671.
124. Alexander Maconochie to Lord Sidmouth, 22 December 1816, NA, HO 102/26, f. 721.
125. *State Trials* vol. 33, col. 14.
126. Alexander Maconochie to Lord Sidmouth, 7 December 1816, NA, HO 102/26, ff. 591–2; Lord Sidmouth to Alexander Maconochie, 11 December 1816, NA, HO 79/1.
127. For the genesis and content of this information see the voluminous correspondence between Alexander Maconochie, Lord Sidmouth, James Reddie, Robert Hamilton, Kirkman Finlay, James Black and others, NA, HO 102/26, ff. 625–839. McKay is identified as 'A.B.', Captain Brown as 'C.D.', Richmond as 'E.F.' and Biggar as 'G.H.' or 'B.'. Richmond's own account is in his *Narrative*, pp. 59–86. See also the declarations of James Finlayson and John Campbell, NA, HO 102/28, ff. 10–19, 539–90.
128. W. M. Roach, 'Alexander Richmond and the Radical Reform Movements in Glasgow in 1816–17', *Scottish Historical Review*, 51 (1972), pp. 1–19.
129. Richmond, *Narrative*, p. 75.
130. Alexander Maconochie to Lord Sidmouth, 25 December 1816 and 'Information by E.F.', 26 December 1816, HO 102/26, ff. 731, 772.
131. Declaration of John Maclachlan, 12 March 1817, NAS, Crown Office Depositions, AD 14/17/8, ff. 128–46.
132. Alexander Maconochie to Lord Sidmouth, 1 January 1817, NA, HO 102/26, f. 815.
133. See depositions at NAS, Crown Office Precognitions, AD 14/16/8. In many ways the conspiracy is a good fit with the 'traditional community' mode of radicalism explored in Calhoun, *The Question of Class Struggle*, ch. 6.

134. For a good account of the involvement of Irish immigrants and the links with former United Irishmen see, M. J. Mitchell, *The Irish in the West of Scotland 1797–1848* (Edinburgh: John Donald, 1998), pp. 90–2.
135. Alexander Maconochie to Lord Sidmouth, 16 January 1817 and Information of B., 9 February 1817, NA, HO 102/27, ff. 101, 292–3.
136. One of the Prisoners at that Period [Hugh Dickson], *The Criterion, or Richmond's Narrative Exposed. Being a Correct Detail of the Whole Proceedings as Delivered by the Delegates of Those Treasonable Societies said to Exist in Glasgow and its Suburbs in the Years 1816 and 1817* (Glasgow, 1825); A Ten Pounder [P. Mackenzie], *An Exposure of the Spy System Pursued in Glasgow During the Years 1816–20* (Glasgow: Muir, Gowans & Co., 1832).
137. Alexander Maconochie to Lord Sidmouth, 1 and 8 January 1817 and Kirkman Finlay to Lord Sidmouth, 28 January 1817, NA, HO 102/27, ff. 5–7, 36, 175–6.
138. Robert Hamilton to Alexander Maconochie, 11 February 1817, NA, HO 102/27, ff. 294–5.

2 Loyalism and Whiggism in Scotland

1. James Reddie to Lord Sidmouth, 8 November 1816, NA, HO 102/26, f. 552.
2. Some highlights of the literature on loyalism in the 1790s are H. T. Dickinson, 'Popular Loyalism in Britain in the 1790s', in E. Hellmuth (ed.), *The Transformation of Political Culture: England and Germany in the Late Eighteenth Century* (Oxford: Oxford University Press, 1990), pp. 503–33; N. Rogers, Burning Tom Paine: Loyalism and Counter-Revolution in Britain, 1792–1793, *Social History*, 32 (1999), pp. 139–71; K. Gilmartin, 'In the Theater of Counterrevolution: Loyalist Association and Conservative Opinion in the 1790s', *Journal of British Studies*, 41 (2002), pp. 291–328; M. S. Smith, 'Anti-Radicalism and Popular Politics in an Age of Revolution', *Parliamentary History*, 24, supplement (2005), pp. 71–92; F. O'Gorman, 'The Paine Burnings of 1792–1793', *Past and Present*, 193 (2006), pp. 111–56. For Scotland see A. Wold, 'Loyalism in Scotland in the 1790s', in U. Broich, H. T. Dickinson, E. Hellmuth (eds), *Reactions to Revolutions: The 1790s and their Aftermath* (Münster: LIT, 2007), pp. 109–35; Harris, *The Scottish People*, ch. 4. Available narratives for the politics of the 1815–1820 period are R. J. White, *Waterloo to Peterloo* (London: William Heinemann Ltd, 1957); Thomis and Holt, *Threats of Revolution*, chs 3–4; J. R. Dinwiddy, *From Luddism to the First Reform Bill* (Oxford: Basil Blackwell, 1986), chs 1–2; Thompson, *The Making*, chs 15–16.
3. M. Philp, 'The Fragmented Ideology of Reform', in M. Philp (ed.), *The French Revolution and British Popular Politics* (Cambridge: Cambridge University Press, 1991), pp. 50–77; M. Philp, 'Disconcerting Ideas: Explaining Popular Radicalism and Popular Loyalism in the 1790s', in G. Burgess and M. Festenstein (eds), *English Radicalism, 1550–1850* (Cambridge: Cambridge University Press, 2007), pp. 157–89; Fulcher, 'Contests', pp. 62–129.
4. Harris, *The Scottish People*, ch. 4.
5. Poole, *The Politics of Regicide*, pp. 144–50.
6. Thompson, *The Making*, pp. 153–9.
7. [H. Brougham], 'History of the Alarms', *Edinburgh Review*, 28 (March 1817), pp. 59–83.
8. William Kerr to Francis Freeling, 7 December 1816, NA, HO 102/26, f. 599.
9. *Parl. Debs.*, vol. 35, col. 446.

10. [H. Brougham], 'On the Present State of Public Affairs', *Edinburgh Review*, 28 (August 1817), p. 532; *Parl. Debs.*, vol. 36, col. 1090. A report on the Spa Fields riots in the *Observer*, 8 December 1816, claimed that among the propaganda distributed by the 'emissaries of mischief' were claims that Duke Nicholas was coming to Britain with 15,000 Russian soldiers, that the Irish of St Giles were ripe for rebellion and that 'the people had risen in Scotland, and that the soldiers called them "their brothers" and refused to act'.
11. G. W. T. Omond, *The Lord Advocates of Scotland*, 2 vols (Edinburgh: David Douglas, 1883), vol. 2, pp. 237–9; *Parl. Debs.*, vol. 35, cols 709–10, 728–30.
12. Alexander Maconochie to Lord Sidmouth, 7 December 1816, NA, HO 102/26, f. 590.
13. James Reddie to Alexander Maconochie, 12, 13 and 27 December 1816, NA, HO 102/26, ff. 643–4, 654, 758.
14. Lord Sidmouth to Alexander Maconochie, 11 December 1816, NA, HO 79/2.
15. Copy letter from Lord Sidmouth to Lords Lieutenant, NA, HO 102/27, f. 121; Lord Sidmouth to Alexander Maconochie 24 December 1816 and 1 January 1817, NA, HO 79/2.
16. Alexander Maconochie to Lord Sidmouth, 17 January 1817, NA, HO 102/27, f. 120.
17. Alexander Maconochie to Robert Hamilton, 27 January 1817, NA, HO 102/27, f. 169.
18. Alexander Maconochie to Lord Sidmouth, 24 November 1 and 25 December 1816, NA, HO 102/26, ff. 569–70, 577, 731–2.
19. Alexander Maconochie to Lord Sidmouth, 17 January 1817, NA, HO 102/27, ff. 119–20.
20. Alexander Maconochie to Lord Sidmouth, 10 January 1817, NA, HO 102/27, f. 41; Lord Sidmouth to Alexander Maconochie, 1 January 1817, NA, HO 79/2.
21. Letters between Lord Sidmouth and Duke of Buccleuch, 27 August, 21 September and 23 November 1817, DRO, 152M/C1817/OZ; W. Scott, *The Letters of Sir Walter Scott*, ed. H. J. C. Grierson, 12 vols (London: Constable, 1932–7), vol. 4, p. 369; A. Aspinall, *Politics and the Press c.1780–1850* (London: Home & Van Thal, 1949), pp. 95–8.
22. Cowan, *The Newspaper in Scotland*, pp. 20–1, 33–6, 38–9.
23. [R. Southey], 'Parliamentary Reform', *Quarterly Review*, 16 (October 1816), pp. 225–79; Lord Liverpool to Lord Sidmouth, 17 November 1816, DRO, 152M/C1816/OH1.
24. 'The *Quarterly Review*. No. 31', *Blackwood's*, 1 (April 1817), p. 85.
25. Rev. G. J. C. Duncan, *Memoir of the Reverend Henry Duncan, Minister of Ruthwell* (Edinburgh: W. Oliphant & Sons, 1848), pp. 69–73. See for examples, *Address to the Labouring Classes of Britain on the Questions of an Equality in Property and Universal Suffrage* (Edinburgh: Doig & Stirling, 1817); A. Telfer, *An Illustration of the Mistaken Notions Entertained with Respect to the Price of Provisions, and the Oppression of Taxation* (Glasgow: J. Steven, 1817).
26. *Comic Poems of the Years 1685, and 1793; On Rustic Scenes in Scotland, at the Times to which they Refer* (Edinburgh, 1817), pp. 105–50.
27. A Society of Clergymen in Dumfries-shire, *The Scotch Cheap Repository Tracts: Containing Moral Tales, for the Instruction of the Young*, 2nd edn (Edinburgh: Oliphant, Waugh & Innes, 1815), p. iii; 'The Scotch Cheap Repository Tracts', *Eclectic Review*, 8 (October 1817), pp. 376–7. For Hannah More's tracts see F. K. Brown, *Fathers of the Victorians: The Age of Wilberforce* (Cambridge: Cambridge University Press, 1961), pp. 134–55; S. Pedersen, 'Hannah More Meets Simple Simon: Tracts, Chapbooks, and Popular Culture in Late Eighteenth-Century England', *Journal of British Studies*, 25 (1986), pp. 84–113.

28. Rev. H. Duncan, *The Cottage Fireside; or, The Parish School Master: A Moral Tale*, 2nd edn (Edinburgh, 1815).
29. *Sawney and Donnel's Exploits at Waterloo: To which are Added, My Country and my Lass, The Broadsword of Scotland and We've aye been Provided for* (Falkirk: T. Johnston, 1817).
30. M. Philp, 'Vulgar Conservatism, 1792–3', *English Historical Review*, 110 (1995), pp. 42–69.
31. [J. Struthers], *An Essay on the State of the Labouring Poor, with some Hints for its Improvement*, 2nd edn (Glasgow: W. Turnbull, 1816), pp. 14–17.
32. A Forfarshire Justice of Peace, *A Conversation on the Causes of our Present Distress and on the Remedies for it* (Dundee, 1817).
33. *At a Meeting of Faculty of Procurators in Paisley* (Paisley, 1817) [printed bill].
34. Rev. W. Hanna, *Memoirs of Thomas Chalmers, D.D. LL.D.*, 2 vols (Edinburgh: T. Constable & Co., 1854), vol. 1, pp. 453–6.
35. T. Chalmers, 'A Sermon Delivered in the Tron Church, Glasgow, on Wednesday, Nov. 19, 1817, the Day of the Funeral of Her Royal Highness the Princess Charlotte of Wales', in *The Works of Thomas Chalmers D. D., Minister of the Tron Church, Glasgow*, 3 vols (Hartford, 1822), vol. 3, p. 390.
36. Ibid., vol. 3, pp. 387, 396–7.
37. J. Epstein, 'Narrating Liberty's Defense: T. J. Wooler and the Law', in his *Radical Expression: Political Language, Ritual, and Symbol in England, 1790–1850* (Oxford: Oxford University Press, 1994), pp. 29–69; J. Epstein, '"Our Real Constitution": Trial Defence and Radical Memory in the Age of Revolution', in Vernon (ed.), *Re-reading the Constitution*, pp. 22–51; M. Davis, 'Prosecution and Radical Discourse during the 1790s: The Case of the Scottish Sedition Trials', *International Journal of the Sociology of Law*, 33 (2005), pp. 148–58; Gilmartin, *Print Politics*, ch. 3.
38. *State Trials*, vol. 33, cols 1–144. The trial was published separately as *Trial of Alexander McLaren and Thomas Baird, before the High Court of Justiciary, at Edinburgh, on the 5th and 7th March 1817, for Sedition* (Edinburgh: J. Robertson, 1817).
39. *State Trials*, vol. 33, cols 6–14.
40. Ibid., cols 41, 84–6.
41. 'To hell, allegiance', *Hamlet*, IV:5. For the reference to *Hamlet* in the trials please see *State Trials*, vol. 33, cols 23–4.
42. Ibid., cols 83, 105.
43. For a discussion linking petitioning and contract theory see Poole, *The Politics of Regicide*, pp. 7–17.
44. *State Trials*, vol. 33, col. 97.
45. Ibid., cols 633–82. The trial was published separately as *Trial of the Rev. Niel Douglas, before the High Court of Justiciary, at Edinburgh, on the 26th May 1817, for Sedition* (Edinburgh: J. Robertson, 1817).
46. P. Mackenzie, *Old Reminiscences of Glasgow and the West of Scotland*, 3rd edn, 2 vols (Glasgow: J. P. Forrester, 1890), vol. 1, p. 452.
47. J. Christodoulou, 'The Glasgow Universalist Church and Scottish Radicalism from the French Revolution to Chartism: A Theology of Liberation', *Journal of Ecclesiastical History*, 43 (1992), pp. 608–13; Harris, *The Scottish People*, pp. 60–1; G. Pentland, 'Patriotism, Universalism and the Scottish Conventions, 1792–1794', *History*, 89 (2004), pp. 356–7.
48. *State Trials*, vol. 33, cols 634, 639, 653.
49. Ibid., cols 633–5.

50. Ibid., col. 77.
51. Ibid., col. 647. For a fascinating discussion of the politically-charged and changing uses of the concept of 'imagination' during the 1790s see J. Barrell, *Imagining the King's Death: Figurative Treason, Fantasies of Regicide 1793–1796* (Oxford: Oxford University Press, 2000).
52. *State Trials*, vol. 33, col. 675.
53. Ibid., cols 677–80; N. Douglas, *Strictures on the Author's Trial, Declaration Before the Sheriff, Remarks on the Crown evidence, and some Important Information Respecting the Cause of Reform* (Glasgow, 1818).
54. Declaration of David Smith, 6 March 1817, NAS, Crown Office Precognitions, AD 14/17/8, ff. 118–21.
55. *State Trials*, vol. 33, cols 600–1. The proceedings were published separately as *Trial of Andrew M'Kinley* [sic], *before the High Court of Justiciary, at Edinburgh, on the 26th July 1817, for Administering Unlawful Oaths: With the Antecedent Proceedings against William Edgar, John Keith, and Andrew M'Kinley. Taken in Short Hand, by John Dow* (Edinburgh: Manners & Miller, 1818).
56. *State Trials*, vol. 33, cols 293–4.
57. Alexander Maconochie to Samuel Shepherd, 4 June 1817, NA, HO 102/28, ff. 178–9.
58. *State Trials*, vol. 33, cols 584–95. The law officers' version of events is in Alexander Maconochie to Lord Sidmouth, 20 July 1817, NA, HO 102/28, ff. 268–73.
59. Information of B., 9 February 1817, NA, HO 102/27, f. 292.
60. Cockburn, *Memorials*, pp. 334–5; Mackenzie, *Old Reminiscences*, vol. 1, pp. 119–20.
61. *State Trials*, vol. 33, col. 622.
62. Ibid., col. 632.
63. Alexander Maconochie to Lord Sidmouth, 20 July 1817, NA, HO 102/28, f. 268.
64. Gilmartin, *Print Politics*, p. 115.
65. N. Douglas, *An Address to the Judges and Jury, in a Case of Alleged Sedition, on 26th May, 1817, which was Intended to be Delivered before Passing Sentence* (Glasgow, 1817).
66. See, for example, *Morning Chronicle*, 28 July 1817.
67. 'Triumphs of the People', *Hone's Reformists' Register*, 9 August 1817.
68. 'Ministerial Artifices Defeated in Scotland', *Black Dwarf*, 30 July 1817.
69. Cited in Gilmartin, *Print Politics*, p. 123.
70. Alexander Maconochie to Lord Sidmouth, 21 May 1817, NA, HO 102/28, f. 135.
71. Hay, *The Whig Revival*, p. 50; Fontana, *Rethinking*, ch. 4.
72. [Brougham], 'On the Present State of Public Affairs', p. 522.
73. [J. Allen], 'Parliamentary Reform', *Edinburgh Review*, 28 (1817), p. 126.
74. [Brougham], 'On the Present State of Public Affairs', p. 523.
75. [Brougham], 'History of the Alarms', pp. 59–83.
76. *State Trials*, vol. 33, cols 71–4, 96.
77. Ibid., col. 100; [Allen], 'Parliamentary Reform', pp. 126–50.
78. *State Trials*, vol. 33, cols 74, 93.
79. Ibid., col. 285.
80. For an excellent analysis of the relationships between written and spoken language and politics for this period see O. Smith, *The Politics of Language, 1791–1819* (Oxford: Clarendon Press, 1984).
81. Pentland, *Radicalism*, pp. 7–25.
82. M. Fry, 'The Whig Interpretation of Scottish History', in I. Donnachie and C. Whatley (eds), *The Manufacture of Scottish History* (Edinburgh: Polygon, 1992), pp. 72–89.

83. N. Phillipson, *The Scottish Whigs and the Reform of the Court of Session, 1785–1830* (Edinburgh: Stair Society, 1990).
84. *Parl. Debs.*, vol. 2, cols 787–817; Omond, *The Lord Advocates*, vol. 2, pp. 209–12.
85. *State Trials*, vol. 33, col. 571.
86. W. Cobbett, *The Parliamentary History of England, from the Earliest Period to the Year 1803*, 36 vols (London, 1806–20), vol. 30, cols 1300, 1563.
87. *Parl. Debs.*, vol. 36, cols 1078–81.
88. For the Lord Advocate's defence see ibid, vol. 36, cols 1250–2.
89. *Parl. Debs.*, vol. 37, cols 268–83.
90. A. Nicholson, *Memoirs of Adam Black* (Edinburgh: Adam & Charles Black, 1885), p. 55.
91. M. Magnusson et al., *The Glorious Privilege: The History of 'The Scotsman'* (London: Thomas Nelson & Sons, 1967), ch. 1; Cowan, *The Newspaper in Scotland*, pp. 36–7, 49–50; Hay, *The Whig Revival*, ch. 2.
92. See for example, *Scotsman*, 29 July 1817.
93. The moderate case for reforming Scotland's burghs was advanced in Thomas McGrugar's pseudonymous *Letters of Zeno to the Citizens of Edinburgh on the Present Mode of Electing a Member of Parliament for the City* (Edinburgh, 1783); H. Meikle, *Scotland and the French Revolution* (Glasgow: James Maclehose & Sons, 1912), pp. 16–24; D. I. Fagerstrom, 'Scottish Opinion and the American Revolution', *William and Mary Quarterly*, 3rd series, 11 (1954), pp. 252–75.
94. For summaries of the representative system in the Scottish burghs see D. W. Hayton (ed.), *The History of Parliament: The House of Commons, 1690–1715*, 5 vols (Cambridge: Cambridge University Press, 2002), vol. 1, pp. 161–77; E. Porrit, *The Unreformed House of Commons: Parliamentary Representation before 1832*, 2 vols (Cambridge: Cambridge University Press, 1903), vol. 2, pp. 115–42.
95. Nicholson, *Memoirs*, p. 58.
96. Mathieson, *Church and Reform in Scotland*, pp. 170–1.
97. R. G. Thorne (ed.), *The History of Parliament: The House of Commons, 1790–1820*, 5 vols (London: Secker & Warburg, 1986), vol. 1, pp. 78–9.
98. For the Lord Advocate's lengthy defence of the precedents used and the policy of issuing crown warrants, see *Parl. Debs.*, vol. 39, cols 1287–1333; Mathieson, *Church and Reform*, pp. 172–6.
99. Nicholson, *Memoirs*, pp. 60–2.
100. *Parl. Debs.*, vol. 39, cols 1286–7, 1351.
101. Ibid., vol. 40, cols 178–86.
102. *Borough Reform or a Peep at the Glasgow Freemen* (Paisley, 1817); *Borough Reform; and City Deformity; A Dramatic Poem*, 2nd edn (Edinburgh, 1818).
103. 'Scotch Reform', *Black Dwarf*, 11 November 1818.
104. For summaries of the election see Thorne (ed.), *The History of Parliament*, vol. 1, pp. 253–77; *The Late Elections. An Impartial Statement of all Proceedings Connected with the Progress and Result of the Late Elections* (London: Pinnock & Maunder, 1818).
105. *The Late Elections*, p. 431.

3 Scotland and the Mass Platform

1. Colonel Brown to Sir Herbert Taylor, 22 April 1820, DRO, 152M/C1820/OI26.
2. T. Carlyle, *Reminiscences*, ed. J. A. Froude (London, 1881), p. 120.
3. J. Chandler, *England in 1819: The Politics of Literary Culture and the Case of Romantic Historicism* (Chicago, IL: University of Chicago Press, 1999).
4. Cockburn, *Memorials*, p. 325.
5. *Parl. Debs.*, vol. 41, col. 1224.
6. R. Saunders, 'Chartism from Above: British Elites and the Interpretation of Chartism', *Historical Research*, 81 (2008), pp. 463–84.
7. *Parl. Debs.*, vol. 41, cols 921–2.
8. Calhoun, *The Question of Class Struggle*, ch. 6; R. Poole, 'The March to Peterloo: Politics and Festivity in Late Georgian England', *Past and Present*, 192 (2006), pp. 109–53.
9. [Parkhill], *The Life and Opinions*, p. 68.
10. The case for the overwhelming importance of Scottish-English connections in both print and personnel during the 1790s is made persuasively in Harris, 'Scottish-English Connections', pp. 189–212.
11. Fulcher, 'Contests', pp. 225–6.
12. Ibid., pp. 224–66.
13. *Parl. Debs.*, vol. 40, cols 919–23; Cookson, *Lord Liverpool's Administration*, pp. 168–72.
14. *Parl. Debs.*, vol. 40, cols 933, 955.
15. 'More Taxes: Address to the Public', *Black Dwarf*, 16 June 1819.
16. *Parl. Debs.*, vol. 40, cols 1442, 1458.
17. Thorne, *The History of Parliament*, vol. 1, p. 100. The seven were Ronald Ferguson (Dysart Burghs), Joseph Hume (Aberdeen Burghs), Thomas Kennedy (Ayr Burghs), John Maxwell (Renfrewshire), Dudley North (Haddington Burghs), John Pringle (Linlithgow Burghs) and George Sinclair (Caithness).
18. See, for example *Scotsman*, 12 June 1819.
19. *Scotsman*, 26 June 1819.
20. 'Meeting for Reform', *Black Dwarf*, 14 July 1819.
21. 'State of Public Opinion in Scotland', *Black Dwarf*, 4 August 1819.
22. *Caledonian Mercury*, 21 June 1810; *Morning Chronicle*, 30 June 1819.
23. 'Emigration', *Black Dwarf*, 17 March 1819. For examples of interest in the question see letters from A. MacDonald and David McAdam to Lord Sidmouth, 15 March and 20 June 1815, DRO, 152M/C1815/OH32-4.
24. For the Blanketeers see S. Bamford, *Passages in the Life of a Radical*, ed. W. H. Chaloner (Oxford: Oxford University Press, 1984), pp. 29–37; Thompson, *The Making*, pp. 711–12; White, *Waterloo to Peterloo*, ch. 13.
25. *Caledonian Mercury*, 21 June 1819.
26. *Morning Chronicle*, 30 June 1819.
27. *Parl. Debs.*, vol. 41, cols 1217–23, 1383–400; An Inhabitant, *A Short Address to the Weavers of Paisley and the Neighbourhood: (Suggesting a Plan for their Relief)* (Paisley: S. Young, 1819).
28. *Caledonian Mercury*, 21 June 1819.
29. *Parl. Debs.*, vol. 40, col. 915.
30. *Scotsman*, 3 July 1819.
31. *Caledonian Mercury*, 16 September 1819.
32. See for examples, *Scotsman*, 26 June 1819; *Morning Chronicle*, 1 July 1819.

33. William Rae to Lord Sidmouth, 3 August 1819, NA, HO 102/30, ff. 465–8.
34. Henry Monteith, James Reddie and William Rae to Lord Sidmouth, 6, 10 and 13 August 1819, NA, HO 102/30, ff. 475–6, 487–8, 497–8.
35. For Peterloo see D. Read, *Peterloo: The Massacre and its Background* (Manchester: Manchester University Press, 1958); Thompson, *The Making*, pp. 745–56; R. Poole, '"By the Law or the Sword": Peterloo Revisited', *History*, 91 (2006), pp. 254–76; M. Bush, *The Casualties of Peterloo* (Lancaster: Carnegie, 2005).
36. Fulcher, 'Contests', p. 274.
37. *Proclamation by the Sheriff of Renfrewshire, and by the Provost and Magistrates of Paisley ... 9th Sept. 1819* (Paisley, 1819).
38. *Scotsman*, 25 September 1819.
39. Robert Hamilton to Lord Sidmouth, 22 August 1819, NA, HO 102/30, ff. 522–3.
40. *Scotsman*, 18 September 1819.
41. Copy report of Lieut.-Col. Hastings, 2 a.m., 12 September 1819, NA, HO 102/30, ff. 571–2.
42. See for examples, *Caledonian Mercury*, 16 September 1819; *Scotsman*, 18 September 1819; *Morning Chronicle*, 21 September 1819; *Observer*, 20 September 1819; 'Magisterial Wisdom Spreading from Lancashire to Scotland', *Cap of Liberty*, 22 September 1819; 'Observations on the Conduct of the Scotch Magistrates, as evinced at the last Paisley Meeting', *Medusa*, 25 September 1819.
43. William Rae to Lord Sidmouth, 15 September 1819, NA, HO 102/30, f. 589.
44. Lord Sidmouth to Prince Regent, 17 September 1819 and Sir George Cockburn to Lord Sidmouth, 18 September 1819, DRO, 152M/C1819/OH34, 36.
45. William Rae to Lord Sidmouth, 15 September 1819, NA, HO 102/30, ff. 589–90.
46. *Scotsman*, 2 and 16 October 1819. James Mackintosh later contrasted the sound common sense and good conduct of the magistrates of Glasgow and Paisley in permitting 'every thing short of actual violence, rather than spill the blood of their fellow-countrymen' with the conduct of the authorities at Manchester, *Parl. Debs.*, vol. 41, col. 116.
47. *Caledonian Mercury*, 27 September 1819.
48. Lord Sidmouth to Lord Melville, 30 September 1819, DRO, 152M/C1819/OH38.
49. 'Magisterial Wisdom', *Cap of Liberty*, 22 September 1819.
50. 'Call of the Corruptionists for Armed Societies Against the People', *Black Dwarf*, 6 October 1819.
51. Donnelly, 'General Rising', pp. 163–6; Thompson, *The Making*, pp. 764–6; William Rae to Lord Sidmouth, 29 October 1819, DRO, 152M/C1819/OH39. For Hunt's letter see *Scotsman*, 30 October 1819.
52. J. Begg, *Memoirs of James Begg*, ed. T. Smith, 2 vols (Edinburgh: J. Gemmell, 1885–8), vol. 1, p. 7.
53. Notebook 'Weather Airdrie 1799–1826', North Lanarkshire Council Archives, Mack Family Papers, U122 2/01. For the attack on magistrates see the depositions at NAS, Crown Office Precognitions, AD 14/19/10.
54. *Parl. Debs.*, vol. 41, col. 2.
55. 'Address of the Inhabitants of Paisley and its Vicinity in Public Meeting Assembled to the Nation', *Black Dwarf*, 11 August 1819.
56. *Spirit of the Union*, 30 October 1819. For Richard Carlile see J. H. Wiener, *Radicalism and Freethought in Nineteenth-Century Britain: The Life of Richard Carlile* (Westport, CT: Greenwood Press, 1983).

57. Precognitions against Margaret Marshall, Andrew Marshall for Sedition and Blasphemy and against Matthew Shiels for Blasphemy, NAS, Crown Office Precognitions, AD 14/19/33 and 301. For some radical discussion of Carlile's publications and ideas see the speech of Robert Steele at Newmilns in Ayrshire, *Proceedings &c* [of meeting at Newmilns] (Glasgow, n.d.), pp. 26–8.
58. Though for an argument that some caution ought to be exercised in taking such public pronouncements at face value see Philp, 'Disconcerting Ideas'.
59. *The Proceedings of a Meeting that took place at Linktown of Kirkcaldy, on the third November, 1819, to take into Consideration the Proceedings at Manchester* (Edinburgh, 1819), p. 18.
60. Declaration of William Rodger, 3 December 1819, NAS, Crown Office Precognitions AD 14/19/10 ff. 17–18.
61. *Scotsman*, 31 July 1819.
62. 'Address of the Inhabitants', *Black Dwarf*, 11 August 1819.
63. *An Account of the Proceedings of a Meeting Held at Dundee, on Wednesday, 10th November, 1819* (Newcastle: J. Marshall, 1821), p. 19; *Dundee, Perth and Cupar Advertiser*, 12 November 1819.
64. 'Clay-Knowes Reform Meeting', *Spirit of the Union*, 6 November 1819.
65. *Caledonian Mercury*, 27 September 1819; 'Call of the Corruptionists', *Black Dwarf*, 6 October 1819.
66. For example, 'A Parody on the Address of Bruce to His Army', 'Parody on Scots Wha' Hae' Wi' Wallace Bled', 'Address', *Black Dwarf*, 18 March 1818, 24 March and 17 November 1819. C. Kidd, 'The English Cult of Wallace and the Blending of Nineteenth-Century Britain', in E. J. Cowan (ed.), *The Wallace Book* (Edinburgh: John Donald, 2007), pp. 136–50.
67. 'A Caledonian Appeal to the Friends of Freedom', *Black Dwarf*, 10 March 1819.
68. Memorandum of an unidentified Kilmarnock businessman, 13 September 1819, NAS, GD 1/1147, f. 36; Precognition against David Potter for selling seditious publications, NAS, Crown Office Precognitions, AD 14/21/213. The inventory of the contents of Potter's shop in February 1820 offers a good sample of the works that were available. Periodical publications included, *A Key to the House of Commons, Black Dwarf, Peterloo Massacre, Chronicles of the Kings of England, Dolby's Parliamentary Register, Cobbett's Weekly Political Register, Manchester Observer, British Luminary, Irishman*; pamphlets and books included W. Hone, *The Political House that Jack Built*, D. I. Eaton, *The Catechism of Man*, T. Paine, *Dissertation on the First Principles of Government* and both Sherwin's and Hone's editions of *Wat Tyler*.
69. See for example 'Meeting of Radical Reformers at Broxbrae Stirlingshire', *Spirit of the Union*, 11 December 1819.
70. Gilmartin, *Print Politics*, ch. 2.
71. *Caledonian Mercury*, 26 August 1819.
72. Declaration of William Symington, 13 April 1820, NAS, Crown Office Precognitions, AD 14/19/209, f. 1.
73. 'Letter of the Spirit of the Union to the Repressed Spirit of Reform in Edinburgh', *Spirit of the Union*, 6 November 1819.
74. Roach, 'Radical Reform Movements', pp. 177–84; William Rae to Lord Sidmouth, 12 October 1819, NA, HO 102/31, f. 39. Brayshaw certainly addressed the Newmilns meeting in late September, *Proceedings &c.*, p. 22.

75. 'Statement of Joseph Brayshaw', *Republican*, 4 October 1822; J. Brayshaw, *An Appeal to the People of England, on the Necessity of Parliamentary Reform* (Newcastle: J. Marshall, 1819).
76. J. Brayshaw, *Remarks upon the Character and Conduct of the Men who met under the Name of the British Parliament at the latter End of the Year 1819, with an Account of the Manner in which they Obtained their Seats. To which is added, a Letter to the Lord Advocate on the State of that Country* (Newcastle: J. Marshall, 1820).
77. For these accounts of Union Societies see J. Paterson, *Autobiographical Reminiscences: Including Recollections of the Radical Years, 1819–20, in Kilmarnock* (Glasgow, 1871), pp. 65–70; C. J. Green, *Trials for High Treason, in Scotland, under a Special Commission, held at Stirling, Glasgow, Dumbarton, Paisley, and Ayr, in the year 1820*, 3 vols (Edinburgh: Manners & Miller, 1825), vol. 2, pp. 135–6, 143–4; Declaration of William Symington, 13 April 1820, NAS, Crown Office Precognitions, AD 14/20/209, ff. 1–2.
78. Epstein, *Radical Expression*; P. Pickering, 'Class without Words: Symbolic Communication in the Chartist Movement', *Past and Present*, 112 (1986), pp. 144–62.
79. Poole, 'The March to Peterloo', p. 116.
80. The best account of the militarized nature of the platform so far is S. H. Myerly, *British Military Spectacle: From the Napoleonic Wars through the Crimea* (Cambridge, MA: Harvard University Press, 1996), pp. 133–8. See also G. Pentland, 'Militarization and Collective Action in Great Britain, 1815–1820', in M. T. Davis and B. Bowden (eds), *Disturbing the Peace: Collective Action in Britain and France, 1381 to the Present* (Basingstoke: Palgrave Macmillan, forthcoming).
81. Bamford, *Passages in the Life of a Radical*, p. 132.
82. Diary of C. H. Hutcheson, 1820–48, NLS, MSS 2773, pp. 14–17, 24.
83. Thompson, *The Making*, p. 746.
84. *Parl. Debs.*, vol. 41, col. 392.
85. Bamford, *Passages in the Life of a Radical*, pp. 132–3.
86. [Parkhill], *The Life and Opinions*, p. 76.
87. Green, *Trials for High Treason*, vol. 3, p. 272.
88. Declaration of Robert McCreath, 8 November 1819, NAS, Crown Office Precognitions, AD 14/19/312, ff. 25–6; *Scotsman*, 6 November 1819.
89. [Parkhill], *The Life and Opinions*, p. 79.
90. *Proceedings of a Meeting ... at Linktown*, pp. 9–10; *Proceedings &c.*, p. 23.
91. Bamford, *Passages in the Life of a Radical*, p. 146.
92. I. Haywood, *Bloody Romanticism: Spectacular Violence and the Politics of Representation, 1776–1832* (London: Palgrave Macmillan, 2006), p. 196; M. T. Davis, 'The Mob Club? The London Corresponding Society and the Politics of Civility in the 1790s', in M. T. Davis and P. A. Pickering (eds), *Unrespectable Radicals? Popular Politics in the Age of Reform* (Aldershot: Ashgate, 2008), pp. 21–40.
93. A. Clark, *The Struggle for the Breeches: Gender and the Making of the British Working Class* (Berkeley, CA: University of California Press, 1995), ch. 9.
94. I. Haywood, *The Revolution in Popular Literature: Print, Politics and the People, 1790–1860* (Cambridge: Cambridge University Press, 2004), pp. 95–8.
95. K. Navickas, 'The Search for 'General Ludd': The Mythology of Luddism', *Social History*, 30 (2005), pp. 290–1.
96. [Parkhill], *The Life and Opinions*, p. 76.

97. Diary of C. H. Hutcheson, p. 17; K. O. Fox, *Making Life Possible: A Study of Military Aid to the Civil Power in Regency England* (Kineton: K. O. Fox, 1982), pp. 160–1.
98. Cookson, *The British Armed Nation*, p. 182.
99. *Parl. Debs.*, vol. 41, col. 528.
100. *Glasgow Chronicle*, 14 December 1819.
101. S. Connolly, '"Under the Banners of Death": Iconoclasm, Iconophobia and the Scopic Vocabularies of English Popular Politics, 1789–1821' (PhD dissertation, University of Manchester, 2009).
102. *Scotsman*, 31 July, 28 August, 30 October and 6 November 1819.
103. Memorandum of an unidentified Kilmarnock Businessman, 18 September 1819, NAS, GD 1/1147 f. 37; *Scotsman*, 25 September 1819.
104. See for example, Declaration of Andrew Fergus, 11 December 1819, NAS, Crown Office Precognitions, AD 14/19/301.
105. J. Epstein, 'Understanding the Cap of Liberty: Symbolic Practice and Social Conflict in Early-Nineteenth-Century England', *Past and Present*, 122 (1989), pp. 96–100.
106. Declarations of George Webster and Robert Martin, 8 November 1819, NAS, Crown Office Precognitions, AD 14/19/312, ff. 3, 17.
107. *Scotsman*, 6 November 1819.
108. Declaration of George Webster, 8 November 1819, NAS, Crown Office Precognitions, AD 14/19/312, f. 5.
109. Declaration of Peter Barbour, 8 November 1819, NAS, Crown Office Precognitions, AD 14/19/312, ff. 18–19.
110. *Scotsman*, 30 October 1819; Declaration of Andrew Fergus 11 December 1819, NAS, Crown Office Precognitions, AD 14/19/301.
111. *Spirit of the Union*, 30 October 1819; *Scotsman*, 6 November 1819.
112. *Caledonian Mercury*, 15 November 1819; *Dundee, Perth and Cupar Advertiser*, 12 November 1819.
113. *Scotsman*, 6 November 1819; Declaration of George Webster, NAS, Crown Office Precognitions, AD 14/19/312, f. 5; A. Rodger, *Poems and Songs, Humorous and Satirical* (Glasgow: D. Robertson, 1838), pp. 29–33.
114. *Caledonian Mercury*, 15 November 1819.
115. R. Chalmers, *Autobiography of Robert Chalmers, the Old Social and Political Reformer* (Dundee, 1872), p. 25; Declaration of Andrew Fergus, 11 December 1819, NAS, Crown Office Precognitions, AD 14/19/301.
116. Clark, *The Struggle for the Breeches*, p. 161.
117. *Scotsman*, 18 December 1819.
118. *Spirit of the Union*, 30 October 1819; Epstein, 'Understanding the Cap of Liberty', p. 86.
119. 'The Warder. No. II', *Blackwood's Edinburgh Magazine*, 6 (1819), p. 323. It has not been possible to identify the authorship of the series of letters from 'The Warder', which appeared in *Blackwood's* between 1819 and 1821. The last was certainly by George Croly and the style of the others is identified with John Gibson Lockhart in A. L. Strout, *A Bibliography of Articles in Blackwood's Magazine, Volumes I through XVIII, 1817–1825*, Library Bulletin no. 5 (Lubbock, TX: Texas Technical College, 1959), p. 61. Eldon confessed 'I may look at what is passing in the Country with the jaundiced Eye of an ultra Alarmist', in Lord Eldon to Lord Sidmouth, 20 September 1819, DRO, 152M/C1819/OH86.
120. For the historiography of loyalism see ch. 2, n. 2. For a stimulating treatment of the ideological traditions from which it sprang see P. Schofield, 'Conservative Political Thought

in Britain in Response to the French Revolution', *Historical Journal*, 29 (1986), pp. 601–22.
121. For loyalist rejection of both dialogic and middle-class-centred perceptions of the social order during the 1790s see Wahrman, *Imagining*, pp. 83–107.
122. [J. Wilson], 'The Radical's Saturday Night', *Blackwood's Edinburgh Magazine*, 6 (1819), pp. 257–62.
123. *Parl. Debs.*, vol. 41, col. 924. For other examples of this emphasis see resolutions of and debate at the Fife county meeting in *Caledonian Mercury*, 20 November 1819; John Monteath to Lord Sidmouth, 6 January 1820, NA, HO 102/32, ff. 34–7; 'A North Briton' to Lord Liverpool, 4 December 1819, BL, Liverpool Papers, Add MSS 38281, ff. 219–20.
124. G. Claeys, *The French Revolution Debate in Britain: The Origins of Modern Politics* (Basingstoke: Palgrave Macmillan, 2007), ch. 5.
125. *Caledonian Mercury*, 23 October 1819.
126. Charles Hope to Viscount Melville, 9 November 1819, NLS, Melville Letters 1817–19, MS10, f. 197.
127. 'The Warder. No. I', *Blackwood's Edinburgh Magazine*, 6 (1819), pp. 208–12. For Lockhart's hounding of the Whigs see A. Lang, *The Life and Letters of John Gibson Lockhart* 2 vols (London: J. C. Nimmo, 1897), vol. 1, chs 5–8.
128. Alexander Boswell to Lord Sidmouth, 24 October 1819, DRO, 152M/C1819/OZ.
129. Gilmartin, *Print Politics*, p. 52.
130. 'The Warder. No. I', p. 211.
131. Connolly, 'Under the Banners of Death', chs 1–4; J. Barrell, 'Radicalism, Visual Culture, and Spectacle in the 1790s', *Romanticism on the Net*, 46 (May 2007), at http://www.erudit.org/revue/ron/2007/v/n46/016131ar.html [accessed 14/10 2010].
132. Diary of C. H. Hutcheson, 1820–48, pp. 5–6.
133. *Parl. Debs.*, vol. 41, cols 924–5.
134. 'The Warder. No. III', *Blackwood's Edinburgh Magazine*, 6 (1819), pp. 334–5.
135. Scott, *The Letters*, vol. 5, pp. 485–6; *Edinburgh Weekly Journal*, 24 August 1819.
136. E. A. Wasson, 'The Great Whigs and Parliamentary Reform, 1809–30', *Journal of British Studies*, 24 (1985), pp. 434–64.
137. Mitchell, *The Whigs in Opposition*, ch. 6; J. J. Sack, *The Grenvillites 1801–29: Party Politics and Factionalism in the Age of Pitt and Liverpool* (Urbana, IL: University of Illinois Press, 1979), pp. 184–95.
138. *Parl. Debs.*, vol. 41, col. 75.
139. [J. Maxwell], *A Letter Addressed to the Honest Reformers of Scotland; with Remarks on the Poor Rates, Corn Law, Religious Establishment, Right of Property, Equality of Ranks, and Revolution* (Glasgow: A. & J. M. Duncan, 1819), p. 9. The *Letter* provoked a furious response and attack on 'this *pretended* Reformer', in *Spirit of the Union*, 13 November 1819.
140. [Maxwell], *A Letter*, pp. 31, 33.
141. *Hints Addressed to Radical Reformers* (Glasgow: W. Lang, 1819), p. 21.
142. Ibid., p. 5. See also the analysis of Sir John Sinclair in the *Caledonian Mercury*, 22 November 1819.
143. *Scotsman*, 16 October 1819.
144. Prince Regent to Lord Sidmouth, 24 October 1819, DRO, 152M/C1819/OH100.

145. William Rae to Lord Sidmouth, 27 October 1819, HO102/31 ff. 51–2; Scott, *The Letters*, vol. 6, p. 16; Charles Hope to Lord Melville, 9 November 1819, NLS, Melville Letters 1817–19, MS 10, ff. 197–8; W. Scott, *The Visionary*, ed. P. Garside (Cardiff: University College Cardiff Press, 1984), p. vii.
146. Duke of Hamilton to Lord Liverpool, 15 November and 6, 13 and 16 December 1819, BL, Liverpool Papers, Add MSS 38281, ff. 53–4, 225, 287, 305–6.
147. See for example, Alexander Boswell and Lord Cassilis to Lord Sidmouth, 27 and 19 December 1819, DRO, 152M/C1819/OH44, 46; 'On the means of employing the people now out of work' by Sir John Sinclair, 14 December 1819, BL, Liverpool Papers, Add MSS 38281, ff. 295ff.
148. Mitchell, *The Whigs in Opposition*, p. 135.
149. R. Hole, 'British Counter-Revolutionary Popular Propaganda in the 1790s', in C. Jones (ed.), *Britain and Revolutionary France: Conflict, Subversion and Propaganda* (Exeter: University of Exeter, 1983), pp. 53–69; Harris, *The Scottish People*, pp. 132–5.
150. T. Shuttle, *The Marrow of Radical Reform; or A Dialogue Between Tam Shuttle and John Turnip* (Glasgow: T. Ogilvie, 1819).
151. A volunteer [George Bruce], *Patie and Nelly or, The Radical Reformation: A True Tale* (Edinburgh, 1820), p. 7.
152. *Better Thole than Be Rash, or, A Crack on the Times* (Edinburgh: W. Blackwood, 1819); *A Brief Argument for those who Think Christianity a Fable* (Edinburgh: W. Whyte, 1820); *A Second Brief Argument for those who Think Christianity a Fable* (Edinburgh: W. Whyte, 1820).
153. *Spirit of the Union*, 4 December and 1 January 1820. For an example of an anti-Cobbett tract circulated in Scotland see *Political Death of Mr William Cobbett* (Edinburgh: W. Blackwood, 1820).
154. Shuttle, *The Marrow*, pp. 11, 14.
155. A. Fairly, *A Half Hour's Crack with a Glasgow Radical Reformer: Rehearsed in a Letter to a Friend* (Edinburgh: W. Whyte, 1820).
156. Rev. H. Duncan, *The Young South Country Weaver; or, A Journey to Glasgow: A Tale for the Radicals*, 2nd edn (Edinburgh: Waugh & Innes, 1821).
157. Scott, *The Letters*, vol. 6, p. 30.
158. Duncan, *The Young South Country Weaver*, pp. iii–iv.
159. Scott, *The Letters*, vol. 6, pp. 30–2, 58; Lord Sidmouth to Lord Melville, 30 September 1819, 152M/C1819/OH38.
160. Scott, *The Letters*, vol. 6, p. 58.
161. It was widely reprinted, including in the *Glasgow Herald* and the *Kelso Mail* and attracted considerable comment. 'The Radical Visionary' responded to the 'boroughmongering visionary', in the *Spirit of the Union*, 18 December 1819.
162. *On the Use and Abuse of Charity; Earnestly Addressed to Associations for Relief of the Distressed throughout the Country* (Edinburgh: W. Blackwood, 1819), pp. 10–11.
163. Wahrman, *Imagining*, ch. 6.
164. Scott, *The Letters*, vol. 6, p. 31.
165. Covering letters enclosing addresses to the Prince Regent of various dates between 13 October and 31 December 1819, NA, HO 102/31, ff. 315–527.
166. *Spirit of the Union*, 13 November 1819.
167. See, for examples, address from the Edinburgh Town Council and the resolutions at Berwickshire county meeting, *Caledonian Mercury*, 1 and 6 November 1819.

168. Mitchell, *The Whigs in Opposition*, pp. 125–8; J. Beckett to Lord Sidmouth, 7 October 1819, DRO, 152M/C1819/OH18.
169. *Scotsman*, 13 November 1819.
170. *Caledonian Mercury*, 20 November 1819.
171. Cockburn, *Memorials*, p. 364.
172. *Scotsman*, 2 October 1819; *Black Dwarf*, 17 November and 1 December 1819.
173. *Spirit of the Union*, 4 December 1819, 1 January 1820.
174. A. Hendrikson, 'Loyalism in Scotland, 1816–1820' (MSc dissertation, University of Edinburgh, 2007).
175. Charles Hope to Viscount Melville, 9 November and 12 December 1819, NLS, Melville Letters 1817–1819, MS10, ff. 197–201, 203–4.
176. Mackenzie, *Old Reminiscences*, vol. 1, pp. 219–20.
177. Memorandum of an unidentified Kilmarnock Businessman, 1 December 1819, NAS, GD 1/1147. ff. 50–1.
178. Cookson, *The British Armed Nation*, passim.
179. *Black Dwarf*, 10 November 1819.
180. *Scotsman*, 20 November 1819.
181. Scott, *The Letters*, vol. 6, pp. 79–80.
182. Ibid., vol. 6, pp. 98–105.
183. The 'Six Acts' were: 60 Geo. III & 1 Geo IV, c. 1, 'An Act to prevent the Training of Persons to the Use of Arms, and to the Practice of Military Evolutions and Exercise' [11 December 1819]; c. 2, 'An Act to Authorise Justices of the Peace, in certain disturbed Counties, to seize and detain Arms collected or kept for purposes dangerous to the Public Peace; to continue in force until the Twenty fifth Day of *March* One thousand eight hundred and twenty two' [18 December 1819]; c. 4, 'An Act to prevent Delay in the Administration of Justice in Cases of Misdemeanour' [23 December 1819]; c. 6, 'An Act for more effectually preventing Seditious Meetings and Assemblies; to continue in force until the End of the Session of Parliament next after Five Years from the passing of the Act' [24 December 1819]; c. 8, 'An Act for the more effectual Prevention and Punishment of blasphemous and seditious Libels' [30 December 1819]; c. 9, 'An Act to subject certain Publications to the Duties of Stamps upon Newspapers, and to make other Regulations for restraining the Abuses arising from the Publication of blasphemous and seditious Libels' [30 December 1819].
184. Fulcher, 'Contests', pp. 13, 199–305.
185. Lord Sidmouth to Lord Eldon, 1 October 1819, DRO, 152M/C1819/OH93. For the prolonged debate see Lord Eldon to Lord Sidmouth, 16, 20, 29 September and 4 October 1819, DRO, 152M/C1819/OH84, 86–7, 96.
186. 60 Geo. III & 1 Geo. IV, c. 1.
187. 60 Geo. III & 1 Geo. IV, c. 4.
188. *Parl. Debs.*, vol. 41, col. 390.

4 The 'General Rising' of 1820

1. Scott, *The Letters*, vol. 6, p. 175.
2. J. Stevenson, *A True Narrative of the Radical Rising in Strathaven, in Vindication of the Parties Concerned, as also of the Martyred James Wilson, in Answer to McKenzie's Exposure of the 'Spy System', and the Rev. Mr Proudfoot, in the 'Statistics of Scotland'* (Glasgow: W. & W. Miller, 1835), p. 8.

3. Thomis and Holt, *Threats of Revolution*, p. 8; D. R. Fisher (ed.), *The History of Parliament: The House of Commons 1820–1832*, 7 vols (Cambridge: Cambridge University Press, 2009), vol. 1, p. 100.
4. This is the view sketched in Whatley, *Scottish Society*, pp. 307–27.
5. Whatley, *Scottish Society*, p. 309.
6. Sir Thomas Bradford to General Torrens, 9 November 1819, NA, HO 102/31, f. 120.
7. Charles Hope to Lord Melville, 9 November 1819, NLS, MS 10, f. 197.
8. Lord Sidmouth to Earl of Lonsdale, 8 December 1819, DRO, 152M/C1819/OH123; 'Benevolus' to Lord Sidmouth, 18 December 1819, NA, HO 102/31, ff. 242–3.
9. Charles Hope to Lord Melville, 14 December 1819, NLS, Melville Letters 1817–19, MS 10, f. 205. Similar claims that three hundred armed radicals had marched from Kilbarchan on Monday 13 December were vociferously denied in 'To the Lord President', *Spirit of the Union*, 25 December 1819.
10. Lord Cassillis to Lord Sidmouth, 29 December 1819, DRO, 152M/C1819/OH46.
11. Henry Hobhouse to Sir Thomas Bradford, 23 December 1819, NA, HO 79/4, f. 40.
12. William Rae to Lord Sidmouth, 13 August 1819, NA, HO 102/30, ff. 497–8.
13. Ibid.; William Rae to Henry Hobhouse, 8 September 1820, Captain Brown to Rae, 25 August 1820, NA, HO 102/33, ff. 282–7.
14. William Rae to Lord Sidmouth, 29 October 1819, DRO, 152M/C1819/OH39.
15. Letters from Robert Hamilton, Henry Monteith and William Rae to Lord Sidmouth, 23 and 25 February 1820, NA, HO 102/32, ff. 186–97; *Glasgow Chronicle*, 24 and 29 February 1820; *Manchester Observer*, 4 March 1820.
16. Ellis and Mac a'Ghobhainn, *The Scottish Insurrection*, pp. 140–1.
17. Robert Hamilton to Lord Sidmouth, 1 March 1820, NA, HO 102/32, f. 216.
18. Deposition of A.B., 7 March 1820, NA, HO 102/32, ff. 235–6. For the public aims of the Union Societies see Brayshaw, *Remarks upon the Character and Conduct*, pp. 36–9.
19. Lord Sidmouth to Sir Benjamin Bloomfield, 13 March 1820, DRO, 152M/C1820/OH52.
20. J. Stanhope, *The Cato Street Conspiracy* (London: Jonathan Cape, 1962); Lord Sidmouth to Sir Charles Grant, 24 February 1820, DRO, 152M/C1820/OH2.
21. Robert Hamilton to Lord Sidmouth, 1 March 1820, NA, HO 102/32, f. 216.
22. J. Brayshaw, 'Account of the Missions', *Republican*, 30 August 1822.
23. Henry Monteith to Lord Sidmouth, 2 March 1820, NA, HO 102/32, f. 224.
24. John Wilson to Lord Sidmouth, 2 March 1820, NA, HO 40/11, f. 77.
25. Lord Sidmouth to Sir Benjamin Bloomfield, 3 March 1820, DRO, 152M/C1820/OH18.
26. Henry Monteith to Lord Sidmouth and Henry Hobhouse to Henry Monteith, 17 and 22 March 1820, NA, HO 102/32, f. 255, HO 79/4, f. 54.
27. Information of Daniel White, 3 March 1820, NA, HO 40/11, ff. 91–2; Thomas Sharp to Henry Monteith, 12 March 1820, ML, G1/2.
28. 'A Briton' to Lord Sidmouth, 1 March 1820, NA, HO 102/32, f. 211.
29. *Dundee, Perth and Cupar Advertiser*, 11 February 1820.
30. Precognition against Alexander Martin, George Fisher and James Scott, NAS, Crown Office Precognitions, AD 14/20/228.
31. [G. Canning], *The Principles and Tendency of Radical Reform* (London: W. Clowes, 1820); 'The Warder. No. VI', *Blackwood's Edinburgh Magazine*, 7 (1820), pp. 11–21.
32. Fisher (ed.), *History of Parliament*, vol. 1, pp. 218–19; *Dundee, Perth and Cupar Advertiser*, 17 March 1820.

33. George Napier to Henry Monteith, 16 March 1820, ML, Monteith Correspondence, G1/2/22.
34. Henry Monteith to Lord Sidmouth, 26 March 1820, NA, HO 102/32, f. 275.
35. C. Esdaile, *Spain in the Liberal Age: From Constitution to Civil War, 1808–1939* (Oxford: Blackwell, 2000), ch. 3.
36. Sir Howard Douglas to Lord Sidmouth, 19 March, DRO, 152M/C1820/OF7.
37. Ibid., 23 March 1820, 152M/C1820/OF9.
38. Alexander Boswell to Lord Sidmouth, 31 March 1820, NA, HO 102/32, f. 280.
39. See for examples, 'On the Lawfulness of our Insurrection', *Republican*, 10 March 1820, pp. 261–6; *Scotsman*, 11 March 1820; *Dundee, Perth and Cupar Advertiser*, 24 March 1820; *Manchester Observer*, 25 March 1820.
40. I. McCalman, 'New Jerusalems: Prophecy, Dissent and Radical Culture in England, 1786–1830', in K. Haakonssen (ed.), *Enlightenment and Religion: Rational Dissent in Eighteenth-Century Britain* (Cambridge: Cambridge University Press, 1996), pp. 312–35; McCalman, *Radical Underworld*, ch. 3; J. F. C. Harrison, *The Second Coming: Popular Millenarianism 1780–1850* (London: Routledge, 1979).
41. A. Mason, *An Inquiry into the Times that shall be Fulfilled at Antichrist's Fall* (Glasgow, 1818).
42. J. Scott, *The Present Revolutions in Europe, and other Signs of the Times, Compared with Scripture Predictions and History, Shewing that in 1822 the Regeneration of the European Dynasties will be Completed* (Glasgow: W. Lang, 1820). I am grateful to Dr Valerie Wallace for pointing out this work to me and offering me a chance to read her unpublished paper 'Presbyterian Prophecy and Political Radicalism in Scotland and Ulster, c.1790–1848'.
43. [J. Scott], *Answers to the Queries, by the Author of the Pamphlet Entitled the 'Present Revolutions in Europe, and other Signs of the Times'* (Glasgow: W. Lang, n.d.), pp. 3–4.
44. *Scotsman*, 11 March 1820.
45. Lord Sidmouth to Sir Benjamin Bloomfield, DRO, 152M/C1820/OH24; *Scotsman*, 1 April 1820.
46. Henry Monteith to Lord Sidmouth, 17 March 1820 and Henry Hobhouse to Henry Monteith, 22 March 1820, NA, HO 103/32, f. 255 and HO 79/4.
47. Thomas Sharp to Henry Monteith, 12 March 1820, ML, Monteith Correspondence, G1/2/20; Report of Monteath, 31 March 1820, NA, HO 102/32, ff. 284–5. See *Dreadful Fray, which Took Place at Culrain near Gladsfield in Ross-shire: With an Account of the Killed and Wounded on Both Sides* (n.p., n.d.).
48. P. K. Monod, 'Dangerous Merchandise: Smuggling, Jacobitism and Commercial Culture in Southeast England, 1690–1760', *Journal of British Studies*, 30 (1991), pp. 150–82.
49. James Inglis, Alexander Williamson, Donald Carmichael and John Grieg to commissioner of excise, 20, 22 and 26 March 1820, NA, HO 102/32, ff. 407–11.
50. *The Trial of Henry Hunt esq., Jno. Knight, Jos. Johnson, Jno. Thacker Saxton, Samuel Bamford, Jos. Healey. James Moorhouse, Robert Jones, Geo Swift, and Robert Wylde for an Alleged Conspiracy to Overturn the Government* (London: T. Dolby, 1820), pp. 298–309. See also Bamford, *Passages in the Life of a Radical*, pp. 179–272. For the important role of the trial in changing definitions of 'political crime' see M. Lobban, 'From Seditious Libel to Unlawful Assembly: Peterloo and the Changing Face of Political Crime, 1770–1820', *Oxford Journal of Legal Studies*, 10 (1990), pp. 307–52.
51. Lord Sidmouth to James Scarlett, 29 March 1820, DRO, 152M/C1820/OH42.

52. Thomas Sharp to Henry Monteith, 20 March 1820, ML, G1/2/25; Mr Chippendale to General Byng, 1 April 1820, NA, HO 40/12, f. 4; Thomas Sharp to Lord Sidmouth, 19 March 1820, NA, HO 40/11, f. 221.
53. Henry Hobhouse to William Rae, 5 April 1820, NA, HO 79/4, f. 56.
54. *The Following is a Correct Account of the Trial and Sentence of Henry Hunt, Esq., James Moorhouse, John T. Saxton, George Swift, Robert Jones, Robert Wilde, Joseph Johnson, Joseph Healey, John Knight and Samuel Bamford: For Unlawfully, Maliciously, and Seditiously Meeting and Assembling* (Glasgow: M. Robertson, 1820).
55. See for example *Manchester Observer*, 25 March 1820.
56. Thomas Sharp to Henry Monteith, 5 April 1820, ML, Monteith Correspondence, G1/2/38.
57. Copy of magistrates' resolutions 31 July 1820 in consequence of the speech of the Lord Advocate as the close of the treason trials in Glasgow, NA, HO 102/33, f. 241.
58. 'Address to the Inhabitants of Great Britain and Ireland' [printed], NA, HO, 102/32, f. 296.
59. Matthew Stevenson to William Kerr, 3 April 1820, HO 102/32, f. 326; Green, *Trials for High Treason*, vol. 3, p. 49.
60. Green, *Trials for High Treason*, vol. 2, pp. 61, 429; J. Hamilton, *Poems, Sketches and Essays*, 2nd edn (Glasgow: J. Maclehose, 1885), pp. 406–7.
61. Green, *Trials for High Treason*, vol. 1, pp. 142–52.
62. Henry Monteith to Lord Sidmouth, 4 April 1820, Dugald Bannatyne to William Kerr, 4 April 1820, NA, HO 102/32, ff. 317, 328.
63. Green, *Trials for High Treason*, vol. 2, p. 434.
64. Ibid., vol. 3, p. 32.
65. Ibid., vol. 2, pp. 420–542; J. C. Colquhoun to Duke of Montrose, 16 April 1820, NA, HO 102/32, f. 425.
66. John Morison to Henry Monteith, 4 April 1820, ML, Monteith Correspondence, G1/2/36; Diary of C. H. Hutcheson, p. 23.
67. Lord Blantyre to Lord Sidmouth, 5 April 1820, NA, HO 102/32, f. 335; Parkhill, *The Life and Opinions*, pp. 89–91; Oliver Jamieson to Henry Monteith, 4 April 1820, ML, Monteith Correspondence, G1/2/35.
68. Diary of C. H. Hutcheson, p. 28.
69. Hamilton, *Poems*, p. 408.
70. Oliver Jamieson to Henry Monteith, 3 April 1820, ML, Monteith Correspondence, G1/2/33–4; Lord Blantyre to Sidmouth, 5 April 1820, NA, HO 102/32, ff. 335–7.
71. Diary of C. H. Hutcheson, p. 23; Dugald Bannatyne to William Kerr, 4 April 1820, NA, HO 102/32, f. 328.
72. This is the central thesis explored in Donnelly, 'General Rising'.
73. The trials and sentences of the 'Bonnymuir radicals' occupy the entire first volume of Green, *Trials for High Treason*.
74. Green, *Trials for High Treason*, vol. 1, pp. 187–9.
75. Roach, 'Radical Reform Movements', pp. 215–28; 'Progress of Revolution', *Republican*, 21 April 1820.
76. Green, *Trials for High Treason*, vol. 1, p. 422.
77. William Rae to Lord Sidmouth, 5 April 1820, NA, HO 102/32, f. 351. See also the account in the *Edinburgh Weekly Journal*, 12 April 1820.

78. Green, *Trials for High Treason*, vol. 2, pp. 1–394; Precognition against James Donald, 18–31 May 1820, NAS, Crown Office Precognitions, AD 14/20/208. For a radical participant's later account see Stevenson, *A True Narrative*.
79. *Glasgow Chronicle*, 8 April 1820.
80. William Rae to Lord Sidmouth, 6 April 1820, NA, HO 102/32, f. 353.
81. William Rae to Lord Sidmouth, 7 April 1820, NA, HO 102/32, ff. 367–8.
82. Alexander Boswell to Lord Sidmouth, 11 April 1820, DRO, 152M/C1820/OH55.
83. Henry Monteith to Lord Sidmouth, 9 April 1820, NA, HO 102/32, ff. 377–8; Declarations and other papers relative to affair in Greenock, NA, HO 102/32, ff. 481–583; *Glasgow Chronicle*, 11 April 1820.
84. General Byng to Lord Sidmouth, 22 April 1820, NA, HO 40/12, f. 282.
85. Mackenzie, *Old Reminiscences*, vol. 1, p. 134. For Mackenzie's interpretation of the 'Radical War' see pp. 124–6.
86. Ellis and Mac a'Ghobhainn, *The Scottish Insurrection*, p. 25.
87. Donnelly, 'General Rising', pp. 370–1.
88. Stevenson, *A True Narrative*, pp. 4–5; Green, *Trials for High Treason*, vol. 1, pp. 216–17, vol. 3, pp. 201–46.
89. See for examples Brayshaw, *Remarks upon the Character and Conduct*, p. 36; 'Discovery of a Spy Among the Unions', *Spirit of the Union*, 1 January 1820.
90. Green, *Trials for High Treason*, vol. 2, p. 383.
91. William Rae to Lord Sidmouth, 15 July 1820, NA, HO 102/33, ff. 168–9.
92. Roach, 'Radical Reform Movements', p. 223.
93. Lord Sidmouth to William Rae, 31 October 1819, NA, HO 41/5.
94. 'A Briton' to Lord Sidmouth, 1 March 1820, NA, HO 102/32, ff. 207–8.
95. M. and A. Macfarlane, *The Scottish Radicals Tried and Transported for Treason in 1820*, 2nd edn (Stevenage: SPA, 1981), pp. 24–5.
96. Stevenson, *A True Narrative*, p. 8; [Parkhill], *The Life and Opinions*, p. 93.
97. Lord Blantyre to Lord Sidmouth, 5 April 1820, NA, HO 102/32, f. 335; Green, *Trials for High Treason*, vol. 3, pp. 270–3.
98. Declaration of A.B., 7 March 1820, NA, HO 102/32, f. 235.
99. Calhoun, *The Question of Class Struggle*, pp. 72–94.
100. Alexander Boswell to Lord Sidmouth, 4 February 1820, DRO, 152M/C1820/OH49.
101. [Parkhill], *The Life and Opinions*, p. 74.
102. Donnelly, 'General Rising', pp. 158–79.
103. Lord Blantyre to Lord Sidmouth, 5 April 1820, NA, HO 102/32, ff. 335–6.
104. Dugald Bannatyne to William Kerr, 4 April 1820, NA, HO102/32, f. 328.
105. Calhoun, *The Question of Class Struggle*, pp. 79–80.
106. Some of these 'idle stories' were collected in the *Glasgow Chronicle*, 4 April 1820.
107. 'Account of the Missions', *Republican*, 4 October 1822, pp. 582–90.
108. Alexander Boswell to Lord Sidmouth, 4 February 1820, DRO, 152M/C1820/OH49.
109. James Norris to Lord Sidmouth, 3 April 1820, NA, HO 40/12, f. 43.
110. Henry Hobhouse to William Rae, 5 April 1820, HO 79/4, f. 57.
111. Sir James Lyon and Mr Chippendale to General Byng, 1 April 1820, NA, HO 40/12, ff. 1–4.
112. Deposition of John Mitchell, weaver in West Rising, Barnsley, NA, HO 40/12, f. 256. [*c*. April 1820]
113. [Parkhill], *The Life and Opinions*, p. 77.
114. General Byng to Lord Sidmouth, 16 April 1820, NA, HO 40/12, f. 240.
115. Henry Monteith to Lord Sidmouth, 6 April 1820, NA, HO 102/32, ff. 355–6.

Conclusion

1. Marquis of Huntly to Lord Sidmouth, 25 November 1820, DRO, 152M/C1820/OZ.
2. T. Chalmers, *The Importance of Civil Government to Society, and the Duty of Christians in Regard to It. A Sermon Preached in St. John's Church, Glasgow, on Sabbath, 30th April, 1820*, 2nd edn (Glasgow: Chalmers & Collins, 1820); G. Ewing, *The Testimony of God Against Massacre and Rapine: A Sermon, Preached in Nile Street Meeting-House, on Sabbath the Ninth of April, 1820* (Glasgow, 1820).
3. Alexander Boswell to Lord Sidmouth, 8 November 1820, DRO, 152M/C1820/OH61.
4. Prospectus of the Clydesdale Journal [printed], NA, HO 102/32, f. 288; Cowan, *The Newspaper in Scotland*, pp. 60–2.
5. Alexander Boswell to Lord Sidmouth, 26 April 1820, DRO, 152M/C1820/OZ.
6. James Reddie to Lord Advocate, 3 July 1820, NAS, Crown Office Precognitions, AD 14/20/225; General Reynell to Lord Sidmouth, NA, HO 102/33, ff. 148–9; *Scotsman*, 1 July 1820.
7. Information of William Telfer, 5 December 1820, NA, HO 102/33, f. 444.
8. John Stirling to Sidmouth, 3 October 1820, NA, HO 102/33, f. 308.
9. Green, *Trials for High Treason*, vol. 3, pp. 490–1.
10. The Crown remitted the part of the sentence that dictated the body be quartered, Lord Sidmouth to Sheriff Deputies of Lanarkshire and Stirlingshire and Lord Provosts and Magistrates of Glasgow and Stirling, 23 and 25 August 1820, NA, HO 104/5, ff. 341–2, 353–4.
11. P. Harling, 'The Law of Libel and the Limits of Repression, 1790–1832', *Historical Journal*, 44 (2001), pp. 107–34.
12. Lord Eldon to Lord Sidmouth, 20 September 1819, DRO, 152M/C1819/OH86.
13. Green, *Trials for High Treason*, vol. 1, p. 121.
14. William Rae to Henry Hobhouse, 23 June 1820, NA, HO 102/33, f. 138; Charles Hope to William Rae, 23 January 1821, NA, HO 102/34, ff. 32–3.
15. Green, *Trials for High Treason*, vol. 3, p. 483.
16. Ibid., vol. 3, pp. 473–4; J. R. Fraser, *Memoir of John Fraser, Newfield, Johnstone* (Paisley: T. & J. Cook, 1879), pp. 28–9.
17. William Rae to Lord Sidmouth, 25 July 1820, NA, HO 102/33, f. 199.
18. B. Gibson to P. Dealtry, 2 June 1820, NA, KB 33/8/5.
19. Green, *Trials for High Treason*, vol. 1, p. 92.
20. Fry, 'The Whig Interpretation', pp. 72–89.
21. G. Pentland, 'The Debate on Scottish Parliamentary Reform, 1830–32', *Scottish Historical Review*, 85 (2006), pp. 102–32.
22. Mackenzie, *Old Reminiscences*, col. 1, p. 155.
23. Charles Hope to William Rae, 23 January 1821, NA, HO 102/34, f. 32.
24. Green, *Trials for High Treason*, vol. 1, pp. 256, 459–61.
25. Ibid., vol. 1, pp. 241–2, See also pp. 455–7.
26. Ibid., vol. 1, p. 456.
27. Ibid., vol. 2, p. 264.
28. *Parl. Debs.*, new series, vol. 3, cols 756–66; *Morning Chronicle*, 12 December 1820.
29. William Rae to Henry Hobhouse, 29 October 1820 and copy of affidavits respecting the printing of the proclamation, NA, HO 102/33, ff. 341–54, 357–72.
30. 'A Letter to Lord Lauderdale', *Pol. Reg.*, 21 October 1820.
31. Spater, *William Cobbett*, vol. 2, pp. 398–408.

32. E. A. Smith, *A Queen on Trial: The Affair of Queen Caroline* (Stroud: Sutton Publishing, 1993); J. Robins, *Rebel Queen: How the Trial of Caroline Brought England to the Brink of Revolution* (London: Simon & Schuster, 2006).
33. Hay, *The Whig Revival*, p. 120.
34. Nicholson, *Memoirs*, pp. 66–7. Cockburn was similarly millenarian in his later account of the event, *Memorials*, pp. 373–8.
35. *Scotsman*, 23 December 1820. For a similar meeting in Glasgow see Mackenzie, *Old Reminiscences*, vol. 1, pp. 305–10.
36. See Scoto-Britannus [T. McCrie], *Free Thoughts on the Late Religious Celebration of the Funeral of her Royal Highness the Princess Charlotte of Wales; and on the Discussion to which it has given rise in Edinburgh* (Edinburgh: Macreadie & Co., 1817); Candidus, *Observations on a Letter by Lucius, to the Rev. Andrew Thomson, Minister of St George's Church* (Edinburgh: Macreadie & Co., 1817).
37. *John Bull*, 21 January 1821.
38. T. Creevey, *The Creevey Papers: A Selection from the Correspondence and Diaries of the Late Thomas Creevey, M. P.*, ed. H. Maxwell, 3rd edn (London: John Murray, 1912), pp. 319–20; *Glasgow Herald*, 21 August 1820; A Presbyterian, *Vindication of the Ministers of the Church of Scotland, who have Prayed for the Queen by Name, Notwithstanding the Order in Council on that Subject*, 2nd edn (Edinburgh: D. Brown, 1820); Mackenzie, *Old Reminiscences*, vol. 1, p. 283; J. Nightingale, *Memoirs of her Late Majesty, Queen Caroline, Consort of King George the Fourth*, 2 vols (London: J. Robins & Co. Albion Press, 1821), vol. 1, pp. 625–6.
39. *Parl. Debs.*, new series, vol. 4, cols 147–8, 689–715.
40. John Alston to Lord Sidmouth, 17 November 1820 and William Kerr to William Rae, 17 November 1820, NA, HO 102/33, ff. 393–7; *Glasgow Herald*, 17 November 1820.
41. *Scotsman*, 2 December 1820.
42. *Parl. Debs.*, new series, vol. 4, cols 228–36.
43. [G. Croly], 'The Queen's Trial', *Blackwood's Edinburgh Magazine*, 8 (November 1820), p. 217.
44. J. Fulcher, 'The Loyalist Response to the Queen Caroline Agitations', *Journal of British Studies*, 34 (1995), pp. 481–502.
45. Mackenzie, *Old Reminiscences*, vol. 1, pp. 277–81, 305–7.
46. Ibid., vol. 1, pp. 276–7.
47. *Scotsman*, 18 November 1820.
48. Fair Play, *Marvellous and Disinterested Patriotism of Certain Learned Whigs, Illustrated in Prose and Rhyme, for the Use of the 'Inhabitants of Edinburgh'*, 3rd edn (Edinburgh: D. Stevenson & Co., 1820), pp. 13–15.
49. [G. Croly], 'Domestic Politics', *Blackwood's Edinburgh Magazine*, 8 (December 1820), p. 337.
50. Pentland, *Radicalism*, pp. 51–2.
51. Rev. James Donaldson to Lord Sidmouth, 31 January 1821, NA, HO 102/34, f. 29.
52. C. M. M. Macdonald, 'Abandoned and Beastly? The Queen Caroline Affair in Scotland', in Y. Galloway Brown and R. Ferguson (eds), *Twisted Sisters: Women Crime and Deviance in Scotland since 1400* (East Linton: Tuckwell Press, 2002), p. 103. Robins gives figures of 8,300 signatures to the address from the 'Ladies of Edinburgh' and 35,718 and 6,000 to the addresses from the inhabitants of Glasgow and Paisley respectively, see *Rebel Queen*, p. 237.
53. Alexander Boswell to Sidmouth, 8 November 1820, DRO, 152M/C1820/OH61.

54. F. Fraser, *The Unruly Queen: The Life of Queen Caroline* (London: Macmillan, 1996), pp. 431–2.
55. Examples of earthenware dishes from the east coast potteries around Edinburgh are found in the National Museums of Scotland collections.
56. This remained a highly contested aspect of the agitation. The *Scotsman* reported on loyalist attempts via the Police Superintendent in Edinburgh to ensure that as many 'abandoned females' as possible signed the address to the Queen and so compromised the addressers claims to respectability. See the *Scotsman*, 25 November 1820.
57. Creevey, *The Creevey Papers*, vol. 1, p. 332.
58. T. W. Laqueur, 'The Queen Caroline Affair: Politics as Art in the Reign of George IV', *Journal of Modern History*, 54 (1982), pp. 417–66.
59. See Thompson's dismissive comments in *The Making*, p. 778.
60. Calhoun, *The Question of Class Struggle*, pp. 105–15.
61. J. Stevenson, 'The Queen Caroline Affair', in J. Stevenson (ed.), *London in the Age of Reform* (Oxford: Blackwell, 1977), pp. 117–48; I. Prothero, *Artisans and Politics in Early Nineteenth-Century London: John Gast and his Times* (Folkestone: William Dawson & Son, 1979), ch. 7; McCalman, *Radical Underworld*, pp. 162–77; N. Rogers, *Crowds, Culture and Politics in Georgian Britain* (Oxford: Clarendon Press, 1998), ch. 8; A. Clark, 'Queen Caroline and the Sexual Politics of Popular Culture in London, 1820', *Representations*, 31 (1990), pp. 31–68; A. Clark, *Scandal: The Sexual Politics of the British Constitution* (Princeton, NJ: Princeton University Press, 2004), ch. 8.
62. Wahrman, 'Public Opinion', pp. 83–122; Macdonald, 'Abandoned and Beastly?', pp. 101–13.
63. Fulcher, 'The Loyalist Response', pp. 492–502.
64. Howie, *Historical Account of Ayr*, p. 79.
65. *Glasgow Herald*, 27 October 1820.
66. *Black Dwarf*, 30 November 1820.
67. For examples, see the *Morning Chronicle*, 20 September 1820 and the *Caledonian Mercury*, 23 September 1820. Though see Macdonald, 'Abandoned and Beastly?', p. 108.
68. 'Her Majesty's Answers to Addresses', *Pol. Reg.*, 21 October 1820.
69. [J. W. Croker], *A Letter from the King to his People*, 13th edn (London: W. Sams, 1820). The publication ran to at least twenty-three editions.
70. *Glasgow Chronicle*, 24 October 1820; *Glasgow Herald*, 27 October 1820.
71. *The Queen's Answer to the Address of the Loyal Inhabitants of Paisley, Presented to Her Majesty 18th Oct. 1820* (Paisley: J. Weir, 1820).
72. J. Parry, *The Rise and Fall of Liberal Government in Victorian Britain* (New Haven, CT, & London: Yale University Press, 1993), ch. 1; P. Mandler, *Aristocratic Government in the Age of Reform: Whigs and Liberals, 1830–1852* (Oxford: Oxford University Press, 1990), pp. 21–31; S. M. Lee, *George Canning and Liberal Toryism, 1801–1827* (Woodbridge: Boydell & Brewer, 2008), ch. 6.
73. Fulcher, 'Contests', p. 411.
74. Pentland, *Radicalism*, pp. 37–9, 51–61.
75. Fulcher, 'The Loyalist Response', p. 483.
76. Marquis of Huntly to Lord Sidmouth, 20 November 1820, DRO, 152M.
77. Fulcher, 'The Loyalist Response', pp. 497–502.
78. James Cleland to Lord Sidmouth, 20 July 1821, NA, HO 102/34, f. 283.
79. Wasson, 'The Great Whigs', pp. 434–64.
80. Pentland, *Radicalism*, pp. 10–25.

81. Wahrman, 'Public Opinion', p. 116.
82. Belchem argues that the 1819–20 period exposed the weaknesses rather than the strengths of popular constitutionalism, *'Orator' Hunt*, ch. 4.
83. Kirkman Finlay to Henry Hobhouse, 6 May 1822, NA, HO 40/17, f. 236.
84. Belchem, *'Orator' Hunt*, ch. 5.
85. Pentland, *Radicalism*, ch. 1.
86. See for example, James Mitchell to John Vickery, 14 December 1819, ML, Letter Book of Clerk of Police 1816–25, E 2/1/1; 'Petition of the undersigned feuars of Balfron', 20 April 1820, NA, HO 102/33, f. 56.
87. 'A Briton' to Lord Sidmouth, 1 March 1820, NA, HO 102/32, f. 207.
88. J. C. D. Clark, *Our Shadowed Present: Modernism, Postmodernism and History* (London: Atlantic Books, 2003), ch. 4.
89. Fulcher, 'Contests', pp. 310–11.
90. Green, *Trials for High Treason*, vol. 1, p. 540.

Epilogue: The Legacies of 1820

1. *Official Report of Scottish Parliament*, 5 September 2001, col. 2251. Online at www.scottish.parliament.uk/business/officialReports/meetingsParliament/or-01/sor0905-01.htm [accessed 8/2/2008].
2. *Official Report of Scottish Parliament*, cols. 2255–6.
3. For an account of the Calton weavers' strike see K. Logue, *Popular Disturbances in Scotland, 1780–1815* (Edinburgh: John Donald, 1979), pp. 155–60.
4. *Official Report of Scottish Parliament*, cols. 2252–3.
5. Ibid., cols. 2254–5.
6. Ibid., cols. 2257–8.
7. P. Connerton, *How Societies Remember* (Cambridge: Cambridge University Press, 1989); J. Fentress and C. Wickham, *Social Memory* (Oxford: Blackwell, 1992); E. Hobsbawm and T. Ranger (eds), *The Invention of Tradition* (Cambridge: Cambridge University Press, 1983); G. L. Mosse, *The Nationalization of the Masses: Political Symbolism and Mass Movements in Germany from the Napoleonic Wars through the Third Reich* (New York, NJ: H. Fertig, 1975); P. Nora (ed.), *Realms of Memory: Rethinking the French Past*, trans. A. Goldhammer, 3 vols (New York, NJ: Columbia University Press, 1996–8).
8. A. Ben-Amos, *Funerals, Politics, and Memory in Modern France, 1789–1996* (Oxford: Oxford University Press, 2000), pp. 1–15; Fentress and Wickham, *Social Memory*, pp. 127–37. The literature is large and expanding but some exemplary works include J. Wolffe, *Great Deaths: Grieving, Religion, and Nationhood in Victorian and Edwardian Britain* (Oxford: Oxford University Press, 2000); H. Hoock (ed.), *History, Commemoration and National Preoccupation: Trafalgar 1805–2005*, British Academy Occasional Paper, 8 (Oxford: Oxford University Press, 2007); J. Winter, *Sites of Memory, Sites of Mourning: The Great War in European Cultural History* (Cambridge: Cambridge University Press, 1995), ch. 4.
9. R. Samuel, *Theatres of Memory*, 2 vols (London: Verso, 1994–8), vol. 1, p. 17.
10. T. J. O' Keefe, 'The 1898 Efforts to Celebrate the United Irishmen: The '98 Centennial', *Éire-Ireland*, 23 (1988), pp. 51–73; R. Foster, 'Remembering 1798', in Ian McBride (ed.), *History and Memory in Modern Ireland* (Cambridge: Cambridge University Press, 2001), pp. 67–94; A. Dolan, *Commemorating the Irish Civil War: History and Memory, 1923–2000* (Cambridge: Cambridge University Press, 2003). See also the innovative

approach in G. Beiner, *Remembering the Year of the French: Irish Folk History and Social Memory* (Madison, WI: University of Wisconsin Press, 2007).
11. See esp. P. A. Pickering and A. Tyrell (eds), *Contested Sites: Commemoration, Memorial and Popular Politics in Nineteenth-Century Britain* (Aldershot: Ashgate, 2004); special issue of *Humanities Research*, 10 (2003).
12. Eley, 'Nations, Publics, and Political Cultures', p. 307.
13. For a good exploration of that 'usability' of various aspects of Scottish history see the essays in E. J. Cowan and R. J. Finlay (eds), *Scottish History: The Power of the Past* (Edinburgh: Edinburgh University Press, 2002). See also D. McCrone, *The Sociology of Nationalism: Tomorrow's Ancestors* (London: Routledge, 1998), pp. 44–63.
14. Connerton, *How Societies Remember*, pp. 57–65.
15. Thompson, *The Making*, p. 660.
16. *The Bonny Bridge of Findhorn, The Radical Battle at Bonny-Muir, and Up in the Morning* (Falkirk: T. Johnston, 1820).
17. Roach, 'Radical Reform Movements', p. 244; *Memoirs and Portraits of One Hundred Glasgow Men*, 2 vols (Glasgow, 1886), vol. 2, pp. 199–202.
18. Mackenzie, *Old Reminiscences*, vol. 1, pp. 261–310.
19. Correspondence from Francis Jeffrey, Lord Advocate, William Patrick Library, Kirkintilloch, Peter Mackenzie Papers, GD185/7.
20. See, for example, the reports of demonstrations across Scotland in the *Scotsman*, 16 and 19 May 1832.
21. *Reformers' Gazette*, 12 May 1832.
22. P. Mackenzie, *The Life of Thomas Muir, Esq., Advocate, younger of Huntershill, near Glasgow* (Glasgow: W. R. McPhun, 1831); Mackenzie, *An Exposure of the Spy System*; P. Mackenzie, *The Trial of James Wilson for High Treason, with an Account of his Execution at Glasgow, September, 1820* (Glasgow: Muir, Gowans & Co., 1832).
23. 'A Copy of the Narrative of James Wilson By Himself', William Patrick Library, Peter Mackenzie Papers, GD185/12/11.
24. Stevenson, *A True Narrative*. See also Roach, 'Radical Reform Movements', pp. 244–8.
25. Ellis and Mac a'Ghobhainn, *The Scottish Insurrection*, pp. 270–1; Stevenson, *A True Narrative*, pp. 13–14.
26. *Reformers' Gazette*, 3 November 1832.
27. Ibid., 10 November 1832; Ellis and Mac a'Ghobhainn, *The Scottish Insurrection*, pp. 289–90.
28. For the resolutions, see H. Cockburn, *Examination of the Trials for Sedition which have hitherto Occurred in Scotland*, 2 vols (Edinburgh: David Douglas, 1888), vol. 2, pp. 247–52; Joseph Hume to Peter Mackenzie, 20 December 1836, William Patrick Library, Peter Mackenzie Papers, GD185/4/18. For an excellent discussion of the monuments to the Scottish martyrs, see A. Tyrell with M. T. Davis, 'Bearding the Tories: The Commemoration of the Scottish Political Martyrs of 1793–4', in Pickering and Tyrell (eds), *Contested Sites*, pp. 25–56.
29. *Scottish Patriot*, 8 February 1840. During George Julian Harney's tour of Scotland, he frequently parodied Mackenzie's position and at Glasgow cries of 'burn the paper of the canting turn-coat' were acted upon. Mackenzie had warned that Chartists would become tools of Tory radicals, A. Wilson, *The Chartist Movement in Scotland* (Manchester: Manchester University Press, 1970), p. 56.

Notes to pages 132–6 175

30. E. Yeo, 'Culture and Constraint in Working Class Movements, 1830–1855', in E. Yeo and S. Yeo (eds), *Popular Culture and Class Conflict 1590–1914: Explorations in the History of Labour and Leisure* (Brighton: Harverster, 1981), pp. 155–86.
31. M. Chase, *Chartism: A New History* (Manchester: Manchester University Press, 2007), p. 102.
32. Wilson, *The Chartist Movement*, p. 63; *Glasgow Saturday Post*, 7 September 1844.
33. *Scottish Patriot*, 4 January 1840.
34. Green, *Trials for High Treason*, vol. 3, pp. 129–37.
35. Fraser, *Memoir of John Fraser*, pp. 20–9; *True Scotsman*, 19 January 1839.
36. Wilson, *The Chartist Movement*, ch. 8; Chase, *Chartism*, pp. 45–56.
37. See, for example, Cockburn, *Examination*, vol. 2, p. 232; *Scotsman*, 14 June 1848.
38. Belchem, 'Republicanism, Popular Constitutionalism and the Radical Platform', pp. 1–32.
39. T. Brotherstone (ed.), *Covenant, Charter and Party: Traditions of Revolt and Protest in Modern Scottish History* (Aberdeen: Aberdeen University Press, 1989); Pentland, 'Scotland and the Creation of a National Reform Movement', pp. 1018–22.
40. *Scottish Patriot*, 21 March 1840.
41. Ibid., 25 January 1840. The Chartists themselves frequently appeared on later platforms and played similar roles, see A. Taylor, '"The Old Chartist": Radical Veterans on the Late Nineteenth- and Early Twentieth-Century Political Platform', *History*, 95 (2010), pp. 458–76.
42. *Scottish Patriot*, 25 January 1840.
43. Ibid., 26 September 1840. This relic reappears intermittently, and seems to have shared similar functions with relics such as the bloodied flags of the Covenanters, which were frequently carried at radical demonstrations; see, for example, Fraser, *Memoir of John Fraser*, p. 30. For political relics in the Irish context see G. Beiner, 'Negotiations of Memory: Rethinking 1798 Commemorations', *Irish Review*, 26 (2000), pp. 62–9.
44. *Glasgow Saturday Post*, 5 September 1846. For the greater part of his speech, Stevenson seems to have relied on the text of his earlier pamphlet.
45. *Scotsman*, 14 June 1848. For a detailed study of this crucial year see J. Saville, *1848: The British State and the Chartist Movement* (Cambridge: Cambridge University Press, 1987).
46. *Scotsman*, 29 July and 2 August 1848; *Glasgow Herald*, 31 July 1848.
47. The letter is reproduced in L. C. Wright, *Scottish Chartism* (Edinburgh: Oliver & Boyd, 1953), pp. 229–30. See also Rankine's speech reported in the *Scotsman*, 26 July 1848.
48. J. Campbell, *Recollections of Radical Times Descriptive of the Last Hour of Baird and Hardie and the Riots in Glasgow, 1848* (Glasgow, 1880).
49. It was a strange claim given that Freir's son evidently followed the trade and became President of the West of Scotland Power Loom Tenters' Society, which had been founded by his father; W. Freer [sic], *My Life and Memories* (Glasgow: Civic Press, 1929), p. 66.
50. White was another of the Bonnymuir radicals who apparently returned to Scotland. Freir stated that he was buried with Baird and Hardie at Sighthill on his death in 1872; Campbell, *Recollections*, pp. 13–15.
51. Freer, *My Life*, p. 12; Campbell, *Recollections*, pp. 8–9.
52. *Scotsman*, 24 July 1847.
53. Campbell, *Recollections*, pp. 9–12.
54. Wilson, *The Chartist Movement*, ch. 17.
55. Chase, *Chartism*, pp. 284–5.

56. *Glasgow Saturday Post*, 14 March 1846.
57. *The Statistical Account of Scotland*, 15 vols (Edinburgh: W. Blackwood, 1834–5), vol. 6, p. 305; I. Bayne, 'Scotland Free or a Desert: A Note on the James Wilson Monument at Strathaven', *Scottish Labour History*, 33 (1998), pp. 116–9.
58. *Glasgow Saturday Post*, 5 September 1846.
59. After prolonged legal and political contest the 90-ft monument had been completed in September 1845; Tyrell and Davis, 'Bearding the Tories', pp. 42–3.
60. The Moore statue, by John Flaxman, was erected in 1819, the Watt statue, by Francis Chantrey, in 1832.
61. G. Blair, *Biographic and Descriptive Sketches of Glasgow Necropolis* (Glasgow: Ogle & Murray, 1857), p. vii. See also R. Scott, *Death By Design: The True Story of the Glasgow Necropolis* (Edinburgh: Black & White, 2005).
62. J. Cookson, 'The Edinburgh and Glasgow Duke of Wellington Statues: Early Nineteenth-Century Unionist-Nationalism as a Tory Project', *Scottish Historical Review*, 83 (2004), pp. 23–40. Both of these statues continue to be sites of contest of varying types. In Glasgow, the city authorities consistently warn about the damage caused by the tradition of the statue always wearing a traffic cone as additional headgear. In Edinburgh, the SNP proposal to replace the Duke of Wellington with a statue of Robert Burns caused some controversy.
63. *Scottish Patriot*, 22 February 1840.
64. Wolffe, *Great Deaths*, chs 1–2.
65. Campbell, *Recollections*, p. 9; Freer, *My Life*, p. 13.
66. Rutherfurd's letter and the inscriptions on the monument are reproduced in Rev. C. Rogers, *Monuments and Monumental Inscriptions in Scotland*, 2 vols (London: Grampian Club, 1871–2), vol. 1, pp. 495–6.
67. Campbell, *Recollections*, p. 12.
68. *Glasgow Saturday Post*, 14 March 1846.
69. See especially the speech delivered by Matthew Cullen in the *Glasgow Saturday Post*, 11 September 1847.
70. Rogers, *Monuments*, vol. 1, p. 430. For a similar process, whereby the radical past was turned into a 'Liberal success story' see A. Taylor, 'Radical Funerals, Burial Customs and Political Commemoration: The Death and Posthumous Life of Ernest Jones', *Humanities Research*, 10 (2003), pp. 29–39. For wider political developments see M. Taylor, *The Decline of British Radicalism, 1847–1860* (Oxford: Clarendon Press, 1995); E. F. Biagini, *Liberty Retrenchment and Reform: Popular Liberalism in the Age of Gladstone, 1860–1880* (Cambridge: Cambridge University Press, 1992).
71. *Lennox Herald*, 13 September 1884. I am very grateful to Dr Mark Nixon for this reference.
72. *Hamilton Advertiser*, 4 November 1865. I am indebted to an article by Ian Bayne for the reference to this, though I disagree with his interpretation that this was simply 'a sop to allay any suspicion of a radical resurgence which a more robust inscription might have stimulated'; Bayne, 'Scotland Free or a Desert', p. 119.
73. For a similar but later event organized by the Trades Union Congress see C. Griffiths, 'Remembering Tolpuddle: Rural History and Commemoration in the Inter-war Labour Movement', *History Workshop Journal*, 44 (1997), pp. 144–69.
74. J. J. Smyth, *Labour in Glasgow 1896–1936: Socialism, Suffrage, Sectarianism* (East Linton: Tuckwell, 2000); A. McKinlay and R. J. Morris (eds), *The ILP on Clydeside, 1893–1932: From Foundation to Disintegration* (Manchester: Manchester University

Press, 1991); C. M. M. Macdonald, *The Radical Thread: Political Change in Scotland. Paisley Politics, 1885–1924* (East Linton: Tuckwell, 2000).
75. G. Morton, 'The First Home Rule Movement in Scotland 1886–1918', in H. T. Dickinson and M. Lynch (eds), *The Challenge to Westminster: Sovereignty, Devolution and Independence* (East Linton: Tuckwell, 2000), pp. 113–22; R. J. Finlay, *A Partnership for Good? Scottish Politics and the Union since 1880* (Edinburgh: John Donald, 1997), chs 1–3; M. G. H. Pittock, *Scottish Nationality* (Basingstoke: Palgrave, 2001), chs 3–4.
76. T. Johnston, *The History of the Working Classes in Scotland* (Glasgow: Forward Publishing Co., 1920), pp. 236–44.
77. Ibid., 240.
78. Executive Council Minute Book (1919–22), 28 May 1920, ML, Independent Labour Party (ILP) Glasgow Federation Archive, G329/9 (SR).
79. W. Stewart, *Fighters for Freedom in Scotland: The Days of Baird and Hardie* (London: Independent Labour Party, 1908), pp. 25–9.
80. Ibid., p. 28.
81. Ibid., 1920 edn, p. 46.
82. 'Bloody Friday', 31 January 1919, was an iconic event of Red Clydeside, when police charged 60,000 demonstrators, who had turned out in support of the Forty Hours' Strike; I. McLean, *The Legend of Red Clydeside* (Edinburgh: John Donald, 1983), ch. 11.
83. *Forward*, 8 February 1919. In the following week, Stewart made similar points in an article on the centenary of Peterloo.
84. Executive Council Minute Book, 16 April and 31 May 1920, ML, ILP Glasgow Federation Archive.
85. *Forward*, 7 August 1920; J. M. Bryson, *Handbook to Strathaven and its Vicinity: With 'The Pioneers: A Tale of the Radical Rising at Strathaven in 1820' and 'Fossils of the District'*, by *J. B. Dalzell* (Strathaven: M. W. Bryson, 1905). *The Pioneers* was originally published in Glasgow in 1843–4 and was reprinted separately a number of times, including in 1920.
86. Executive Council Minute Book, 28 May and 25 June 1920, ML, ILP Glasgow Federation Archive.
87. *Forward*, 26 June, 7 and 28 August 1920.
88. Smyth, *Labour in Glasgow*, ch. 3.
89. *Forward*, 11 September 1920.
90. Smyth, *Labour in Glasgow*, p. 95.
91. I. S. Wood, 'Hope Deferred: Labour in Scotland in the 1920s', in I. Donnachie, C. Harvie and I. S. Wood (eds), *Forward! Labour Politics in Scotland 1888–1898* (Edinburgh: Polygon, 1989), pp. 30–48; I. S. Wood, 'The ILP and the Scottish national question', in D. James, T. Jowitt and K. Laybourn (eds), *The Centennial History of the Independent Labour Party* (Halifax: Ryburn, 1992), pp. 63–74.
92. *Forward*, 5 April 1919.
93. For examples see Wood, 'Hope Deferred', pp. 36–7.
94. Lectures Committee Minute Book (1918–23), 11 August 1920, ML, ILP Glasgow Federation Archive. The ILP inscription was only discovered when the monument was carefully restored during subsequent attempts to commemorate the martyrs, see *Glasgow Herald*, 5 June 1986.
95. *Glasgow Herald*, 8 September 1920.
96. *Forward*, 11 September 1920 claimed an attendance of 5,000 while the *Glasgow Herald*, 8 September 1920 claimed only 2,000 were present.

97. A. Calder, 'The Scottish National War Memorial', in W. Kidd and B. Murdoch (eds), *Memory and Memorials: The Commemorative Century* (Aldershot: Ashgate, 2004), pp. 61–74.
98. The *Glasgow Herald*, for example, had a regular column 'War Memorials', which detailed this activity.
99. *Forward*, 11 September 1920; Lectures Committee Minute Book, 11 August 1920, ML, ILP Glasgow Federation Archive.
100. The banner is in Glasgow's Burrell Collection.
101. *Liberty*, 2 October 1920 cited in R. J. Finlay, *Independent and Free: Scottish Politics and the Origins of the Scottish National Party, 1918–1945* (Edinburgh: John Donald, 1994), pp. 38–9.
102. Finlay, *Independent and Free*, ch. 2.
103. The first of these was H. Shapiro, *Background to Revolt: A Short Study in the Social and Economic Conditions that led to the 'Radical Revolt' on Clydeside in 1820 and of the Part Played in that Rising by James, Perley, Wilson and the Strathaven Weavers* (Glasgow, 1945).
104. F. A. Sherry, *The Rising of 1820* (Glasgow: William Maclellan, 1968), pp. 1–2.
105. Ibid., p. 11.
106. See, for example, Peter Holt's review in *Scottish Labour History Society Journal*, 3 (1970), pp. 34–9.
107. There is a short account of the Committee (which became the 1820 Society) at www.scotsindependent.org/features/orgs/1820.htm [accessed 23/1/2007].
108. N. Easton, 'Message from the new Honorary Secretary', *1820 Society Newsletter* (Summer 1977).
109. Ellis and Mac a'Ghobhainn, *The Scottish Insurrection*, pp. 3–5. See also the new preface to the 2001 edition, pp. xi–xiii.
110. *1820 Society Newsletter* (Summer 1977).
111. Ellis and Mac a'Ghobhainn, *The Scottish Insurrection*, 2001 edn, p. xiii. This notion of 'commemorating the commemorators' had an interesting precedent in the offer made to Edward Freir of 'sharing the martyrs lair', an offer his family refused; Freer, *My Life*, p. 13.
112. A. Busby, 'Activities in 1981', *1820 Society Newsletter* (Winter 1981). During the run-up to the 1979 referendum the slogan was frequently daubed on prominent roadside locations. I am indebted to Ewen Cameron for this information.
113. *Scots Independent*, November 1996.
114. J. C. Halliday, *1820 Rising: The Radical War* (Stirling: Scots Independent, 1993), p. 1. For examples of poems and plays see T. Leonard, 'First Poster Poem against the Criminal Injustice Bill', in his *Access to the Silence: Poems and Posters 1984–2004* (Buckfastleigh: Etruscan Books, 2004), p. 30; T. Lannon, *The Boys from Bonnymuir* (Edinburgh: Albyn Press, 1985); J. Kelman, *Hardie and Baird and other Plays* (London: Secker & Warburg, 1991), pp. 105–80; *Glasgow 800 Theatre Company Present The Rising by Hector MacMillan* (Glasgow: Glasgow 800 Theatre Company, 1975).
115. *The People's Palace History Paintings: A Short Guide* (Glasgow: Glasgow Museums & Art Galleries 1990), pp. 19–25.
116. For these phenomena see P. A. Pickering and A. Tyrell, 'The Public Memorial of Reform: Commemoration and Contestation', in Pickering and Tyrell (eds), *Contested Sites*, p. 5; D. Cannadine, 'The Context, Performance and Meaning of Ritual: The British Monarchy and the 'Invention of Tradition', *c.* 1820–1977', in Hobsbawm and Ranger (eds), *Invention of Tradition*, pp. 133–50.
117. G. Morton, *William Wallace: Man and Myth* (Stroud: Sutton Publishing, 2001).

WORKS CITED

Manuscript Sources

Airdrie Public Library, Mack Family Papers.

British Library, London, Liverpool Papers.

Devon Record Office, Exeter, Addington Papers

Mitchell Library, Glasgow

    Independent Labour Party (ILP) Glasgow Federation Archive.

    Letter Book of Clerk of Police, 1816–25.

    Monteith Correspondence.

National Library of Scotland, Edinburgh

    Diary of C. H. Hutcheson, 1820–48.

    Melville Letters 1817–19.

National Archives, London

    Home Office: Disturbances Correspondence.

    Home Office: Disturbances Entry Books.

    Home Office: Private and Secret Entry Books.

    Home Office (Scotland): Correspondence and Papers.

    Home Office (Scotland): Domestic Entry Books.

    Home Office (Scotland): Criminal Entry Books.

    Court of King's Bench: Notes concerning Searches in the Baga de Secretis for Treason Cases.

National Archives Scotland

    Crown Office Precognitions.

    Memorandum of an Unidentified Kilmarnock Businessman.

William Patrick Library (Kirkintilloch), East Dunbartonshire, Peter Mackenzie Papers.

Newspapers and Periodicals

1820 Society Newsletter.
Black Dwarf.
Blackwood's Edinburgh Magazine.
Caledonian Mercury.
Cap of Liberty.
Cobbett's Weekly Political Register.
Dundee, Perth and Cupar Advertiser.
Eclectic Review.
Edinburgh Review.
Edinburgh Weekly Journal.
Forward.
Glasgow Chronicle.
Glasgow Herald.
Glasgow Saturday Post.
Hone's Reformists' Register.
John Bull.
Lennox Herald.
Manchester Observer.
Medusa.
Morning Chronicle.
Observer.
Quarterly Review.
Reformers' Gazette.
Republican.
Scots Independent.
Scotsman.
Scottish Patriot.
Spirit of the Union.

Primary Sources

An Account of the Proceedings of a Meeting Held at Dundee, on Wednesday, 10th November, 1819 (Newcastle: J. Marshall, 1821).

Account of the Proceedings of the Public Meeting of the Burgesses, Householders, and Inhabitants of the Royal Burgh of Renfrew, held on the 23d November, 1816, Respecting the Distresses of the Country with a Full Report of the Speeches Delivered on that Occasion (Glasgow: W. Lang, 1816).

Address to the Labouring Classes of Britain on the Questions of an Equality in Property and Universal Suffrage (Edinburgh: Doig & Stirling, 1817).

An Address to the Public in Behalf of the Operative Weavers (Kilmarnock: H. Crawford, 1816).

Affairs Being now Settled ABROAD, 'tis High Time to Look at HOME (Glasgow: W. Lang, 1815).

Bamford, S., *Passages in the Life of a Radical*, ed. W. H. Chaloner (Oxford: Oxford University Press, 1984).

Begg, J., *Memoirs of James Begg*, ed. T. Smith, 2 vols (Edinburgh: J. Gemmell, 1885–8).

Better Thole than Be Rash, or, A Crack on the Times (Edinburgh: W. Blackwood, 1819).

Blair, G., *Biographic and Descriptive Sketches of Glasgow Necropolis* (Glasgow: Ogle & Murray, 1857).

The Bonny Bridge of Findhorn, The Radical Battle at Bonny-Muir, and Up in the Morning (Falkirk: T. Johnston, 1820).

Borough Reform; and City Deformity; A Dramatic Poem, 2nd edn (Edinburgh, 1818).

Borough Reform or a Peep at the Glasgow Freemen (Paisley, 1817).

Brayshaw, J., *An Appeal to the People of England, on the Necessity of Parliamentary Reform* (Newcastle: J. Marshall, 1819).

—, *Remarks upon the Character and Conduct of the Men who met under the Name of the British Parliament at the latter End of the Year 1819, with an Account of the Manner in which they Obtained their Seats. To which is Added, a Letter to the Lord Advocate on the State of that Country* (Newcastle: J. Marshall, 1820).

—, 'Account of the Missions', *Republican*, 30 August 1822.

A Brief Argument for those who think Christianity a Fable (Edinburgh: W. Whyte, 1820).

[Bruce, G.], *Patie and Nelly or, The Radical Reformation: A True Tale* (Edinburgh, 1820).

Bryson, J. M., *Handbook to Strathaven and its Vicinity: With 'The Pioneers: A Tale of the Radical Rising at Strathaven in 1820' and 'Fossils of the District', by J. B. Dalzell* (Strathaven: M. W. Bryson, 1905).

Campbell, J., *Recollections of Radical Times Descriptive of the Last Hour of Baird and Hardie and the Riots in Glasgow, 1848* (Glasgow, 1880).

Candidus, *Observations on a Letter by Lucius, to the Rev. Andrew Thomson, Minister of St George's Church* (Edinburgh: Macreadie & Co., 1817).

[Canning, G.], *The Principles and Tendency of Radical Reform* (London: W. Clowes, 1820).

Carlyle, T., *Reminiscences*, ed. J. A. Froude (London, 1881).

Cartwright, J., *Letter, &c.* (London, 1815).

—, *Life and Correspondence of Major Cartwright*, ed. F. D. Cartwright, 2 vols (London, 1826).

Chalmers, R., *Autobiography of Robert Chalmers, the Old Social and Political Reformer* (Dundee, 1872).

Chalmers, T., *The Importance of Civil Government to Society, and the Duty of Christians in Regard to It. A Sermon Preached in St. John's Church, Glasgow, on Sabbath, 30th April, 1820*, 2nd edn (Glasgow: Chalmers & Collins, 1820).

—, 'A Sermon Delivered in the Tron Church, Glasgow, on Wednesday, Nov. 19, 1817, the Day of the Funeral of Her Royal Highness the Princess Charlotte of Wales', in *The Works of Thomas Chalmers D. D., Minister of the Tron Church, Glasgow*, 3 vols (Hartford, 1822), pp. 377–410.

Chronicles of the Isles (Glasgow: W. Duncan, n.d.).

Cobbett, W. (ed.), *The Parliamentary History of England, from the Earliest Period to the Year 1803*, 36 vols (London, 1806–20).

Cockburn, H., *Memorials of his Time* (Edinburgh: Adam & Charles Black, 1856).

—, *Examination of the Trials for Sedition which have hitherto Occurred in Scotland*, 2 vols (Edinburgh: David Douglas, 1888).

Comic Poems of Rustic Scenes in Scotland, at the Times to which they Refer (Edinburgh, 1817).

Cooper, W. S., *A History of the Ayrshire Yeomanry Cavalry* (Edinburgh: David Douglas, 1881).

Creevey, T., *The Creevey Papers: A Selection from the Correspondence and Diaries of the Late Thomas Creevey, M. P.*, ed. H. Maxwell, 3rd edn (London: J. Murray, 1912).

[Croker, J. W.], *A Letter from the King to his People*, 13th edn (London: W. Sams, 1820).

[Dickson, H.], *The Criterion, or Richmond's Narrative Exposed. Being a Correct Detail of the Whole Proceedings as Delivered by the Delegates of Those Treasonable Societies said to Exist in Glasgow and its Suburbs in the Years 1816 and 1817* (Glasgow, 1825).

Douglas, N., *An Address to the Judges and Jury, in a Case of Alleged Sedition, on 26th May, 1817, which was Intended to be Delivered before Passing Sentence* (Glasgow, 1817).

—, *Strictures on the Author's Trial, Declaration Before the Sheriff, Remarks on the Crown Evidence, and some Important Information Respecting the Cause of Reform* (Glasgow, 1818).

Dreadful Fray, which Took Place at Culrain near Gladsfield in Ross-shire: With an Account of the Killed and Wounded on Both Sides (n.p., n.d.).

Duncan, Rev. G. J. C., *Memoir of the Reverend Henry Duncan, Minister of Ruthwell* (Edinburgh: W. Oliphant & Sons, 1848).

Duncan, Rev. H., *The Cottage Fireside; or, The Parish School Master: A Moral Tale*, 2nd edn (Edinburgh, 1815).

—, *The Young South Country Weaver; or, A Journey to Glasgow: A Tale for the Radicals*, 2nd edn (Edinburgh: Waugh & Innes, 1821).

Ewing, G., *The Testimony of God Against Massacre and Rapine: A Sermon, Preached in Nile Street Meeting-House, on Sabbath the Ninth of April, 1820* (Glasgow, 1820).

Fairly, A., *A Half Hour's Crack with a Glasgow Radical Reformer: Rehearsed in a Letter to a Friend* (Edinburgh: W. Whyte, 1820).

Fair Play, *Marvellous and Disinterested Patriotism of Certain Learned Whigs, Illustrated in Prose and Rhyme, for the Use of the 'Inhabitants of Edinburgh'*, 3rd edn (Edinburgh: D. Stevenson & Co., 1820).

The Following is a Correct Account of the Trial and Sentence of Henry Hunt, Esq., James Moorhouse, John T. Saxton, George Swift, Robert Jones, Robert Wilde, Joseph Johnson, Joseph Healey, John Knight and Samuel Bamford: For Unlawfully, Maliciously, and Seditiously Meeting and Assembling (Glasgow: M. Robertson, 1820).

A Forfarshire Justice of Peace, *A Conversation on the Causes of our Present Distress and on the Remedies for it* (Dundee, 1817).

Fraser, J. R., *Memoir of John Fraser, Newfield, Johnstone* (Paisley: T. & J. Cook, 1879).

Freer, W., *My Life and Memories* (Glasgow: Civic Press, 1929).

Gilchrist, J. B., *Parliamentary Reform, on Constitutional Principles; or, British Loyalty against Continental Royalty, the Whole Host of Sacerdotal Inquisitors in Europe, and every Iniquitous Judge, Corrupt Ruler, Venal Corporation, Rotten Borough, Slavish Editor, or Jacobitical Toad-Eater within the British Empire* (Glasgow: W. Lang, 1815).

Glasgow 800 Theatre Company Present The Rising by Hector MacMillan (Glasgow: Glasgow 800 Theatre Company, 1975).

Green, C. J., *Trials for High Treason, in Scotland, under a Special Commission, held at Stirling, Glasgow, Dumbarton, Paisley, and Ayr, in the year 1820*, 3 vols (Edinburgh: Manners & Miller, 1825).

Hamilton, J., *Poems, Sketches and Essays*, 2nd edn (Glasgow: J. Maclehose, 1885).

Hanna, Rev. W., *Memoirs of Thomas Chalmers, D.D. LL.D.*, 2 vols (Edinburgh: T. Constable & Co., 1854).

Hansard, T. C. (ed.), *The Parliamentary Debates from the Year 1803 to the Present Time* (London, 1812–).

Hints Addressed to Radical Reformers (Glasgow: W. Lang, 1819).

Howell, T. J. (ed.), *Complete Collection of State Trials and Proceedings for High Treason and other Crimes and Misdemeanours*, 33 vols (London, 1809–28).

Howie, J., *Historical Account of the Town of Ayr for the Last Fifty Years* (Kilmarnock: J. McKie, 1861).

An Inhabitant, *A Short Address to the Weavers of Paisley and the Neighbourhood: (Suggesting a Plan for their Relief)* (Paisley: S. Young, 1819).

Journals of the House of Commons, 119 vols (London, 1628–).

Kelman, J., *Hardie and Baird and other Plays* (London: Secker & Warburg, 1991).

Lang, A., *The Life and Letters of John Gibson Lockhart*, 2 vols (London: J. C. Nimmo, 1897).

Lannon, T., *The Boys from Bonnymuir* (Edinburgh: Albyn Press, 1985).

The Late Elections. An Impartial Statement of all Proceedings Connected with the Progress and Result of the Late Elections (London: Pinnock & Maunder, 1818).

Leonard, T., 'First Poster Poem against the Criminal Injustice Bill', in T. Leonard, *Access to the Silence: Poems and Posters 1984–2004* (Buckfastleigh: Etruscan Books, 2004), p.30.

[McCrie, T.], *Free Thoughts on the Late Religious Celebration of the Funeral of her Royal Highness the Princess Charlotte of Wales; and on the Discussion to which it has given rise in Edinburgh. By Scoto-Britannus* (Edinburgh: Macreadie & Co., 1817).

[McGrugar, T.], *Letters of Zeno to the Citizens of Edinburgh on the Present Mode of Electing a Member of Parliament for the City* (Edinburgh, 1783).

McKay, A., *Burns and his Kilmarnock Friends* (Kilmarnock, 1874).

Mackenzie, P., *The Life of Thomas Muir, Esq., Advocate, younger of Huntershill, near Glasgow* (Glasgow: W. R. McPhun, 1831).

—, *The Trial of James Wilson for High Treason, with an Account of his Execution at Glasgow, September, 1820* (Glasgow: Muir, Gowans & Co., 1832).

[—], *An Exposure of the Spy System Pursued in Glasgow During the Years 1816–20* (Glasgow: Muir, Gowans & Co., 1832).

—, *Old Reminiscences of Glasgow and the West of Scotland*, 3rd edn, 2 vols (Glasgow: J. P. Forrester, 1890).

Margarot, M., *Proposal for a Grand National Jubilee; Restoring to Every Man his own, and thereby Extinguishing both Want and War* (Sheffield, 1812).

—, *Thoughts on Revolution* (Harlow, 1812).

Mason, A., *An Inquiry into the Times that shall be Fulfilled at Antichrist's Fall* (Glasgow, 1818).

[Maxwell, J.], *A Letter Addressed to the Honest Reformers of Scotland; with Remarks on the Poor Rates, Corn Law, Religious Establishment, Right of Property, Equality of Ranks, and Revolution* (Glasgow: A. & J. M. Duncan, 1819).

Memoirs and Portraits of One Hundred Glasgow Men, 2 vols (Glasgow: J. Maclehose, 1886).

Nicholson, A., *Memoirs of Adam Black* (Edinburgh: Adam & Charles Black, 1885).

Nightingale, J., *Memoirs of her Late Majesty, Queen Caroline, Consort of King George the Fourth*, 3 vols (London: J. Robins & Co. Albion Press, 1821–2).

Official Report of Scottish Parliament, 5 September 2001, col. 2251. Online at http://www.scottish.parliament.uk/business/officialReports/meetingsParliament/or-01/sor0905-01.htm [accessed 8/2/2008].

On the Use and Abuse of Charity; Earnestly Addressed to Associations for Relief of the Distressed throughout the Country (Edinburgh: W. Blackwood, 1819).

[Parkhill, J.], *The Life and Opinions of Arthur Sneddon* (Paisley: J. Cook, 1860).

Paterson, J., *Autobiographical Reminiscences: Including Recollections of the Radical Years, 1819–20, in Kilmarnock* (Glasgow, 1871).

Political Death of Mr William Cobbett (Edinburgh: W. Blackwood, 1820).

Populis, A., *Letter Addressed to Sir Thomas Cochrane, Commonly Called Lord Cochrane, on his Conduct in the Meeting at the London Tavern, on the 29th July 1816, Met for the Purpose of Taking into Consideration the Distress of the Country, and the Means of Relief* (Paisley: R. Smith, 1816).

A Presbyterian, *Vindication of the Ministers of the Church of Scotland, who have Prayed for the Queen by Name, Notwithstanding the Order in Council on that Subject*, 2nd edn (Edinburgh: D. Brown, 1820).

Proceedings &c [of meeting at Newmilns] (Glasgow, n.d.).

The Proceedings of a Meeting that took place at Linktown of Kirkcaldy, on the third November, 1819, to take into Consideration the Proceedings at Manchester (Edinburgh, 1819).

Proclamation by the Sheriff of Renfrewshire, and by the Provost and Magistrates of Paisley ... 9th Sept. 1819 (Paisley, 1819).

The Queen's Answer to the Address of the Loyal Inhabitants of Paisley, Presented to Her Majesty 18th Oct. 1820 (Paisley: J. Weir, 1820).

Reid, W. H., *Memoirs of the Life of Colonel Wardle* (London: T. Kelly, 1809).

Report of the Meeting Held in the Relief Church, Kilbarchan on 21st December 1816, to Consider the Distresses of the Country, and the Propriety of Petitioning the Prince Regent and the Legislature for Reform (Paisley, 1817).

Report of the Meeting Held in the Relief Church, Paisley, On Saturday the 5th October, 1816, to Consider the Present Distresses of the Country, their Causes, and Probable Remedies (Paisley: R. Smith, 1816).

Report of the Proceedings of the Crawfordsdyke Meeting Convened for the Purpose of Taking into Consideration the Propriety of Petitioning the Prince Regent on the Distresses of the Country (Greenock: Donaldson & Macfarlan, 1817).

Richmond, A. B., *Narrative of the Condition of the Manufacturing Population; and the Proceedings of Government which led to the State Trials in Scotland* (London: J. Miller, 1824).

Rodger, A., *Poems and Songs, Humorous and Satirical* (Glasgow: D. Robertson, 1838).

Rogers, Rev. C., *Monuments and Monumental Inscriptions in Scotland*, 2 vols (London: Grampian Club, 1871–2).

Sawney and Donnel's Exploits at Waterloo: To which are Added, My Country and my Lass, The Broadsword of Scotland and We've aye been Provided for (Falkirk: T. Johnston, 1817).

Scott, J., *The Present Revolutions in Europe, and other Signs of the Times, compared with Scripture Predictions and History, Shewing that in 1822 the Regeneration of the European Dynasties will be completed* (Glasgow: W. Lang, 1820).

—, *Answers to the Queries, by the Author of the Pamphlet Entitled the "Present Revolutions in Europe, and other Signs of the Times"* (Glasgow: W. Lang, n.d.).

Scott, W., *The Letters of Sir Walter Scott*, ed. H. J. C. Grierson, 12 vols (London: Constable, 1932–7).

—, *The Visionary*, ed. P. Garside (Cardiff: University College Cardiff Press, 1984).

A Second Brief Argument for those who Think Christianity a Fable (Edinburgh: W. Whyte, 1820).

Shuttle, T., *The Marrow of Radical Reform; or A Dialogue between Tam Shuttle and John Turnip* (Glasgow: T. Ogilvie, 1819).

A Society of Clergymen in Dumfries-shire, *The Scotch Cheap Repository Tracts: Containing Moral Tales, for the Instruction of the Young*, 2nd edn (Edinburgh: Oliphant, Waugh & Innes, 1815).

The Statistical Account of Scotland, 15 vols (Edinburgh: W. Blackwood, 1834–5).

Stevenson, J., *A True Narrative of the Radical Rising in Strathaven, in Vindication of the Parties Concerned, as also of the Martyred James Wilson, in Answer to McKenzie's Exposure of the 'Spy System,' and the Rev. Mr Proudfoot, in the 'Statistics of Scotland'* (Glasgow: W. & W. Miller, 1835).

[Struthers, J.], *An Essay on the State of the Labouring Poor, with some Hints for its Improvement*, 2nd edn (Glasgow: W. Turnbull, 1816).

Telfer, A., *An Illustration of the Mistaken Notions Entertained with Respect to the Price of Provisions, and the Oppression of Taxation* (Glasgow: J. Steven, 1817).

Thaumaturgus; or, the Wonders of the Magic Lantern; Exhibiting at one View the Distresses of the Country, and some of the Consequences of the Late Just and Necessary War; in which some Living Characters are set off in a Stile Entirely New (Edinburgh, 1816).

Trial of Alexander McLaren and Thomas Baird, before the High Court of Justiciary, at Edinburgh, on the 5th and 7th March 1817, for Sedition (Edinburgh: J. Robertson, 1817).

Trial of Andrew M'Kinley [sic], *before the High Court of Justiciary, at Edinburgh, on the 26th July 1817, for Administering Unlawful Oaths: With the Antecedent Proceedings against William Edgar, John Keith, and Andrew M'Kinley. Taken in Short Hand, by John Dow* (Edinburgh: Manners & Miller, 1818).

Trial of Henry Hunt esq., Jno. Knight, Jos. Johnson, Jno. Thacker Saxton, Samuel Bamford, Jos. Healey. James Moorhouse, Robert Jones, Geo Swift, and Robert Wylde for an Alleged Conspiracy to Overturn the Government (London: T. Dolby, 1820).

Trial of the Rev. Niel Douglas, before the High Court of Justiciary, at Edinburgh, on the 26th May 1817, for Sedition (Edinburgh: J. Robertson, 1817).

Turner, J., *Recollections of James Turner, Esq., of Thrushgrove*, ed. J. Smith (Glasgow, 1858).

Secondary Sources

Aspinall, A., *Politics and the Press c.1780–1850* (London: Home & van Thal, 1949).

Barrell, J., *Imagining the King's Death: Figurative Treason, Fantasies of Regicide 1793–1796* (Oxford: Oxford University Press, 2000).

—, 'Radicalism, Visual Culture, and Spectacle in the 1790s', *Romanticism on the Net*, 46 (May 2007), http://www.erudit.org/revue/ron/2007/v/n46/016131ar.html [accessed 14/10/2010].

Bayne, I., 'Scotland Free or a Desert: A Note on the James Wilson Monument at Strathaven', *Scottish Labour History*, 33 (1998), pp. 116–19.

Beiner, G., 'Negotiations of Memory: Rethinking 1798 Commemorations', *Irish Review*, 26 (2000), pp. 62–9.

—, *Remembering the Year of the French: Irish Folk History and Social Memory* (Madison, WI: University of Wisconsin Press, 2007).

Belchem, J., 'Republicanism, Popular Constitutionalism and the Radical Platform in Early Nineteenth-Century England', *Social History*, 6 (1981), pp. 1–32.

—, *'Orator' Hunt: Henry Hunt and English Working-Class Radicalism* (Oxford: Clarendon Press, 1985).

Ben-Amos, A., *Funerals, Politics, and Memory in Modern France, 1789–1996* (Oxford: Oxford University Press, 2000).

Biagini, E. F., *Liberty Retrenchment and Reform: Popular Liberalism in the Age of Gladstone, 1860–1880* (Cambridge: Cambridge University Press, 1992).

Bowen, H. V., *War and British Society 1688–1815* (Cambridge: Cambridge University Press, 1998).

Brock, M., *The Great Reform Act* (London: Hutchinson & Co., 1973).

Brotherstone, T. (ed.), *Covenant, Charter and Party: Traditions of Revolt and Protest in Modern Scottish History* (Aberdeen: Aberdeen University Press, 1989).

Brown, F. K., *Fathers of the Victorians: The Age of Wilberforce* (Cambridge: Cambridge University Press, 1961).

Bush, M., *The Casualties of Peterloo* (Lancaster: Carnegie, 2005).

Calder, A., 'The Scottish National War Memorial', in W. Kidd and B. Murdoch (eds), *Memory and Memorials: The Commemorative Century* (Aldershot: Ashgate, 2004), pp. 61–74.

Calhoun, C., *The Question of Class Struggle: Social Foundations of Popular Radicalism during the Industrial Revolution* (Oxford: Blackwell, 1982).

Cannadine, D. 'The Context, Performance and Meaning of Ritual: The British Monarchy and the "Invention of Tradition", c. 1820–1977', in Hobsbawm and Ranger (eds), *Invention of Tradition*, pp. 133–50.

Chandler, J., *England in 1819: The Politics of Literary Culture and the Case of Romantic Historicism* (Chicago, IL: University of Chicago Press, 1999).

Chase, M., *The People's Farm: English Radical Agrarianism 1775–1840* (Oxford: Clarendon Press, 1988).

—, 'From Millennium to Anniversary: The Concept of Jubilee in Late Eighteenth- and Nineteenth-Century England', *Past and Present*, 129 (1990), pp. 132–47.

—, *Chartism: A New History* (Manchester: Manchester University Press, 2007).

Christodoulou, J., 'The Glasgow Universalist Church and Scottish Radicalism from the French Revolution to Chartism: A Theology of Liberation', *Journal of Ecclesiastical History*, 43 (1992), pp. 608–13.

Claeys, G., *The French Revolution Debate in Britain: The Origins of Modern Politics* (Basingstoke: Palgrave Macmillan, 2007).

Clark, A., 'Queen Caroline and the Sexual Politics of Popular Culture in London, 1820', *Representations*, 31 (1990), pp. 31–68.

—, *The Struggle for the Breeches: Gender and the Making of the British Working Class* (Berkeley, CA: University of California Press, 1995).

—, *Scandal: The Sexual Politics of the British Constitution* (Princeton, NJ: Princeton University Press, 2004).

Clark, J. C. D., *Our Shadowed Present: Modernism, Postmodernism and History* (London: Atlantic Books, 2003).

Clive, J., *Scotch Reviewers: The 'Edinburgh Review' 1802–1815* (London: Faber & Faber, 1957).

Colley, L., 'The Reach of the State, the Appeal of the Nation: Mass Arming and Political Culture in the Napoleonic Wars', in L. Stone (ed.), *An Imperial State at War: Britain from 1689 to 1815* (London: Routledge, 1994), pp. 165–84.

Connerton, P., *How Societies Remember* (Cambridge: Cambridge University Press, 1989).

Connolly, S., '"Under the Banners of Death": Iconoclasm, Iconophobia and the Scopic Vocabularies of English Popular Politics, 1789–1821 (PhD dissertation, University of Manchester, 2009).

Cookson, J. E., *Lord Liverpool's Administration, 1815–1822* (Edinburgh and London: Scottish Academic Press, 1975).

—, *The British Armed Nation, 1793–1815* (Oxford: Clarendon Press, 1997).

—, 'The Edinburgh and Glasgow Duke of Wellington Statues: Early Nineteenth-Century Unionist-Nationalism as a Tory Project', *Scottish Historical Review*, 83 (2004), pp. 23–40.

Cowan, E. J., and R. J. Finlay (eds), *Scottish History: The Power of the Past* (Edinburgh: Edinburgh University Press, 2002).

Cowan, R. M. W., *The Newspaper in Scotland: A Study of its First Expansion, 1816–1860* (Glasgow: George Outram & Co. Ltd, 1946).

Daunton, M., *Trusting Leviathan: The Politics of Taxation in Britain, 1799–1914* (Cambridge: Cambridge University Press, 2001).

—, 'The Fiscal-Military State and the Napoleonic Wars: Britain and France Compared', in D. Cannadine (ed.), *Trafalgar in History: A Battle and its Afterlife* (Basingstoke: Palgrave Macmillan, 2006), pp. 18–43.

Davidson, N., 'Class Consciousness and National Consciousness in the Scottish General Strike of 1820', in K. Flett and D. Renton (eds), *New Approaches to Socialist History* (London: New Clarion Press, 2003), pp. 133–48.

Davis, M. T., 'Prosecution and Radical Discourse during the 1790s: The Case of the Scottish Sedition Trials', *International Journal of the Sociology of Law*, 33 (2005), pp. 148–58.

—, 'The Mob Club? The London Corresponding Society and the Politics of Civility in the 1790s', in M. T. Davis and P. A. Pickering (eds), *Unrespectable Radicals? Popular Politics in the Age of Reform* (Aldershot: Ashgate, 2008), pp. 21–40.

Dickinson, H. T., 'Popular Loyalism in Britain in the 1790s', in E. Hellmuth (ed.), *The Transformation of Political Culture: England and Germany in the Late Eighteenth Century* (Oxford: Oxford University Press, 1990), pp. 503–33.

Dinwiddy, J. R., 'Luddism and Politics in the Northern Counties', *Social History*, 4 (1979), pp. 33–63.

—, *From Luddism to the First Reform Bill* (Oxford: Basil Blackwell, 1986).

Dolan, A., *Commemorating the Irish Civil War: History and Memory, 1923–2000* (Cambridge: Cambridge University Press, 2003).

Donnelly, F. K., 'The General Rising of 1820: A Study of Social Conflict in the Industrial Revolution' (PhD dissertation, University of Sheffield, 1975).

—, 'The Scottish Rising of 1820: A Reinterpretation', *Scottish Tradition*, 6 (1976), pp. 27–37.

Eckersley, R. E., 'The Drum Major of Sedition: The Political Life and Career of John Cartwright' (PhD dissertation, University of Manchester, 1999).

—, 'Of Radical Design: John Cartwright and the Redesign of the Reform Campaign, *c.*1800–1811', *History*, 89 (2004), pp. 560–80.

Edwards, O. D., *Burke and Hare*, 2nd edn (Edinburgh: Mercat Press, 1993).

Eley, G., 'Nations, Publics, and Political Cultures: Placing Habermas in the Nineteenth Century', in C. Calhoun (ed.), *Habermas and the Public Sphere* (Cambridge, MA: MIT Press, 1992), pp. 289–339.

Ellis, P. B., and S. Mac a'Ghobhainn, *The Scottish Insurrection of 1820* (London: Victor Gollancz, 1970).

—, *The Scottish Insurrection of 1820*, new edn (1970; Edinburgh: John Donald, 2001).

Emsley, C., *British Society and the French Wars, 1793–1815* (London: Macmillan, 1979).

Epstein, J., 'Understanding the Cap of Liberty: Symbolic Practice and Social Conflict in Early-Nineteenth-Century England', *Past and Present*, 122 (1989), pp. 75–118.

—, 'The Constitutional Idiom: Radical Reasoning, Rhetoric and Action in Early Nineteenth-Century England', *Journal of Social History*, 23 (1990), pp. 553–74.

—, 'Narrating Liberty's Defense: T. J. Wooler and the Law', in his *Radical Expression: Political Language, Ritual, and Symbol in England, 1790–1850*, pp. 29–69.

—, *Radical Expression: Political Language, Ritual, and Symbol in England, 1790–1850* (Oxford: Oxford University Press, 1994).

—, '"Our Real Constitution": Trial Defence and Radical Memory in the Age of Revolution', in Vernon (ed.), *Re-reading the Constitution*, pp. 22–51.

Esdaile, C., *Spain in the Liberal Age: From Constitution to Civil War, 1808–1939* (Oxford: Blackwell, 2000).

Fagerstrom, D. I., 'Scottish Opinion and the American Revolution', *William and Mary Quarterly*, 3rd series, 11 (1954), pp. 252–75.

Fentress J., and C. Wickham, *Social Memory* (Oxford: Blackwell, 1992).

Finlay, R. J., *Independent and Free: Scottish Politics and the Origins of the Scottish National Party, 1918–1945* (Edinburgh: John Donald, 1994).

—, *A Partnership for Good? Scottish Politics and the Union since 1880* (Edinburgh: John Donald, 1997).

Fisher, D. R. (ed.), *The History of Parliament: The House of Commons 1820–1832*, 7 vols (Cambridge: Cambridge University Press, 2009).

Fontana, B., *Rethinking the Politics of Commercial Society: The 'Edinburgh Review' 1802–32* (Cambridge: Cambridge University Press, 1985).

Foster, R., 'Remembering 1798', in I. McBride (ed.), *History and Memory in Modern Ireland* (Cambridge: Cambridge University Press, 2001), pp. 67–94.

Fox, K. O., *Making Life Possible: A Study of Military Aid to the Civil Power in Regency England* (Kineton, K. O. Fox, 1982).

Fraser, F., *The Unruly Queen: The Life of Queen Caroline* (London: Macmillan, 1996).

Fraser, P., 'Public Petitioning and Parliament before 1832', *History*, 46 (1961), pp. 195–211.

Fry, M, 'The Whig Interpretation of Scottish History', in I. Donnachie and C. Whatley (eds), *The Manufacture of Scottish History* (Edinburgh: Polygon, 1992), pp. 72–89.

Fulcher, J. C. S. J., 'Contests over Constitutionalism: The Faltering of Reform in England, 1816–1824' (PhD dissertation, University of Cambridge, 1993).

—, 'The Loyalist Response to the Queen Caroline Agitations', *Journal of British Studies*, 34 (1995), pp. 481–502.

Gash, N., 'After Waterloo: British Society and the Legacy of the Napoleonic Wars', *Transactions of the Royal Historical Society*, 5th series, 28 (1978), pp. 145–57.

Gilmartin, K., *Print Politics: The Press and Radical Opposition in Early Nineteenth-Century England* (Cambridge: Cambridge University Press, 1996).

—, 'In the Theater of Counterrevolution: Loyalist Association and Conservative Opinion in the 1790s', *Journal of British Studies*, 41 (2002), pp. 291–328.

Griffiths, C., 'Remembering Tolpuddle: Rural History and Commemoration in the Inter-war Labour Movement', *History Workshop Journal*, 44 (1997), pp. 144–69.

Halliday, J. C., *1820 Rising: The Radical War* (Stirling: Scots Independent, 1993).

Harling, P., 'The Duke of York Affair (1809) and the Complexities of Wartime Patriotism', *Historical Journal*, 39 (1996), pp. 963–84.

—, 'The Law of Libel and the Limits of Repression, 1790–1832', *Historical Journal*, 44 (2001), pp. 107–34.

Harris, B., 'Scottish-English Connections in British Radicalism in the 1790s', in T. C. Smout (ed.), *Anglo-Scottish relations from 1603 to 1900*, Proceedings of the British Academy, 127 (Oxford: Oxford University Press, 2005), pp. 189–212.

— (ed.), *Scotland in the Age of the French Revolution* (Edinburgh: John Donald, 2005).

—, 'Scotland's Newspapers, the French Revolution and Domestic Radicalism (*c.* 1789–1794)', *Scottish Historical Review*, 84 (2005), pp. 38–62.

—, *The Scottish People and the French Revolution* (London: Pickering & Chatto, 2008).

Harrison, J. F. C., *The Second Coming: Popular Millenarianism 1780–1850* (London: Routledge, 1979).

Hay, W. A., *The Whig Revival, 1808–1830* (Basingstoke: Palgrave Macmillan, 2005).

Hayton, D. W. (ed.), *The History of Parliament: The House of Commons, 1690–1715*, 5 vols (Cambridge: Cambridge University Press, 2002).

Haywood, I., *The Revolution in Popular Literature: Print, Politics and the People, 1790–1860* (Cambridge: Cambridge University Press, 2004).

—, *Bloody Romanticism: Spectacular Violence and the Politics of Representation, 1776–1832* (London: Palgrave Macmillan, 2006).

Hendrikson, A., 'Loyalism in Scotland, 1816–1820' (MSc dissertation, University of Edinburgh, 2007).

Hobsbawm, E.. and T. Ranger (eds), *The Invention of Tradition* (Cambridge: Cambridge University Press, 1983).

Hole, R., 'British Counter-Revolutionary Popular Propaganda in the 1790s', in C. Jones (ed.), *Britain and Revolutionary France: Conflict, Subversion and Propaganda* (Exeter: University of Exeter, 1983), pp. 53–69.

Holt, P., 'Review of The Scottish Insurrection', *Scottish Labour History Society Journal*, 3 (1970), pp. 34–9.

Hone, J. A., *For the Cause of Truth: Radicalism in London, 1796–1821* (Oxford: Clarendon Press, 1982).

Hoock, H. (ed.), *History, Commemoration and National Preoccupation: Trafalgar 1805–2005*, British Academy Occasional Paper, 8 (Oxford: Oxford University Press, 2007).

Johnston, T., *The History of the Working Classes in Scotland* (Glasgow: Forward Publishing Co., 1920).

Jones, G. S., 'Rethinking Chartism', in his *Languages of Class: Studies in English Working Class History, 1832–1982* (Cambridge: Cambridge University Press, 1982), pp. 90–178.

Kidd, C., 'The English Cult of Wallace and the Blending of Nineteenth-Century Britain', in E. J. Cowan (ed.), *The Wallace Book* (Edinburgh: John Donald, 2007), pp. 136–50.

Laqueur, T. W., 'The Queen Caroline Affair: Politics as Art in the Reign of George IV', *Journal of Modern History*, 54 (1982), pp. 417–66.

Lawrence, J., 'Political History', in S. Berger, H. Feldner, K. Passmore (eds), *Writing History: Theory and Practice* (London: Arnold, 2003), pp. 183–202.

Lee, S. M., *George Canning and Liberal Toryism, 1801–1827* (Woodbridge: Boydell & Brewer, 2008).

Lobban, M., 'From Seditious Libel to Unlawful Assembly: Peterloo and the Changing Face of Political Crime, 1770–1820', *Oxford Journal of Legal Studies*, 10 (1990), pp. 307–52.

Logue, K., *Popular Disturbances in Scotland, 1780–1815* (Edinburgh: John Donald, 1979).

McCalman, I., *Radical Underworld: Prophets, Revolutionaries, and Pornographers in London, 1795–1840* (Cambridge: Cambridge University Press, 1988).

—, 'New Jerusalems: Prophecy, Dissent and Radical Culture in England, 1786–1830', in K. Haakonssen (ed.), *Enlightenment and Religion: Rational Dissent in Eighteenth-Century Britain* (Cambridge: Cambridge University Press, 1996), pp. 312–35.

McCrone, D., *The Sociology of Nationalism: Tomorrow's Ancestors* (London: Routledge, 1998).

McLean, I., *The Legend of Red Clydeside* (Edinburgh: John Donald, 1983).

Macdonald, C. M. M., *The Radical Thread: Political Change in Scotland. Paisley Politics, 1885–1924* (East Linton: Tuckwell Press, 2000).

—, 'Abandoned and Beastly? The Queen Caroline Affair in Scotland', in Y. Galloway Brown and R. Ferguson (eds), *Twisted Sisters: Women Crime and Deviance in Scotland since 1400* (East Linton: Tuckwell Press, 2002), pp. 101–13.

Macfarlane, A., and M. Macfarlane, *The Scottish Radicals Tried and Transported for Treason in 1820*, rev. edn (Stevenage: SPA, 1981).

McKinlay, A., and R. J. Morris (eds), *The ILP on Clydeside, 1893–1932: From Foundation to Disintegration* (Manchester: Manchester University Press, 1991).

Macleod, E. V., 'The Scottish Opposition Whigs and the French Revolution', in B. Harris (ed.), *Scotland in the Age of the French Revolution* (Edinburgh: John Donald, 2005), pp. 79–98.

Magnusson, M., et al., *The Glorious Privilege: The History of 'The Scotsman'* (London: Thomas Nelson & Sons, 1967).

Mandler, P., *Aristocratic Government in the Age of Reform: Whigs and Liberals, 1830–1852* (Oxford: Oxford University Press, 1990).

Marwick, A. (ed.), *Total War and Social Change* (Basingstoke: Macmillan, 1988).

Mather, F. C., 'Army Pensioners and the Maintenance of Civil Order in Early Nineteenth Century England', *Journal of the Society of Army Historical Research*, 36 (1958), pp. 110–24.

Mathieson, W. L., *Church and Reform in Scotland 1797–1843* (Glasgow: James Maclehose & Sons, 1916).

Meikle, H., *Scotland and the French Revolution* (Glasgow: James Maclehose & Sons, 1912).

Miller, N. C., 'John Cartwright and Radical Parliamentary Reform, 1808–1819', *English Historical Review*, 83 (1968), pp. 705–28.

Mitchell, A., *The Whigs in Opposition 1815–1830* (Oxford: Clarendon Press, 1967).

Mitchell, M. J., *The Irish in the West of Scotland 1797–1848* (Edinburgh: John Donald, 1998).

Monod, P. K., 'Dangerous Merchandise: Smuggling, Jacobitism and Commercial Culture in Southeast England, 1690–1760', *Journal of British Studies*, 30 (1991), pp. 150–82.

Morton, G., 'The First Home Rule Movement in Scotland 1886–1918', in H. T. Dickinson and M. Lynch (eds), *The Challenge to Westminster: Sovereignty, Devolution and Independence* (East Linton: Tuckwell Press, 2000), pp. 113–22.

—, *William Wallace: Man and Myth* (Stroud: Sutton Publishing, 2001).

Mosse, G. L., *The Nationalization of the Masses: Political Symbolism and Mass Movements in Germany from the Napoleonic Wars through the Third Reich* (New York, NJ: H. Fertig, 1975).

Murray, N., *The Scottish Handloom Weavers, 1790–1850: A Social History* (Edinburgh: John Donald, 1978).

Myerly, S. H., *British Military Spectacle: From the Napoleonic Wars through the Crimea* (Cambridge, MA: Harvard University Press, 1996).

Navickas, K., 'The Search for "General Ludd": The Mythology of Luddism', *Social History*, 30 (2005), pp. 281–95.

—, *Loyalism and Radicalism in Lancashire, 1798–1815* (Oxford: Oxford University Press, 2009).

Nora, P. (ed.), *Realms of Memory: Rethinking the French Past*, trans. A. Goldhammer, 3 vols (New York: Columbia University Press, 1996–8).

O'Brien, P. K., 'Public Finance in the Wars with France, 1793–1815', in H. T. Dickinson (ed.), *Britain and the French Revolution, 1789–1815* (New York: St Martin's Press, 1989), pp. 165–87.

O'Gorman, F., 'The Paine Burnings of 1792–1793', *Past and Present*, 193 (2006), pp. 111–56.

O'Keefe, T. J., 'The 1898 Efforts to Celebrate the United Irishmen: The '98 Centennial', *Éire-Ireland*, 23 (1988), pp. 51–73.

Omond, G. W. T., *The Lord Advocates of Scotland*, 2 vols (Edinburgh: David Douglas, 1883).

Parry, J., *The Rise and Fall of Liberal Government in Victorian Britain* (New Haven, CT, & London: Yale University Press, 1993).

Pedersen, S., 'Hannah More Meets Simple Simon: Tracts, Chapbooks, and Popular Culture in Late Eighteenth-Century England', *Journal of British Studies*, 25 (1986), pp. 84–113.

Pentland, G., 'Patriotism, Universalism and the Scottish Conventions, 1792–1794', *History*, 89 (2004), pp. 340–60.

—, 'Scotland and the Creation of a National Reform Movement, 1830–1832', *Historical Journal*, 48 (2005), pp. 999–1023.

—, 'The Debate on Scottish Parliamentary Reform, 1830–32', *Scottish Historical Review*, 85 (2006), pp. 102–32.

—, *Radicalism, Reform and National Identity in Scotland, 1820–1833* (Woodbridge: Boydell and Brewer, 2008).

—, 'Militarization and Collective Action in Great Britain, 1815–1820', in M. T. Davis and B. Bowden (ed.), *Disturbing the Peace: Collective Action in Britain and France, 1381 to the Present* (Basingstoke: Palgrave Macmillan, forthcoming).

The People's Palace History Paintings: A Short Guide (Glasgow: Glasgow Museums & Art Galleries, 1990).

Phillipson, N., *The Scottish Whigs and the Reform of the Court of Session, 1785–1830* (Edinburgh: Stair Society, 1990).

Philp, M. (ed.), 'The Fragmented Ideology of Reform', in M. Philp (ed.), *The French Revolution and British Popular Politics* (Cambridge: Cambridge University Press, 1991), pp. 50–77.

—, 'Vulgar Conservatism, 1792–3', *English Historical Review*, 110 (1995), pp. 42–69.

—, *Resisting Napoleon: The British Response to the Threat of Invasion, 1797–1815* (Aldershot: Ashgate, 2006).

—, 'Disconcerting Ideas: Explaining Popular Radicalism and Popular Loyalism in the 1790s', in G. Burgess and M. Festenstein (eds), *English Radicalism, 1550–1850* (Cambridge: Cambridge University Press, 2007), pp. 157–89.

Pickering, P., 'Class without Words: Symbolic Communication in the Chartist Movement', *Past and Present*, 112 (1986), pp. 144–62.

Pickering, P., and A. Tyrell (eds), *Contested Sites: Commemoration, Memorial and Popular Politics in Nineteenth-Century Britain* (Aldershot: Ashgate, 2004).

Pittock, M. G. H., *Scottish Nationality* (Basingstoke: Palgrave, 2001).

Poole, R., '"By the Law or the Sword": Peterloo Revisited', *History*, 91 (2006), pp. 254–76.

—, 'The March to Peterloo: Politics and Festivity in Late Georgian England', *Past and Present*, 192 (2006), pp. 109–53.

Poole, S., *The Politics of Regicide in England, 1760–1850* (Manchester: Manchester University Pres, 2000).

Porrit, E., *The Unreformed House of Commons: Parliamentary Representation before 1832*, 2 vols (Cambridge: Cambridge University Press, 1903).

Prothero, I., *Artisans and Politics in Early Nineteenth-Century London: John Gast and his Times* (Folkestone: William Dawson & Son, 1979).

Read, D., *Peterloo: The Massacre and its Background* (Manchester: Manchester University Press, 1958).

Roach, W. M., 'Radical Reform Movements in Scotland from 1815 to 1822 with Particular Reference to Events in the West of Scotland' (PhD dissertation, University of Glasgow, 1970).

—, 'Alexander Richmond and the Radical Reform Movements in Glasgow in 1816–17', *Scottish Historical Review*, 51 (1972), pp. 1–19.

Roberts, M., *Political Movements in Urban England, 1832–1914* (Basingstoke: Palgrave Macmillan, 2009).

Robins, J., *Rebel Queen: How the Trial of Caroline Brought England to the Brink of Revolution* (London: Simon & Schuster, 2006).

Roe, M., 'Maurice Margarot: A Radical in Two Hemispheres, 1792–1815', *Bulletin of the Institute of Historical Research*, 31 (1958), pp. 68–78.

Rogers, N., *Crowds, Culture and Politics in Georgian Britain* (Oxford: Clarendon Press, 1998).

—, Burning Tom Paine: Loyalism and Counter-Revolution in Britain, 1792–1793, *Social History*, 32 (1999), pp. 139–71.

Sack, J. J., *The Grenvillites 1801–29: Party Politics and Factionalism in the Age of Pitt and Liverpool* (Urbana, IL: University of Illinois Press, 1979).

Samuel, R., *Theatres of Memory*, 2 vols (London: Verso, 1994–8).

Saunders, R., 'Chartism from Above: British Elites and the Interpretation of Chartism', *Historical Research*, 81 (2008), pp. 463–84.

Saville, J., *1848: The British State and the Chartist Movement* (Cambridge: Cambridge University Press, 1987).

Schofield, P., 'Conservative Political Thought in Britain in Response to the French Revolution', *Historical Journal*, 29 (1986), pp. 601–22.

Scott, R., *Death By Design: The True Story of the Glasgow Necropolis* (Edinburgh: Black & White, 2005).

Shapiro, H., *Background to Revolt: A Short Study in the Social and Economic Conditions that led to the 'Radical Revolt' on Clydeside in 1820 and of the Part Played in that Rising by James, Perley, Wilson and the Strathaven Weavers* (Glasgow, 1945).

Sherry, F. A., *The Rising of 1820* (Glasgow: William Maclellan, 1968).

Smith, E. A., *A Queen on Trial: The Affair of Queen Caroline* (Stroud: Sutton Publishing, 1993).

Smith, M. S., 'Anti-Radicalism and Popular Politics in an Age of Revolution', *Parliamentary History*, 24, supplement (2005), pp. 71–92.

Smith, O., *The Politics of Language, 1791–1819* (Oxford: Clarendon Press, 1984).

Smyth, J. J., *Labour in Glasgow 1896–1936: Socialism, Suffrage, Sectarianism* (East Linton: Tuckwell Press, 2000).

Southall, H., 'Agitate! Agitate! Organize! Political Travellers and the Construction of a National Politics 1839–1880', *Transactions of the Institute of British Georgraphers*, 21 (1996), pp. 177–93.

Spater, G., *William Cobbett: The Poor Man's Friend*, 2 vols (Cambridge: Cambridge University Press, 1982).

Spence, P., *The Birth of Romantic Radicalism: War, Popular Politics and English Radical Reformism, 1800–1815* (Aldershot: Ashgate, 1996).

Stanhope, J., *The Cato Street Conspiracy* (London: Jonathan Cape, 1962).

Stevenson, J., 'The Queen Caroline Affair', in J. Stevenson (ed.), *London in the Age of Reform* (Oxford: Blackwell, 1977), pp. 117–48.

Stewart, W., *Fighters for Freedom in Scotland: The Days of Baird and Hardie* (London: Independent Labour Party, 1908).

—, *Fighters for Freedom in Scotland: The Days of Baird and Hardie* (1908; Glasgow, 1920).

Strout, A. L., *A Bibliography of Articles in Blackwood's Magazine, Volumes I through XVIII, 1817–1825*, Library Bulletin no. 5 (Lubbock, TX: Texas Technical College, 1959).

Taylor, A., 'Radical Funerals, Burial Customs and Political Commemoration: The Death and Posthumous Life of Ernest Jones', *Humanities Research*, 10 (2003), pp. 29–39.

—, '"The Old Chartist": Radical Veterans on the Late Nineteenth- and Early Twentieth-Century Political Platform', *History*, 95 (2010), pp. 458–76.

Taylor, M., *The Decline of British Radicalism, 1847–1860* (Oxford: Clarendon Press, 1995).

Thomis, M. I., and P. Holt, *Threats of Revolution in Britain 1789–1848* (London: Macmillan, 1977).

Thompson, E. P., *The Making of the English Working Class*, rev. edn (1963; London: Penguin, 1991).

Thorne, R. G. (ed.), *The History of Parliament: The House of Commons, 1790–1820*, 5 vols (London: Secker & Warburg, 1986).

Tilly, C., *Popular Contention in Great Britain, 1758–1834* (Cambridge, MA: Harvard University Press, 1995).

Tyrell, A., and M. T. Davis, 'Bearding the Tories: The Commemoration of the Scottish Political Martyrs of 1793–4', in Pickering and Tyrell (eds), *Contested Sites*, pp. 25–56.

Vernon, J. (ed.), *Re-reading the Constitution: New Narratives in the Political History of England's Long Nineteenth Century* (Cambridge: Cambridge University Press, 1996).

Wahrman, D., *Imagining the Middle Class: The Political Representation of Class in Britain, c. 1780–1840* (Cambridge: Cambridge University Press, 1995).

—, 'Public Opinion, Violence and the Limits of Constitutional Politics', in Vernon (ed.), *Re-reading* pp. 83–122.

Wallace, V., 'Exporting Radicalism within the Empire: Scots Presbyterian Political Values in Scotland and British North America, c.1815–c.1850' (PhD dissertation, University of Glasgow, 2009).

Wasson, E. A., 'The Great Whigs and Parliamentary Reform, 1809–30', *Journal of British Studies*, 24 (1985), pp. 434–64.

Whatley, C. A., *Scottish Society 1707–1830: Beyond Jacobitism, Towards Industrialisation* (Manchester: Manchester University Press, 2000).

White, R. J., *Waterloo to Peterloo* (London: William Heinemann Ltd, 1957).

Wiener, J. H., *Radicalism and Freethought in Nineteenth-Century Britain: The Life of Richard Carlile* (Westport, CT: Greenwood Press, 1983).

Wilson, A., *The Chartist Movement in Scotland* (Manchester: Manchester University Press, 1970).

Winter, J., *Sites of Memory, Sites of Mourning: The Great War in European Cultural History* (Cambridge: Cambridge University Press, 1995).

Wold, A., 'Loyalism in Scotland in the 1790s', in U. Broich, H. T. Dickinson, E. Hellmuth (eds), *Reactions to Revolutions: The 1790s and their Aftermath* (Münster: LIT, 2007), pp. 109–35.

Wolffe, J., *Great Deaths: Grieving, Religion, and Nationhood in Victorian and Edwardian Britain* (Oxford: Oxford University Press, 2000).

Wood, I. S., 'Hope Deferred: Labour in Scotland in the 1920s', in I. Donnachie, C. Harvie and I. S. Wood (eds), *Forward! Labour Politics in Scotland 1888–1898* (Edinburgh: Polygon, 1989), pp. 30–48.

—, 'The ILP and the Scottish national question', in D. James, T. Jowitt and K. Laybourn (eds), *The Centennial History of the Independent Labour Party* (Halifax: Ryburn, 1992), pp. 60–74.

Worrall, D., *Radical Culture: Discourse, Resistance and Survelliance, 1790–1820* (Detroit, MI: Wayne State University Press, 1992).

Wright, L. C., *Scottish Chartism* (Edinburgh: Oliver & Boyd, 1953).

Yeo, E., 'Culture and Constraint in Working Class Movements, 1830–1855', in E. Yeo and S. Yeo (eds), *Popular Culture and Class Conflict 1590–1914: Explorations in the History of Labour and Leisure* (Brighton: Harvester Press, 1981), pp. 155–86.

INDEX

Aberdeen, 20, 50, 93
Age of Reason, 83, 111
Airdrie, 56, 62, 64, 66, 73, 91, 99, 106, 133
Aiton, William, 64, 109
Allen, John, 45, 46
Althorp, John Charles Spencer, Viscount, 71
Angus, 66
Arbroath, Declaration of (1320), 102, 142
Association for the Relief of the Manufacturing and Labouring Poor, 22
Atholl, John Murray, 3rd Duke of, 15
Ayr, 20, 91, 93
Ayrshire, 104, 107

Baird, John, 100, 105, 111, 113, 114, 126, 127, 131, 132, 133, 134, 135, 137, 138, 141, 142, 144
Baird, Thomas, 40, 41, 46
Ballantyne, James, 77
Bamford, Samuel, 68, 69–70, 96
Bannockburn, Battle of (1314), 40, 140
Beacon, 118
Bennet, Henry, 35
Berri, Charles Ferdinand d'Artois, Duc de, 92
Berwick Advertiser, 10
Biggar, George, 30, 31, 35, 43
Birmingham, 92, 120
Black, Adam, 49, 116
Black Book, 65, 67
Black Dwarf, 43, 44, 51, 55, 56, 61–2, 65, 66, 67, 83, 120
Blackwood's Edinburgh Magazine, 37–8, 73, 74, 75, 93
Blair, Robert, 23
Blanketeers, March of the (1817), 57

Bonnymuir, Battle of (1820), 1, 100–1, 103, 113, 114, 128, 130, 133, 135
Borthwick, William Murray, 109
Boswell, Alexander, 75, 94, 101, 106, 109, 110
Bothwell Brig, Battle of (1679), 134
Boyle, David Boyle, Lord (Lord Justice Clerk, 1811–41), 43
Bradford, Major-General Sir Thomas, 90
Brandreth, Jeremiah, 43
Braxfield, Robert Macqueen, Lord, 139
Brayshaw, Joseph, 67, 90, 92, 107
Brewster, Rev. Patrick, 133
Bridgeton, 106
Brougham, Henry, 9, 10, 11, 45, 48, 55
Brown, Capt. James, 30, 91, 110
Bruce, Robert (King of Scots), 25, 120
Buccleuch, Charles Montagu-Scott, 4th Duke of, 37
Buchanan, George, 25
Burdett, Sir Francis, 15, 28, 55, 72
burgh reform, 4, 25, 49–51, 117, 123
Byng, Major-General Sir John, 102, 108

Caledonian Mercury, 16
Calhoun, Craig, 106, 119
Calton, 19, 30, 43, 72, 81, 106, 127, 144
Campbell, John (state prisoner), 42–3
Campbell, John (journalist and author), 134–6
Canada, 56
Canning, George, 93
Carlile, Richard, 44, 62, 63, 67, 82, 100, 111, 125
Carlisle, 57, 92

Caroline, Queen of United Kingdom of Great Britain and Ireland, 2, 5, 110, 115–21, 122, 124, 125, 129, 130
Carron iron works, 100
Cartwright, Major John, 13–18, 21, 27, 28, 45, 64, 72, 92, 120, 123
Cassilis, Archibald Kennedy, 12th Earl of, 90
Castlereagh, Robert Stewart, Viscount, 22, 68
Castle, John, 103
Cato Street Conspiracy (1820), 92, 102, 129
Chalmers, Rev. Thomas, 39
Charles I, King of England, Scotland and Ireland, 65
Chartism/Chartists, 2, 5, 16, 132–4, 136–7
Charlotte, Princess, 39, 116
Church of Scotland, 116–17
Clarke, Mary Anne, 10, 12
Clayknowes, 65
Clelland, James, 105
Clerk, John, 45, 46
Clydesdale Journal, 109, 118
Cobbett, William, 64, 80, 92, 120, 123, 129
Cobbett's Weekly Political Register, 17, 20–1, 23, 26, 37, 65, 115
Cochran, Adam, 99, 105
Cochrane, Thomas *see* Dundonald
Cockburn, Henry, 11, 16, 43, 45, 53, 84, 85, 123
Collins, John, 133
Collins, Wilkie, 135
Collins, William, 138
Colquhoun, Archibald (Lord Advocate, 1807–16), 19
combination laws, 125
commemoration *see* monuments
Commemoration Committee (1820) / 1820 Society, 127, 143
Condorrat, 100, 135
Connell, John, 14
Cookson, J. E., 7, 8, 85
corn laws, 15, 19, 20, 24, 125
Court of Session, 47, 49, 50
Covenanters, 25, 69, 133, 140, 144
  see also Bothwell Brig, Battle of; Drumclog, Battle of
Coventry, 92
Craigend, 99
Cranstoun, George, 42, 44, 46

Creevey, Thomas, 119
Croker, John Wilson, 79, 120
Culrain, 95
Cumbernauld, 138
Cumming, James, 134
Cupar, 93
Currie, Ken, 144

Daily Herald, 140
Dinwiddy, John, 13
Dollan, Patrick 140
Douglas, Niel, 4, 41–2, 43–4, 46
Downie, David, 112
Drumclog, Battle of (1679), 134
Dublin, 120
Dumbarton, 106
Dumfries, 34, 81
Dumfries and Galloway Courier, 10
Duncan, Rev. Henry, 38, 81
Dundee, 20, 27–8, 31, 44–5, 36, 38, 41, 50, 51, 64, 66, 72, 127
Dundee, Perth and Cupar Advertiser, 10, 16
Dundonald, Thomas Cochrane, 10th Earl of, 22
Dunfermline, 10, 83
Duntocher, 99, 106
Dysart, 12

Ecclefechan, 91
Eckersley, Rachel, 14
Edgar, William, 42
Edinburgh, 5, 11, 14, 16, 17, 18, 30, 34, 37, 44, 47, 48, 50, 66, 81, 83, 84, 85, 91, 110, 116, 118, 119, 120, 134, 136, 137
Edinburgh Correspondent, 16
Edinburgh Evening Courant, 37
Edinburgh Gazetteer, 17
Edinburgh Merchant Company, 49
Edinburgh Review, 9–10, 11, 45–6, 47, 75, 123
Edinburgh Weekly Journal, 37, 77, 82
Edwards, George, 92, 103
Elderslie, 24, 69, 91
Eldon, John Scott, 1st Earl of, 73, 86–7, 111
elections
  general, 51, 55, 93–4, 105, 130, 136
  Hamilton by-election (1967), 142
  municipal, 49–50, 140

Index

Eley, Geoff, 5
Elgin, 93
Ellis, Peter Berresford, and Seumas Mac a'Ghobhainn, *The Scottish Insurrection of 1820*
emigration, 56–7, 58
Epstein, James, 28, 39–40, 68
Ewing, Winifred, 142

Fabiani, Linda, 127
Falkirk, 15, 38, 56, 100
Ferrie, Adam, 18
Fife, 66, 83, 128
Finlay, Kirkman, 30, 48, 125
Finalyson, James, 43
Fitzwilliam, William Wentworth, 2nd Earl, 78, 79, 83, 123
Fletcher of Saltoun, Andrew, 18, 25
Forbes, John, 81
Forfar, 15
Forward, 139, 140
Fox, Charles James, 48
Foxbar, 99, 105
Franklin (alias Fletcher; Forbes), William, 114–15
Fraser, John, 132–3
Freeling, Francis, 34
Freir, Edward, 134–5, 137, 144
French Revolution (1789–99), 37, 63, 87
Fulcher, Jonathan, 3, 33, 54, 70, 86, 122, 125
Fyshe Palmer, Thomas, 45, 48

Galashiels, 86
Galloway Levellers, 143
Galston, 106, 118
George III, King of Great Britain and Ireland, 34, 41, 93
George IV, King of Great Britain and Ireland, 28, 29, 34, 40, 41, 56, 61, 63, 64, 65, 79, 93, 94, 115, 118, 120, 122
George V, King of Great Britain and Ireland, 141
Gerrald, Joseph, 134
Gilchrist, John Borthwick, 17–18, 120
Gillespie, Rev. William, 116–17
Gillon, Joseph, 37
Gilmartin, Kevin, 27

Glasgow, 10, 14, 17, 19, 20, 23, 27, 29, 30, 34, 42, 59–62, 63, 66, 72, 76, 79, 84, 90, 91, 92, 93, 97, 99, 103, 106, 107, 110, 111, 117, 119, 120, 122, 129, 130, 136, 137, 138, 143
Glasgow Chronicle, 10, 16, 49, 56, 58, 66, 71, 110
Glasgow Courier, 37
Glasgow Herald, 37, 73, 84, 139
Glasgow Sentinel see Glasgow Chronicle
Glasgow Trades Council, 127
Glencoe Massacre (1692), 69
Gleniffer, 69
'Glorious' Revolution (1688–9), 102, 130
Goldsmiths' Hall Association, 27
Gordon Riots (1780), 70
Grant, John Peter, 45, 118
Greenock, 27, 99, 100
Greenock Advertiser, 10
Grenvillites, 78
Grey, Charles Grey, 2nd Earl, 48, 130

Haddington, 75
Half Hour's Crack with a Glasgow Radical Reformer, 81
Hamilton, 100, 106, 142
Hamilton, Alexander Douglas-Hamilton, 10th Duke of, 48, 61, 79, 123
Hamilton, Lord Archibald, 25, 48, 50, 51, 84, 117
Hamilton, Robert, 30
Hamlet, 40
Hampden, John, 25–6, 65
Hampden Club, 14, 16, 17, 18, 24, 27
Hardie, Andrew, 99, 100, 111, 113, 114, 126, 127, 131, 132, 133, 134, 141, 142, 144
Hardie, James, 99
Hardie, Keir, 139
Harney, George Julian, 133
Harris, Bob, 34
Harrowby, Dudley Ryder, 1st Earl of, 92
Hastie, Archibald, 14
Healy, Joseph, 96
Home Drummond, Henry, 42
Hone, William, 44

Hope, Charles (Lord President of the Court of Session, 1811–41), 46, 75, 79, 84, 90, 111, 113, 126
Hopkirk, Thomas, 61, 65
Hullock, Serjeant John, 112, 113
Hume, Joseph, 51, 93, 114–5, 129, 130, 136
Huddersfield, 96
Hunt, Henry, 28, 59, 62, 64, 70, 71, 72, 73, 92, 96, 112, 125, 129
Hunter, Samuel, 84
Hutcheson, Charles, 68, 76–7

Independent Labour Party, 129, 138–41
Inglis, Rev. John, 81
Inverness, 50

James II and VII, King of England, Scotland and Ireland, 40, 65
Jeffrey, Francis, 9, 40, 41, 45, 46, 83, 112, 113, 118, 130
John Bull, 116
Johnson, Joseph, 96
Johnston, Thomas, 139, 140, 141
Johnston, Capt. William, 17, 18
Johnstone, 28, 99, 106
Jones, Gareth Stedman, 2–3, 9

Kerr, William, 34
Kilbarchan 29, 106
Kilmarnock, 23, 29, 40, 67, 71, 72, 73, 84, 85, 106, 109, 110
Kilsyth, 56, 99
Kinloch, George, 18, 107
Kirkcaldy, 64
Kirkintilloch, 25, 91
Knight, John, 96
Knox, John, 25, 120

Lanark, 93, 109
Lanarkshire, 10, 13, 62
Laing, John, 112
Lang, William, 15, 17, 24, 94
Largs, 99
Lauderdale, Charles Maitland, 8th Earl of, 15
Leeds, 67, 75, 92
Leeds Mercury, 58, 102
Leith, 10
Liberty, 142

Liverpool, Robert Banks Jenkinson, 2nd Earl of, 9, 11, 37, 79, 121, 123
Lochaw, 95
London Corresponding Society, 34
loyalism/loyalists
  addresses/meetings of, 26, 37, 61, 79, 82–3, 117
  character/rhetoric of, 2–4, 8, 16, 33–4, 53–4, 59, 61, 62–3, 73–87, 96, 101, 105, 109, 115, 117–18, 122
  and press, 37–9, 73, 75, 80–2, 116, 118
  and Whigs, 59, 77–80
  see also Six Acts; trials; volunteers
Loyal Reformers' Gazette, 130
Luddism/Luddites, 12–13, 42, 70

McAllion, John, 127
Mac a'Ghobhainn, Seumas *see* Ellis and Mac a'Ghobhainn, *The Scottish Insurrection of 1820*
Macdonald, Catriona, 119
Macdonald, Marshall, 107
McDonald, Ronald, 113
Macdouall, Peter, 133
Macfarlane, Thomas, 133
McKay, Andrew, 30
Mackenzie, Peter, 43, 102, 130–2, 136, 137, 139
McKinlay, Andrew, 4, 42–3, 46, 47, 49
McLaren, Alexander, 40, 41, 46
McLaren, Charles, 48
Maconochie, Alexander (Lord Advocate, 1816–19), 30, 31, 32, 35, 36–7, 43, 44, 47, 48, 111
Magna Carta, 26, 102
Majocchi, Theodore, 118
Manchester, 59, 60, 61, 69, 79, 83, 92, 96, 106, 107, 119, 120
Manchester Gazette, 58
Manchester Observer, 65, 66, 67, 96
Mann, James, 92
Margarot, Maurice, 14–5
Marrow of Radical Reform, 80–1
Mason, Archibald, 94
Mather, F. C., 8
Maxton, James, 140, 141
Maxwell, John, 66, 78
Maybole, 92

Melville, Robert Saunders Dundas, 2nd Viscount, 61
Miller, William, 66, 73
Moffat, William, 14
Moncreiff, James, 118
Montagu, Henry Montagu-Scott, Lord, 85
Monteith, Brian, 128
Monteith, Henry, 93, 94, 108
Montrose, 49–50, 51
Montrose Review, 10
monuments
    at Bonnymuir, 1
    in Edinburgh, 132, 137
    in Glasgow, 129, 131–2, 135–8, 141, 143, 144
    in Paisley, 137, 143
    in Stirling, 143
    in Strathaven, 129, 134–7, 138
Morning Chronicle 56, 58, 60
More, Hannah, 38, 80
Morrison, John, 105
Muir, Thomas, 14, 48, 134, 139, 142, 143
municipal reform *see* burgh reform
Munro, Hugh, 95
Murray, John Archibald, 45, 114

national debt, 11, 22
Newcastle, 85
Newmilns, 106
New Statistical Account, 136
Norris, James, 107
North British Express, 134
Nottingham, 92, 108

Oldham, 96
Oliver the Spy (W. J. Richards), 103
Owenism, 125

Paine, Thomas, 28, 34, 56, 82, 111, 125
Paisley, 10, 14, 22, 23, 39, 56, 58, 59–62, 63, 64, 69, 71, 72, 74, 77, 79, 90, 91, 92, 99, 103, 106, 120, 121, 137, 143
Parkhill, John, 69, 70–1
Parliament
    Scottish, 2, 127–8, 129
    UK, 21, 22, 24–5, 30, 34, 35, 40, 42, 47–8, 50, 54, 55, 57–8, 63, 71, 86, 115, 117, 119, 120, 123

Pate, McDowal, 42
Paterson, Gil, 127
Patie and Nelly, 80
Perth, 15, 31, 99, 120
Peterloo Massacre (1819), 59, 62, 63, 64, 66, 68, 69, 70, 71–2, 79, 83, 84, 86, 90, 95, 96, 100, 111, 120, 124, 132
petitions/petitioning, 16, 18, 19, 28–9, 30, 39, 40–1, 45–51, 57, 64–5, 76, 77, 83, 105, 120, 124
    burgh reform, 50–1
    corn laws, 15, 20
    orders in council, 10, 13
    parliamentary reform, 9, 15, 16, 17–18, 20–8, 35, 40–1, 56–7, 58, 94, 130, 131
    property tax, 10–12, 18, 20, 40–1
    slave trade, 16, 18, 40
Phillipson, Nick, 47
Philp, Mark, 33, 38
Pitt, William, 11, 62
Poole, Robert, 68
Port Glasgow, 100
Primrose, Frederick, 53
Prince Regent *see* George IV
Proudfoot, Rev. James, 136

Quarterly Review, 10, 37
Quinan, Lloyd, 127

radicalism/radicals
    character/rhetoric of, 2–5, 8–9, 10, 12–18, 21–32, 50–1, 53–5, 56–7, 58–73, 86–7, 92, 97–8, 104–8, 109–10, 112, 119–21, 123–6, 130–42
    English connections of, 2, 4, 12–16, 31, 32, 65–6, 92, 96, 107–8
    meetings of, 17–18, 21, 22–4, 25–8, 29, 56–7, 59–60, 62–3, 64, 65, 66, 68–73
    and press, 4, 10, 17, 20–1, 43–4, 48–9, 65–6
    and Union Societies, 66–7, 90, 91–7
    and Whigs, 4, 34, 45–7, 51, 66
    see also Chartism/Chartists; Peterloo Massacre; petitions/petitioning; trials
Rae, William (Lord Advocate, 1819–30), 53, 59, 61, 74–5, 77, 79, 81, 91, 100, 103, 104, 112

Reddie, James, 36, 110
Reform Act, Scotland (1832), 128, 129, 130–1
Reformers' Gazette, 132
Reid, Jimmy, 143
Renfrewshire, 10, 13, 62, 69, 93
Richmond, Alexander, 13, 30, 31, 35, 102
Ritchie, William, 48
Roach, William, 13
Rodger, Alexander, 72
Rodger, William, 64, 66, 73
Ross, 95
Russell, Lord John, 130
Rutherfurd, Andrew, 137
Rutherglen, 25, 72
Rutherglen Reformer, 135

Samuel, Raphael, 128
Scotch Cheap Repository, 38
Scotsman, 48–9, 51, 56, 58, 60, 66, 72, 117, 123
Scott, John, 94
Scott, Walter, 37, 38, 77, 79, 81, 82, 85–6, 128
Scottish Home Rule Association, 138
Scottish Insurrection of 1820, The, 1, 4–5, 89, 102, 131, 143
Scottish National League, 142
Scottish National Party, 1, 127, 142, 143
Selkirk, 93
Sherry, Frank, 142
Sherwin, William, 66
Shields, James, 103
Sidmouth, Henry Addington, Viscount, 13, 20, 30, 36, 37, 61, 64, 81, 86–7, 91, 92, 93, 94, 95, 96, 103, 104, 107, 108, 111, 118, 120
Sidney, Algernon, 26
Six Acts, 63, 78, 80, 86–7, 104, 119
slavery/slave trade, 16, 18, 40
Smellie, John, 105
Smithfield, 64
Southey, Robert, 37
Spa Fields (1816), 27, 28–9, 32, 34, 35
Spain, 9, 94, 142
Speirs, James, 105, 112, 133
Spence, Thomas, 14
spenceans, 28–9

Spirit of the Union, 4, 63, 66, 67, 73, 80, 82, 84
Stevenson, John, 131, 134
Stewart, William, 139, 140, 141
Stirling, 50, 100, 111, 126, 138, 140, 143
Stirlingshire, 66
Strathaven, 67, 91, 101, 103, 105, 106, 108, 114, 127, 129, 131, 134, 136, 137, 138, 140
Struthers, John, 38
Stuart, James, 83

Tannochside, 127
taxation/taxes, 7, 9, 10–12, 18, 22–3, 24, 38, 41, 55–9, 63, 72, 134
Taylor, Dr John, 133
Thaumaturgus, 26
Thistlewood, Arthur, 62, 92, 104
Thompson, E. P., 1, 53, 94, 119, 125, 129
Thomson, Rev. Andrew, 116
Thrushgrove, 25–6, 30, 126, 131, 137
Tierney, George, 55, 78
Tooke, Horne, 18
Toryism/Tories, 9–10, 37, 73–4, 75, 79, 81, 113, 121–2, 127–8, 132, 144
trials
  in 1817, 39–48, 111–12
  in 1820, 110–15
tricolour flag, 73, 79
True Scotsman, 133
Turner, James, 131, 137

Union, Anglo-Scottish (1707), 112–13, 142
Union canal, 17
Union Societies *see* radicalism/radicals
Use and Abuse of Charity, 82

Vansittart, Nicholas, 22, 55
volunteers, 36, 68, 76, 84–6, 90, 100, 102, 109, 118
Visionary, 82

Wade, John, 65
Wahrman, Dror, 82, 119, 124
Wallace, William, 18, 65, 69, 72, 81, 120, 140, 144
war, 7, 26–7, 83, 124, 139
Washington, George, 65
Watson, 'Dr' James, 29, 62

Watt, Robert, 112
Wellington, Arthur Wellesley, 1st Duke of, 22, 137
Whatley, Christopher A., 1
Whiggism/Whigs, 4, 9–11, 34, 44–51, 55, 57–8, 59, 66, 73–4, 75, 77–80, 83–4, 112–17, 123, 124, 125, 131
Whitbread, Samuel, 47
White, Andrew, 135
William III and II, King of England, Scotland and Ireland, 122
William IV, King of Great Britain and Ireland, 130

Wilson, James, 67, 101, 111, 112, 114, 127, 130, 133–4, 136, 138, 139
Wilson, John, 67, 101, 111
Wood, Ian, 140
Wooler, Thomas, 44, 55, 61, 66, 92
Worker, 140
Wroe, James, 65

yeomanry corps *see* volunteers
York, 73, 96, 112, 120
York, Prince Frederick, Duke of, 10, 12, 22
Yorkshire, 78, 83
Young South Country Weaver, 81